eBook and Digital Learning Tools for

Fire in the Streets

The Social Crisis of the 1960s

JOEL M. SIPRESS

Carefully scratch off the silver coating with a coin to see your personal redemption code.

This code can be used only once and cannot be shared!

If the code has been scratched off when you receive it, the code may not be valid. Once the code has been scratched off, this access card cannot be returned to the publisher. You may buy access at **www.oup.com/us/debatingamericanhistory**.

The code on this card is valid for 2 years from the date of first purchase. Complete terms and conditions are available at **https://oup-arc.com.**

Access length: 6 months from redemption of the code.

D1608580

OXFORI
UNIVERSITY PRE

Directions for accessing your **eBook and Digital Learning Tools**

VIA THE OUP SITE

1. Visit **www.oup.com/us/debatingamericanhistory**
2. Select the edition you are using and the student resources for that edition.
3. Click the link to upgrade your access to the student resources.
4. Follow the on-screen instructions.
5. Enter your personal redemption code when prompted on the checkout screen.

VIA YOUR SCHOOL'S LEARNING MANAGEMENT SYSTEM

1. Log in to your instructor's course.
2. When you click a link to a protected resource, you will be prompted to register for access.
3. Follow the on-screen instructions.
4. Enter your personal redemption code when prompted on the checkout screen.

For assistance with code redemption or registration, please contact customer support at **arc.support@oup.com**.

PRAISE FOR *DEBATING AMERICAN HISTORY*

"Debating American History repositions the discipline of history as one that is rooted in discovery, investigation, and interpretation."

—Ingrid Dineen-Wimberly, University of California, Santa Barbara

"Debating American History is an excellent replacement for a 'big assignment' in a course. It offers a way to add discussion to a class, and it is a perfect 'active learning' assignment, in a convenient package."

—Gene Rhea Tucker, Temple College

"The advantage that Debating American History has over other projects and texts currently available is that this brings a very clear and focused organization to the notion of classroom debate. The terms of the debate are clear. The books introduce students to historiography and primary sources. Most of all, the project re-envisions the way that US history should be taught. No other textbook or set of teaching materials does what these books do when taken together as the sum of their parts."

—Ian Hartman, University of Alaska

DEBATING AMERICAN HISTORY

FIRE IN THE STREETS

DEBATING AMERICAN HISTORY

Series Editors: Joel M. Sipress, David J. Voelker

Conflict and Accommodation in Colonial New Mexico
Jonathan Decoster

The Powhatans and the English in the Seventeenth-Century Chesapeake
David J. Voelker

Democracy and the US Constitution
Joel M. Sipress

The Causes of the Civil War
Joel M. Sipress

Emancipation and the End of Slavery
Joel M. Sipress

Industrialization and Social Conflict in the Gilded Age
Joel M. Sipress

A Progressive Era for Whom?: African Americans in an Age of Reform, 1890–1920
Michelle Kuhl

The Politics of Prosperity: Mass Consumer Culture in the 1920s
Kimberley A. Reilly

Fire in the Streets: The Social Crisis of the 1960s
Joel M. Sipress

DEBATING AMERICAN HISTORY

FIRE IN THE STREETS

The Social Crisis of the 1960s

Joel M. Sipress
UNIVERSITY OF WISCONSIN–SUPERIOR

NEW YORK   OXFORD
OXFORD UNIVERSITY PRESS

Oxford University Press is a department of the University of Oxford.
It furthers the University's objective of excellence in research, scholarship,
and education by publishing worldwide. Oxford is a registered trade mark of
Oxford University Press in the UK and certain other countries.

Published in the United States of America by Oxford University Press
198 Madison Avenue, New York, NY 10016, United States of America.

For titles covered by Section 112 of the US Higher Education
Opportunity Act, please visit www.oup.com/us/he for the latest
information about pricing and alternate formats.

Library of Congress Cataloging-in-Publication Data
Names: Sipress, Joel M., author.
Title: Fire in the streets : the social crisis of the 1960s / Joel M.
Sipress.
Description: New York : Oxford University Press, [2021] | Series: Debating
american history | Includes bibliographical references and index. |
Summary: "A higher education History primary source textbook that
embraces an argument based model for teaching history. It is part of the
Debating American History series, and covers the social crisis of the
1960s"— Provided by publisher.
Identifiers: LCCN 2020001505 (print) | LCCN 2020001506 (ebook) | ISBN
9780197519172 (paperback) | ISBN 9780197519189 (epub) | ISBN
9780197527184 c
Subjects: LCSH: United States—Social conditions—1960-1980—Sources. |
Counterculture—United States—History—20th century—Sources. | Protest
movements—United States—History—20th century—Sources. | United
States—History—1961-1969—Sources.
Classification: LCC HN59 .S485 2021 (print) | LCC HN59 (ebook) | DDC
303.48/409046—dc23
LC record available at https://lccn.loc.gov/2020001505
LC ebook record available at https://lccn.loc.gov/2020001506

Printing number: 9 8 7 6 5 4 3 2
Printed by LSC Communications, Inc., United States of America

TABLE OF CONTENTS

LIST OF FIGURES AND TABLES

Figures

Tables

ABOUT THE AUTHOR

Joel M. Sipress received his PhD in United States history from the University of North Carolina at Chapel Hill. He is a Professor of History at the University of Wisconsin–Superior, where he teaches US and Latin American history. He has published articles and book chapters on the history of the US South with a focus on the role of race and class in late nineteenth-century southern politics. He has also written essays on teaching and learning history, including "Why Students Don't Get Evidence and What We Can Do About It," *The History Teacher* 37 (May 2004): 351–363; and "The End of the History Survey Course: The Rise and Fall of the Coverage Model," coauthored with David J. Voelker, *Journal of American History* 97 (March 2011): 1050–1066, which won the 2012 Maryellen Weimer Scholarly Work on Teaching and Learning Award. He serves as coeditor of *Debating American History* with David J. Voelker.

ACKNOWLEDGMENTS

We owe gratitude to Aeron Haynie, Regan Gurung, and Nancy Chick for introducing us and pairing us to work on the Signature Pedagogies project many years ago, as well as to the UW System's Office of Professional and Instructional Development (OPID), which supported that endeavor. Brian Wheel, formerly with Oxford University Press, helped us develop the idea for *Debating American History* and started the project rolling. We want to thank Charles Cavaliere at Oxford for taking on the project and seeing it through to publication. Joel thanks the University of Wisconsin–Superior for support from a sabbatical, and David thanks the University of Wisconsin–Green Bay for support from a Research Scholar grant. David would also like to thank his colleagues in humanities, history, and First Nations Studies, who have been supportive of this project for many years, and Joel thanks his colleagues in the Department of Social Inquiry. Joel also thanks Margaret Engebretson for her feedback on "The Experience of Vietnam" section of this volume. We are also indebted to our colleagues (too numerous to mention) who have advanced the Scholarship of Teaching and Learning within the field of history. Without their efforts, this project would not have been possible. We would also like to thank the reviewers of this edition: Andrew C. Baker, Texas A&M University-Commerce; Maurice Isserman, Hamilton College; Tramaine Anderson, Tarrant County College; Ian Hartman, University of Alaska Anchorage; Michael Holm, Boston University; Matthew Tribbe, Fullerton College; Thomas W. Devine, CSU Northridge; and Robert J. Allison, Suffolk University.

SERIES INTRODUCTION

Although history instruction has grown richer and more varied over the past few decades, many college-level history teachers remain wedded to the coverage model, whose overriding design principle is to cover huge swaths of history, largely through the use of textbooks and lectures. The implied rationale supporting the coverage model is that students must be exposed to a wide array of facts, narratives, and concepts in order to have the necessary background both to be effective citizens and to study history at a more advanced level—something that few students actually undertake. Although coverage-based courses often afford the opportunity for students to encounter primary sources, the imperative to cover an expansive body of material dominates these courses, and the main assessment technique, whether implemented through objective or written exams, is to require students to identify or reproduce authorized knowledge.

Unfortunately, the coverage model has been falling short of its own goals since its very inception in the late nineteenth century. Educators and policymakers have been lamenting the historical ignorance of American youth going back to at least 1917, as Stanford professor of education Sam Wineburg documented in his illuminating exposé of the history of standardized tests of historical knowledge.[1] In 2010, the *New York Times* declared that "History is American students' worst subject," basing this judgment on yet another round of abysmal standardized test scores.[2] As we have documented in our own historical research, college professors over the past century have episodically criticized the coverage model and offered alternatives. Recently, however, college-level history instructors have been forming a scholarly community to improve the teaching of the introductory course

1 Sam Wineburg, "Crazy for History," *Journal of American History* 90 (March 2004): 1401–1414.

2 Sam Dillon, "U.S. Students Remain Poor at History, Tests Show," *New York Times*, June 14, 2011. Accessed online at http://www.nytimes.com/2011/06/15/education/15history.html?emc=eta1&pagewanted=print.

by doing research that includes rigorous analysis of student learning. A number of historians who have become involved in this discipline-based pedagogical research, known as the Scholarship of Teaching and Learning (SoTL), have begun to mount a challenge to the coverage model.[3]

Not only has the coverage model often achieved disappointing results by its own standards, but it also proves to be ineffective at helping students learn how to think historically, which has long been a stated goal of history education. As Lendol Calder argued in a seminal 2006 article, the coverage model works to "cover up" or "conceal" the nature of historical thinking.[4] The eloquent lecture or the unified textbook narrative reinforces the idea that historical knowledge consists of a relatively straightforward description of the past. Typical methods of covering content hide from students not only the process of historical research—the discovery and interpretation of sources—but also the ongoing and evolving discussions among historians about historical meaning. In short, the coverage model impedes historical thinking by obscuring the fact that history is a complex, interpretative, and argumentative discourse.

Informed by the scholarship of the processes of teaching and learning, contemporary reformers have taken direct aim at the assumption that factual and conceptual knowledge must precede more sophisticated forms of historical study. Instead, reformers stress that students must learn to think historically by doing—at a novice level—what expert historians do.[5]

With these ideas in mind, we thus propose an argument-based model for teaching the introductory history course. In the argument-based model, students participate in a contested, evidence-based discourse about the human past. In other words, students are asked to argue about history. And by arguing, students develop the dispositions and habits of mind that are central to the discipline of history.[6] As the former American Historical

---

3 See Lendol Calder, "Uncoverage: Toward a Signature Pedagogy for the History Survey," *Journal of American History* 92 (March 2006): 1358–1370; Joel M. Sipress and David J. Voelker, "The End of the History Survey Course: The Rise and Fall of the Coverage Model," *Journal of American History* 97 (March 2011): 1050–1066; and Penne Restad, "American History Learned, Argued, and Agreed Upon," in *Team-Based Learning in the Social Sciences and Humanities*, ed. Michael Sweet and Larry K. Michaelson, 159–180 (Sterling, VA: Stylus, 2012). For an overview of the Scholarship of Teaching and Learning (SoTL) in history, see Joel M. Sipress and David Voelker, "From Learning History to Doing History: Beyond the Coverage Model," in *Exploring Signature Pedagogies: Approaches to Teaching Disciplinary Habits of Mind*, ed. Regan Gurung, Nancy Chick, and Aeron Haynie, 19–35 (Stylus Publishing, 2008). Note also that the International Society for the Scholarship of Teaching and Learning in History was formed in 2006. See http://www.indiana.edu/~histsotl/blog/.

4 Calder, "Uncoverage," 1362–1363.

5 For influential critiques of the "facts first" assumption, see Sam Wineburg, "Crazy for History," *Journal of American History* 90 (March 2004): 1401–1414; and Calder, "Uncoverage."

6 For discussions of argument-based courses, see Barbara E. Walvoord and John R. Breihan, "Arguing and Debating: Breihan's History Course," in Barbara E. Walvoord and Lucille P. McCarthy, *Thinking and Writing in College: A Naturalistic Study of Students in Four Disciplines* (Urbana, IL: National Council of Teachers of English, 1990), 97–143; Todd Estes, "Constructing the Syllabus: Devising a Framework for Helping Students Learn to Think Like Historians," *History Teacher* 40 (February 2007): 183–201; Joel M. Sipress, "Why Students Don't Get Evidence and What We Can Do About It," *The History Teacher* 37 (May 2004): 351–363; David J. Voelker, "Assessing Student Understanding in Introductory Courses: A Sample Strategy," *The History Teacher* 41 (August 2008): 505–518.

Association (AHA) president Kenneth Pomeranz noted in late 2013, historians should consider seeing general education history courses as valuable "not for the sake of 'general knowledge' but for the intellectual operations you can teach."[7] Likewise, the AHA "Tuning Project" defines the discipline in a way much more consistent with an argument-based course than with the coverage model: "History is a set of evolving rules and tools that allows us to interpret the past with clarity, rigor, and an appreciation for interpretative debate. It requires evidence, sophisticated use of information, and a deliberative stance to explain change and continuity over time. As a profoundly public pursuit, history is essential to active and empathetic citizenship and requires effective communication to make the past accessible to multiple audiences. As a discipline, history entails a set of professional ethics and standards that demand peer review, citation, and toleration for the provisional nature of knowledge."[8] We have designed *Debating American History* with these values in mind.

In the coverage-based model, historical knowledge is seen as an end in itself. In the argument-based model, by contrast, the historical knowledge that students must master serves as a body of evidence to be employed in argument and debate. While the ultimate goal of the coverage approach is the development of a kind of cultural literacy, the argument-based history course seeks to develop historical modes of thinking and to encourage students to incorporate these modes of thinking into their daily lives. Particularly when housed within a broader curriculum that emphasizes engaged learning, an argument-based course prepares students to ask useful questions in the face of practical problems and challenges, whether personal, professional, or civic. Upon encountering a historical claim, such as those that frequently arise in political discussions, they will know how to ask important questions about context, evidence, and logic. In this way, the argument-based course fulfills the discipline's long-standing commitment to the cultivation of engaged and informed citizens.[9]

While there is no single correct way to structure an argument-based course, such courses do share a number of defining characteristics that drive course design.[10] In particular, argument- based courses:

---

7 Kenneth Pomeranz, "Advanced History for Beginners: Why We Should Bring What's Best about the Discipline into the Gen Ed Classroom," *Perspectives on History* (Nov. 2013), at http://www.historians.org/publications-and-directories/perspectives-on-history/november-2013/advanced-history-for-beginners-why-we-should-bring-what's-best-about-the-discipline-into-the-gen-ed-classroom.

8 This definition reflects the state of the Tuning Project as of September 2013. For more information, see "AHA History Tuning Project: 2013 History Discipline Core," at https://www.historians.org/teaching-and-learning/tuning-the-history-discipline/2013-history-discipline-core. Accessed January 31, 2019.

9 As recently as 2006, the AHA's Teaching Division reasserted the importance of history study and scholarship in the development of globally aware citizens. Patrick Manning, "Presenting History to Policy Makers: Three Position Papers," *Perspectives: The Newsmagazine of the American Historical Association* 44 (March 2006), 22–24.

10 Our approach to course design is deeply influenced by Grant Wiggins and Jay McTighe, *Understanding by Design*, 2nd ed. (Upper Saddle River, NJ: Pearson Education, 2006).

1. ARE ORGANIZED AROUND SIGNIFICANT HISTORICAL QUESTIONS ABOUT WHICH HISTORIANS THEMSELVES DISAGREE.

Argument-based courses are, first and foremost, question-driven courses in which "big" historical questions (rather than simply topics or themes) provide the overall organizational structure. A "big" historical question is one about which historians themselves disagree and that has broad academic, intellectual, or cultural implications. Within these very broad parameters, the types of questions around which a course may be organized can vary greatly. The number of "big" questions addressed, however, must be relatively limited in number (perhaps three to five over the course of a typical fifteen-week semester), so that students can pursue the questions in depth.

2. SYSTEMATICALLY EXPOSE STUDENTS TO RIVAL POSITIONS ABOUT WHICH THEY MUST MAKE INFORMED JUDGMENTS.

Argument-based courses systematically expose students to rival positions about which they must form judgments. Through repeated exploration of rival positions on a series of big questions, students see historical debate modeled in way that shatters any expectation that historical knowledge is clear-cut and revealed by authority. Students are thus confronted with the inescapable necessity to engage, consider, and ultimately evaluate the merits of a variety of perspectives.

3. ASK STUDENTS TO JUDGE THE RELATIVE MERITS OF RIVAL POSITIONS ON BASIS OF HISTORICAL EVIDENCE.

To participate in historical argument, students must come see historical argument as more than a matter of mere opinion. For this to happen, students must learn to employ evidence as the basis for evaluating historical claims. Through being repeatedly asked to judge the relative merits of rival positions on the basis of evidence, students come to see the relationship between historical evidence and historical assertions.

4. REQUIRE STUDENTS TO DEVELOP THEIR OWN POSITIONS FOR WHICH THEY MUST ARGUE ON THE BASIS OF HISTORICAL EVIDENCE.

In an argument-based course, the ultimate aspiration should be for students to bring their own voices to bear on historical discourse in a way that is thoroughly grounded in evidence. Students must therefore have the opportunity to argue for their own positions. Such positions may parallel or synthesize those of the scholars with which they have engaged in the course or they may be original. In either case, though, students must practice applying disciplinary standards of evidence.

Learning to argue about history is, above all, a process that requires students to develop new skills, dispositions, and habits of mind. Students develop these attributes through the act of arguing in a supportive environment where the instructor provides guidance and feedback. The instructor is also responsible for providing students with the background, context, and in-depth materials necessary both to fully understand and appreciate each big question and to serve as the body of evidence that forms the basis for judgments and arguments. While argument-based courses eschew any attempt to provide comprehensive coverage, they ask students to think deeply about a smaller number of historical questions, and in the process of arguing about the selected questions, students will develop significant content knowledge in the areas emphasized.

While a number of textbooks and readers in American history incorporate elements of historical argumentation, there are no published materials available that are specifically designed to support an argument-based course. *Debating American History* consists of a series of modular units, each focused on a specific topic and question in American history that will support all four characteristics of an argument-based course noted previously. Each of the modules is designed for a roughly three- to four-week course unit. Instructors will select units that support their overall course design, perhaps incorporating one or two modules into an existing course or structuring an entire course around three to five such units. (Instructors, of course, are free to supplement the modular units with other materials of their choosing, such as additional primary documents, secondary articles, multimedia materials, and book chapters.) By focusing on a limited number of topics, students will be able to engage in in-depth historical argumentation, including consideration of multiple positions and substantial bodies of evidence.

Each unit has the following elements:

1. THE BIG QUESTION

Each unit begins with a brief narrative introduction that poses the central question of the unit and provides general background.

2. HISTORIANS' CONVERSATIONS

This section establishes the debate by providing two or three original essays that present distinct and competing scholarly positions on the Big Question. While these essays make occasional reference to major scholars in the field, they are not intended to provide historiographical overviews, but rather to provide models of historical argumentation through the presentation and analysis of evidence.

3. DEBATING THE QUESTION

Each module includes a variety of materials containing evidence for students to use to evaluate the various positions and develop a position of their own. Materials may include primary source documents, images, a timeline, maps, or brief secondary sources. The specific materials vary depending upon the nature of the question. Some modules include detailed case studies that focus on a particular facet of the Big Question.

For example, one module that we have developed for an early American history course focuses on the following Big Question: "How were the English able to displace the thriving Powhatan people from their Chesapeake homelands in the seventeenth century?" The Historians' Conversations section includes two essays: "Position #1: The Overwhelming Advantages of the English"; and "Position #2: Strategic Mistakes of the Powhatans." The unit materials allow students to undertake a guided exploration of both Powhatan and English motivations and strategies. The materials include two case studies that serve specific pedagogical purposes. The first case study asks the question, "Did Pocahontas Rescue John Smith from Execution?" Answering this question requires grappling with the nature of primary sources and weighing additional evidence from secondary sources; given historians' confidence that Powhatan did adopt Smith during his captivity, the case study also raises important questions about Powhatan strategy. The second case study focuses on the 1622 surprise attack that the Powhatans (led by Opechancanough) launched against the English, posing the question: "What was the Strategy behind the 1622 Powhatan Surprise Attack?" Students wrestle with a number of scholarly perspectives regarding Opechancanough's purpose and the effectiveness of his strategy. Overall, this unit introduces students to the use of primary sources and the process of weighing different historical interpretations. Because of Disney's 1995 film *Pocahontas*, many students begin the unit thinking that they already know about the contact between the Powhatans and the English; many of them also savor the chance to bring critical, historical thinking to bear on this subject, and doing so deepens their understanding of how American Indians responded to European colonization.

Along similar lines, the Big Question for a module on the Gilded Age asks, "Why was industrialization in the late nineteenth century accompanied by such great social and political turmoil?" The materials provided allow students to explore the labor conflicts of the period as well as the Populist revolt and to draw conclusions regarding the underlying causes of the social and political upheavals. Primary sources allow students to delve into labor conflicts from the perspectives of both workers and management, and to explore both Populist and anti-Populist perspectives. Three short case studies allow students to examine specific instances of social conflict in depth. A body of economic data from the late nineteenth century is also included.

Many history instructors, when presented with the argument-based model, find its goals to be compelling, but they fear that it is overly ambitious—that introductory-level students will be incapable of engaging in historical thinking at an acceptable level. But we must ask: how well do students learn under the coverage model? Student performance varies in an argument-based course, but it varies widely in a coverage-based course as well. In our experience, most undergraduate students are capable of achieving a basic level competence at identifying and evaluating historical interpretations and using primary and secondary sources as evidence to make basic historical arguments. We not only have evidence of this success in the form of our own grade books, but we have studied our students' learning to document the success of our approach.[11] Students can indeed learn how to think like historians at a novice level, and in doing so they will gain both an appreciation for the discipline and develop a set of critical skills and dispositions that will contribute to their overall higher education. For this to happen, however, a course must be "backward designed" to promote and develop historical thinking. As historian Lawrence Gipson (Wabash College) asked in a 1916 AHA discussion, "Will the student catch 'historical-mindedness' from his instructor like the mumps?"[12] The answer, clearly, is "no."

11 See Sipress, "Why Students Don't Get Evidence," and Voelker, "Assessing Student Understanding."

12 Lawrence H. Gipson, "Method of the Elementary Course in the Small College," *The History Teacher's Magazine* 8 (April 1917), 128. (The conference discussion took place in 1916.)

In addition to the modular units focused on big questions, instructors will also be provided with a brief instructors' manual, entitled "Developing an Argument-Based Course." This volume will provide instructors with guidance and advice on course development, as well as with sample in-class exercises and assessments. Additionally, each module includes an Instructor's Manual. Together, these resources will assist instructors with the process of creating an argument-based course, whether for a relatively small class at a liberal arts college or for a large class of students at a university. These resources can be used in both face-to-face and online courses.

The purpose of *Debating American History* is to provide instructors with both the resources and strategies that they will need to design such a course. This textbook alternative leaves plenty of room for instructor flexibility, and it requires instructors to carefully choose, organize, and introduce the readings to students, as well as to coach students through the process of thinking historically, even as they deepen their knowledge and understanding of particular eras and topics.

Joel M. Sipress
Professor of History
University of Wisconsin-Superior

David J. Voelker
Professor of Humanities and History
University of Wisconsin-Green Bay

DEBATING AMERICAN HISTORY

FIRE IN THE STREETS

THE BIG QUESTION

WHY DID THE UNITED STATES ENTER A PERIOD OF SOCIAL AND POLITICAL TURMOIL IN A TIME OF UNPRECEDENTED ECONOMIC PROSPERITY?

Heavy snow began to fall on Washington, DC, around noon on January 19, 1961. By evening, blizzard conditions, unusual for the nation's capital, had virtually shut the city down. So severe was the storm that some feared that the next day's presidential inauguration ceremonies might be ruined. As the morning of January 20 dawned, however, the weather broke and Washingtonians were treated to a bright and brisk winter day. A bit after noon, John F. Kennedy took the oath of office and was sworn in as the nation's 35th president. Just forty-three years of age, Kennedy ("JFK" as he was nicknamed) was the youngest candidate ever elected to the presidency. Although having just narrowly defeated Republican Richard Nixon in the 1960 election, Kennedy's boyish good looks and aristocratic charm, along with the stylish elegance of his wife Jacqueline Bouvier Kennedy, had captured the public imagination.

The previous July, in accepting the Democratic Party's nomination for president, JFK had challenged the nation to confront the pressing issues of the day:

> *We stand today on the edge of a New Frontier—the frontier of the 1960s, the frontier of unknown opportunities and perils, the frontier of unfilled hopes and unfilled threats. . . . Beyond that frontier are uncharted areas of science and space, unsolved problems of peace and war, unconquered problems of ignorance and prejudice, unanswered questions of poverty and surplus.*

"Give me your help and your hand and your voice," the candidate urged the American people:

> *Recall with me the words of Isaiah that "They that wait upon the Lord shall renew their strength; they shall mount up with wings as eagles; they shall run and not be weary." As we face the coming great challenge, we too, shall wait upon the Lord, and ask that He renew our strength. Then shall we be equal to the test. Then we shall not be weary. Then we shall prevail.*

Kennedy's message was an optimistic one, and it fit the spirit of the times. Americans of his generation had lived through two great cataclysms, the Great Depression and the Second World War, and the nation had emerged seemingly the stronger for it. The economic collapse of the 1930s had caused untold suffering and shaken the very foundations of the country's economic and political system. Under the leadership of President Franklin Delano Roosevelt, though, the federal government put in place a series of reforms (known as the "New Deal") that stabilized the economy and provided relief and assistance to the elderly, the unemployed, and the impoverished.

Following the Japanese attack on Pearl Harbor in December 1941, the nation found itself involved in the most horrific and destructive war in human history. Americans, however, were spared the unspeakable death tolls and physical devastation suffered by the peoples of Europe and East Asia, where the bulk of the fighting took place. In fact, virtually alone among the nations of the world, the United States emerged from the Second World War economically stronger than it had entered it. Government spending on military equipment and supplies had helped to bring an end to the Great Depression, and with much of the world bankrupted and in ruins, the United States entered the postwar period in a position of unchallenged global economic dominance.

Many feared that the reductions in military spending that followed the surrender of Nazi Germany and Imperial Japan would return the country to the depression conditions of the 1930s. In fact, the postwar period saw an economic boom unprecedented in American history. In the fifteen-year period between the end of the war and JFK's 1960 election victory, the value of all goods and services produced in the United States grew by over 50%. With the exception of a few relatively mild recessions, unemployment remained low throughout the period, and, unlike the booms of the late nineteenth and early twentieth centuries, the fruits of the postwar expansion were broadly shared by workers at all levels. Between 1945 and 1960, the annual income of the typical American family (adjusted for inflation) increased by about 40%, as did workers' wages. Between 1947 and 1960, Congress more than doubled the value of the minimum wage, ensuring that the lowest-earning workers saw their conditions improve especially quickly.

Certainly, the nation faced important challenges. But when it came to the country's most vexing domestic issue—the problem of racial inequality—there, too, seemed reason for hope. In 1954, the United States Supreme Court struck a bold blow for equality by declaring racially segregated public schools to be unconstitutional. Not long afterward, black residents of Montgomery, Alabama, led by a young Baptist minister named Martin Luther King, Jr., waged a successful year-long boycott to bring segregated seating to an end on city buses. Increasingly, the Jim Crow system of the segregated South (the most visible symbol of the nation's racial inequities) seemed a historical anachronism whose days were numbered.

Most Americans, including the new president, assumed that the nation's greatest challenges came from overseas. For over a decade, the United States had found itself locked in a so-called Cold War with the world's other great superpower, the Soviet Union. American leaders cast the U.S.–Soviet rivalry as a global struggle between adherents of American-style democratic capitalism and Soviet-style communism, a social system that American leaders warned threatened the prosperity and freedom not just of Americans, but all the peoples of the world. Yet, while the Soviet Union and its global allies wielded significant military and political might, the prosperity that Americans enjoyed at home provided confidence that the American free enterprise system (particularly as modified by the New Deal reforms of the 1930s) would eventually triumph over Soviet-style communism.

In his inaugural address, President Kennedy called upon his countrymen to rededicate themselves to the cause of human freedom, both at home and abroad:

> *Let every nation know, whether it wishes us well or ill, that we shall pay any price, bear any burden, meet any hardship, support any friend, oppose any foe, in order to assure the survival and the success of liberty.*

In fighting this Cold War, the new president challenged Americans to build a better world for all humanity:

> *Now the trumpet summons us again—not as a call to bear arms, though arms we need; not as a call to battle, though embattled we are—but a call to bear the burden of a long twilight struggle, year in and year out, "rejoicing in hope, patient in tribulation"—a struggle against the common enemies of man: tyranny, poverty, disease, and war itself.*

The inaugural ceremonies of January 20, 1961, captured the confidence and optimism with which most Americans entered the decade of the 1960s. It seemed as if a new era had dawned. By

1970, however, this confidence and optimism had been shattered—torn apart by a series of interlocking social upheavals that left many Americans fearing that the country was in fact coming apart at the seams. At the heart of the upheavals of the sixties lay a series of rebellions against the nation's social and cultural status quo—rebellions that left the country deeply divided and polarized.

The 1960s was a decade, above all, of racial turmoil, as the nation was rocked by a wave of protests against racial inequality. At first these protests were limited largely to the southern states and aimed primarily at overturning that region's system of racial segregation, commonly known as "Jim Crow." In the early 1960s, civil rights protests grew in size and scope, culminating in 1963, when a wave of protest and resistance engulfed the South and compelled the United States Congress to take action. In 1964, Congress passed a civil rights bill that outlawed racial discrimination in education, employment, and public accommodations (private businesses that directly serve the public). The following year, Congress approved a voting rights bill that guaranteed the rights of all American citizens to vote without regard to race or ethnicity.

The victories and achievements of the civil rights movement, however, did not bring the racial crisis of the 1960s to an end. On the contrary, in the mid- to late 1960s, the crisis intensified and spread nationwide. The growing popularity of a set of ideas that came to be known as "black power" inspired more radical forms of protest and politics in African American communities both north and south. Advocates of black power argued that racial oppression and exploitation were woven into the very fabric of American society, and they called for African American people to close ranks, unite, and create social and economic institutions that they themselves controlled. The late 1960s also saw the most destructive wave of urban riots in American history, as residents of African American ghettoes vented their frustrations with the conditions of life to which they were subjected. Between 1965 and 1968, there were roughly three hundred riots and disturbances in African American communities nationwide. While most were relatively minor, major disturbances in Los Angeles, Detroit, Washington, DC, and Newark, New Jersey, left dozens dead (mostly residents who died at the hands of law enforcement), thousands wounded and arrested, and resulted in millions of dollars of property damage.

The 1960s also saw a groundswell of unrest among a significant portion of the nation's white youth. This youth rebellion took two primary forms. The first was a wave of left-wing politics and protest, particularly among the rapidly expanding population of college students. This "New Left" (so-called to distinguish it from older forms of radical politics) had its origins in the early 1960s, as students began to organize in support of the civil rights movement. The size and militancy of the New Left, however, grew rapidly following President Lyndon Johnson's 1965 decision to send large numbers of US combat troops to fight in the Southeast Asian nation of Vietnam. By 1968, roughly half a million US military personnel (many of them draftees) were in Vietnam. In April of that year, a student strike protesting Columbia University's policies toward its surrounding black neighborhood and its ties to the US military shut down the Ivy League campus and forced the cancellation of the spring semester. The Columbia uprising inspired similar protests elsewhere, and by 1969 mass student demonstrations had become common on college and university campuses. Student unrest reached its peak in the spring of 1970 when, in response President Richard Nixon's decision to expand the Vietnam War into the neighboring country of Cambodia, student strikes shut down more than four hundred universities, colleges, and high schools. Youth unrest also took the form of the so-called counterculture of the 1960s, a form of cultural rebellion in which young people, labeled "hippies" or "freaks," rejected mainstream cultural values and norms and embraced ways of living at odds with the mainstream. Although the number of youth who truly "dropped out" of mainstream society was relatively small, the counterculture had reverberations that eventually reached millions of young people and created great unease among the "mainstream."

Additionally, toward the end of the decade, a group of younger, mainly college-educated women began to openly challenge sexism in American culture. Women's rights struggles had a long history in the United States, dating back to 1848, when a group of reformers gathered in the town of Seneca Fall, New York, and issued the famous "Declaration of Sentiments" that called for equality between men and women. After women gained the right to vote in 1920, however, organized women's rights activity in the United States had largely dissipated. Throughout the twentieth century, the numbers of women pursuing formal higher education and working for wages outside the home had steadily climbed. Women, though, faced a job market segregated by gender with the higher paying high-status professions, like medicine and law, reserved almost exclusively for men. At the same time, cultural expectations emphasized a womanly ideal focused almost entirely on the roles of wife and mother. Betty Friedan's 1963 bestselling book, *The Feminine Mystique*, urged women to look beyond the role of housewife for personal satisfaction. In 1966, Friedan helped to organize the National Organization for Women (NOW), an organization dedicated to struggle against discrimination against women. The years that followed saw increasing public protest against a multitude of forms of sexism and discrimination against women. Just as importantly, large numbers of young female college graduates began to defy social convention by pursuing careers in traditionally male-dominated professions. These female pioneers often faced bitter opposition in the workplace, but over time succeeded in opening up new opportunities for women.

The social and political rebellions of the 1960s sparked a vehement backlash that polarized and divided the nation. Increasingly, Americans came to view each other as members of two rival camps—rebels intent on challenging the status quo versus defenders of the traditional social order. Eventually, the country's social divisions undermined the optimism of the postwar period. In 1964, President Lyndon Baines Johnson (who had taken office following the November 1963 assassination of Kennedy) had been re-elected in one of the largest landslides in American history on a promise to make America a "Great Society," free from the scourges of poverty and racism. As the crisis of the 1960s deepened, though, voters increasingly turned to leaders who promised to defend the status quo. In 1966, movie actor Ronald Reagan rode a wave of hostility toward hippies, rioters, and student radicals to the office of governor in the state of California. Two years later, Richard Nixon was elected president as the self-proclaimed candidate of the "silent majority" that neither protested nor rebelled. Public opinion polls revealed intense hatred of anti-war radicals, members of the counterculture, feminists, and black protesters—even among those who agreed with many of their goals. The country's deep divisions came to a head in the spring of 1970, when construction workers in New York City physically assaulted an anti-war demonstration on the streets of the city.

The turmoil of the 1960s brought significant changes to the United States, particularly in the areas of race and gender, but it also left scars that can be felt to this day. Even as the unrest subsided and the sense of crisis receded, Americans continued to debate and to refight the decade's battles. In introducing a 1997 collection of essays entitled *Reassessing the Sixties*, political scientist Stephen Macedo observed that the controversies of the sixties "directly engaged fundamental American ideals of freedom and equality with a vigor and depth rarely matched before or since." The question, Macedo wrote, "is whether the changes associated with that notable decade represent a fuller realization of American ideals or their betrayal."[1]

For historians, though, a key question is *why* these issues came to be debated so ferociously in the 1960s. The racial and gender inequalities that polarized Americans in the 1960s had existed for generations. The Vietnam War was but one of a series of foreign wars fought by the United States, a number of which (including the Korean War of 1950–1953) were deeply unpopular. The 1950s was a decade of relative social calm that gave little indication of the storm that was to come. The United States had previously experienced periods of turmoil and strife. The Civil War of the 1860s left over 700,000 Americans dead. The industrial revolution of the late nineteenth century sparked mass protest among farmers and workers who believed that they were excluded from the benefits of this social and economic transformation. The Great Depression of the 1930s led many to fear for the nation's very survival. The 1960s, however, began as a decade of prosperity and confidence, with rising incomes and an improved standard of living for a wide range of Americans. Why, during this moment of unprecedented economic prosperity, did Americans find themselves so deeply divided?

---

1 Stephen Macedo, ed., *Reassessing the Sixties: Debating the Political and Cultural Legacy* (New York: W.W. Norton, 1997), 16.

TIMELINE

1954
United States Supreme Court's *Brown vs. Board of Education* decision declares racially segregated public schools to be unconstitutional. Orders desegregation of segregated schools with "all deliberate speed."

1955–1956
Montgomery bus boycott. Black residents of Montgomery, Alabama, refuse to ride city buses for a year in a successful protest of segregated seating.

1957
Local opposition to court-ordered desegregation of Central High School in Little Rock, Arkansas, sparks a wave of "massive resistance" to school desegregation across the South.

1960
Wave of sit-ins at segregated facilities across the South marks the emergence of a mass civil rights movement.

1961
President John F. Kennedy dispatches a small force of United States Special Forces troops to Vietnam. By 1963, 11,000 US military personnel are in the country.

1962
Students for a Democratic Society (SDS) holds its first national convention and issues the Port Huron Statement.

1963 (February)—Betty Friedan publishes *The Feminine Mystique*.

1963 (April–May)
Martin Luther King, Jr. leads mass demonstrations against Jim Crow in Birmingham, Alabama. Success of demonstrations inspires similar protests across the South in what King deems "The Year of the Negro Revolution."

1963 (August)
Approximately 225,000 civil rights demonstrators gather in Washington, DC, for a March for Jobs and Freedom. King delivers the "I Have a Dream Speech."

1963 (November)
President John F. Kennedy assassinated. Vice President Lyndon Johnson assumes the presidency.

1964 (July)—Congress passes a civil rights act that bans discrimination on the basis of race, color, religion, sex, or national origin in education, employment, and public accommodations (private businesses that directly serve the public.)

1964 (August)
United States launches first air strikes against Vietnam.

1964 (October–December)
Mass demonstrations against restrictions on political activity at the University of California-Berkeley mark the first of the great student uprisings of the 1960s.

1964 (November)
Lyndon Johnson reelected president in a landslide on a promise to make America a "Great Society" free from poverty and racism.

1965 (March)
First US ground combat forces arrive in Vietnam. By December, nearly 200,000 US ground troops are in Vietnam.

1965 (April)
First major anti-war demonstration, sponsored by SDS, held in Washington, DC.

1965 (July)—Congress passes a voting rights act that outlaws a variety of practices that had been used to deny black southerners the right to vote.

1965 (July)
Watts Riot. Six days of looting and arson in Los Angeles, California, results in thirty-four deaths (most neighborhood residents who died at the hands of law enforcement) and marks the beginning of the most destructive wave of urban riots in the nation's history.

1965–1968
Membership in SDS grows rapidly reaching an estimated 100,000 individuals.

1966 (May)
Stokely Carmichael elected chairman of the Student Nonviolent Coordinating Committee (a major civil rights organization) on a black power platform.

1966 (October)
Formation of the National Organization for Women (NOW).

1966 (October)
Formation of Black Panther Party for Self-Defense in Oakland, California.

1966
Emergence of countercultural scenes in cities such as San Francisco and Los Angeles centered on a newly developed form of "psychedelic" rock music.

1967
US troop strength in Vietnam reaches approximately 500,000.

1967 (May)
Black Panther Party gains national attention after members appear armed (which was allowed by law) at the California State Legislature to protest proposed legislation to ban the public display of firearms in urban areas. In the wake of this protest, the party experiences explosive nationwide growth in membership.

1967 (Summer)
The urban riots of the 1960s reach their peak. Major disturbances in Newark, New Jersey, and Detroit, Michigan, along with smaller incidents in dozens of cities and towns, leave nearly one hundred people dead and result in tens of millions of dollars of property damage.

1967 (Summer)
San Francisco's counterculture scene receives national media attention in what observers dub the "summer of love." Psychedelic rock performers such as the Doors, Jefferson Airplane, and Jimi Hendrix achieve mass commercial success.

1968
Turmoil of 1960s reaches such levels that some fear that the country is coming apart. Military setbacks in Vietnam significantly undermine public support for the war. President Lyndon Baines Johnson announces he will not seek re-election. Assassination of Martin Luther King, Jr. and presidential candidate Robert F. Kennedy shock the nation. King's murder sparks riots in African American communities around the country. Student strike shuts down Columbia University in New York City and helps to inspire a wave of protests on many college campuses. Large anti-war demonstrations outside the Democratic National Convention in Chicago in August met with police violence.

Feminist protests at the Miss America pageant in September gain national attention. Republican Richard M. Nixon elected president in November on a promise to return "law and order" to the country.

1969 (June)
Police harassment of gay and lesbian people in New York City's Greenwich Village leads to two days of mass street protests (the "Stonewall Riots") marking the emergence of the modern gay rights movement.

1969 (July)
Release of the "Redstockings Manifesto" marks the emergence of the women's liberation movement.

1969 (August)
Half a million young people attend the countercultural Woodstock music festival in upstate New York.

1969 (November)
Nearly one million people attend a massive anti-war march in Washington, DC. President Nixon asks for the nation's "silent majority" to support his policies in Vietnam.

1970 (May)
President Nixon expands Vietnam War into the neighboring nation of Cambodia sparking mass protests and student strikes at roughly four hundred university, college, and high school campuses. Ohio National Guard troops open fire on student protesters at Kent State University, leaving four dead. Police fire leaves two students dead at Jackson State College, a historically black campus in Mississippi. Anti-war protesters in New York City attacked by construction workers.

1972
Richard Nixon defeats anti-war candidate George McGovern and secures re-election in one of the largest presidential landslides in American history.

1973
Paris Peace Accords end direct US military involvement in Vietnam

HISTORIANS' CONVERSATIONS

POSITION #1—THE 1960S AND THE STRUGGLE FOR EQUALITY

More than two centuries ago a group of rebels founded a new nation dedicated to the proposition that all men are created equal and are endowed by their creator with certain unalienable rights. Ever since, Americans have struggled to live up to this promise. While this struggle often proceeds quietly, at times the gap between American principles and American practice explodes into turmoil and upheaval. In the 1860s, for instance, a bloody civil war erupted over the practice of human slavery. The industrial boom of the late nineteenth century created a vast and unprecedented gulf between rich and poor and provoked a wave of labor unrest. During the Great Depression of the 1930s, the federal government enacted a series of "New Deal" reforms designed to extend the blessings of American liberty to those who worked for wages. Left unaddressed by the New Deal reforms of the 1930s, however, were the inequalities of race and gender that had characterized the United States since its founding. In the 1960s, the country's racial and gender inequities forced the nation to once again confront the distance between American principles and American practice. Inspired by the southern civil rights movement, more and more people began to question the deeply rooted inequalities of American life. As Terry H. Anderson writes, "The irrepressible issues, the shocking events, forced citizens to consider disturbing questions—was America racist, imperialist, sexist? And the relentless demonstrations, the fires in the streets, forced neighbors to take a stand and decide publicly about policies concerning a legion of new topics—from civil rights to women's liberation."[1]

From the late nineteenth century through the depression decade of the 1930s, issues of labor and social class dominated American public life. The tone was set in July of 1877, when a nationwide strike of railroad workers left over one hundred people, mainly striking workers and their supporters, dead. From that point onward, communities around the United States were regularly rocked by tumultuous and often violent labor conflicts. Despite the efforts of both the union movement and social reformers, the oppressive conditions that produced this strife persisted well into the twentieth century. The economic collapse of the early 1930s forced the nation to finally confront the vast inequalities produced by industrialization. Under the leadership of President Franklin Delano Roosevelt, the nation implemented a series of "New Deal" reforms designed to provide dignity and security to American workers. Private-sector workers received the right to organize unions

1 Terry H. Anderson, *The Movement and the Sixties: Protest in America from Greensboro to Wounded Knee* (New York: Oxford University Press, 1995), xiii.

and bargain collectively, and by the 1950s, roughly one-third of American workers had the benefits of union representation—an all-time high. A social security system provided retirement benefits to the elderly, disability benefits for those unable to work, and unemployment insurance for those suffering from layoffs. The federal government established a minimum wage and declared the forty-hour work week to be the law of the land.

The economic boom of the post–World War II period was unprecedented less for the overall growth in the economy and more for the degree to which, for the first time, the benefits of this growth were broadly shared. This broadly shared prosperity, however, was not equally shared, as long-standing patterns of racial and gender inequality persisted into the postwar period. The most visible expression of these inequalities was the Jim Crow system of the American South, which imposed a form of second-class citizenship on black southerners. Although the open and legally sanctioned racism of Jim Crow was limited to the southern states, systematic job and housing discrimination confined African American people nationwide to overcrowded and decaying ghetto neighborhoods and restricted black access to better paying occupations, both blue and white collar. Women, as well, faced discriminatory attitudes and practices. Even as women's participation in paid employment steadily grew, deeply engrained assumptions that women's proper place was in the home kept college-educated women out of higher status professions (such as law and medicine) and restricted working-class women to lower paid jobs, such as clerical and retail work. Even harsher was the discrimination against gay and lesbian people. All fifty states considered "homosexual" behavior (as it was then called) a criminal offense punishable by imprisonment. Faced with social ostracism, harassment, and even physical violence, gay and lesbian people were forced to either deny their identities or to live double or closeted lives. By the early 1960s, gay and lesbian colonies had developed in a handful of major cities, like New York and San Francisco, but those who migrated there were often forced to sever ties with their previous lives and faced regular harassment from police vice squads who saw "homosexual" behavior as a morally odious illegal activity.

The first major challenge to the inequalities of the postwar period came in the form of a mass civil rights movement that emerged in the American South in the late 1950s and early 1960s. Advocates for racial justice had long struggled to overturn the South's Jim Crow system, but for most of the twentieth century, violence and repression had kept most black southerners from openly confronting their second-class status. In 1955 and 1956, though, virtually the entire African American population of Montgomery, Alabama, refrained from riding segregated city busses for an entire year, providing an example of successful mass resistance to racist oppression. Civil rights demonstrations gained strength across the South in the early 1960s, culminating in a wave of mass protests in the spring and summer of 1963. Civil rights leaders like Martin Luther King, Jr. pushed citizens to examine the gap between American ideals of equality and the nation's practices of racial exclusion.

The victories of the civil rights movement, enshrined in the Civil Rights Act of 1964 and Voting Rights Act of 1965, encouraged black people to challenge racist practices nationwide and helped fuel the rise of black power politics. Black power advocates called upon African American people to unite; to take pride in themselves, their history, and their culture; and to take control of the social, economic, and political institutions under which they lived. As black power advocate Stokely Carmichael put it, "Throughout this country, vast segments of the black communities are beginning to recognize the need to assert their own definitions, to reclaim their history, their culture; to create their own sense of community and togetherness."[2] The ideas of black power helped mobilize African American people to challenge the white power structures that dominated American cities, but resistance was great and change came slowly. In the mid- to late 1960s, years of frustration with the conditions of life within African American ghettoes exploded in a series of urban riots that shook American cities.

The southern civil rights movement inspired other groups to question the inequalities of American life. Idealistic young college students who participated in civil rights organizing, for instance, were some of the most important architects of the early New Left. The civil rights movement also primed many young people to be immediately skeptical of the US war in Vietnam. Government spokespeople justified direct US military intervention in Vietnam, which commenced in earnest in 1965, in terms of American principles of freedom and liberty. For many young people, however, the violence unleashed by the United States government on an impoverished Asian nation seemed more reminiscent of the police dogs and fire hoses used by racist southerners to suppress the civil rights movement. A growing and increasingly militant New Left began to see racism at home and imperialism abroad as two sides of the same coin—both products of an American establishment that would stop at nothing to defend its power and its privilege. The New Left even borrowed some of its most effective tactics, such as the sit-in, from the civil rights movement.

The nation's emerging feminist movement also took inspiration from the civil rights movement. In 1963, the very year of King's "I Have a Dream" speech, magazine writer Betty Friedan published *The Feminine Mystique*, a bestselling critique of a culture that told women that they could fulfill all their human needs solely in the roles of wife and mother. Reflecting the influence of the growing civil rights movement, Friedan urged women to seek an equal place in business, the workplace, politics, and government. Three years later, Friedan was among the founders of the National Organization for Women (NOW), a women's rights organization modeled closely on the National Association for the Advancement of Colored People (NAACP), the country's oldest and most prominent civil rights organization. By the late 1960s, a more radical brand of feminism termed "women's liberation" emerged that had striking similarities to the black power movement. Early leaders of women's liberation, many of whom were veterans of the New Left and civil rights efforts (both of which they had found to be suffused with sexist attitudes and behaviors) called upon women to unite as a sex to challenge the oppression that they saw permeating all aspects of American culture.

By the late 1960s, a host of excluded groups were organizing and demanding change in America. In 1968, for instance, a group of Native American activists gathered in Minneapolis, Minnesota, and founded the American Indian Movement (AIM), an organization that called

2 Stokely Carmichael and Charles V. Hamilton, *Black Power: The Politics of Liberation in America* (New York: Random House, 1967), 37.

for self-determination for native people and employed militant tactics to challenge federal policies that they believed promoted poverty and corruption on Indian reservations. In 1969, a police raid on the Stonewall Inn, a gay bar in New York City, prompted two days of rioting that gave birth to the modern gay and lesbian rights movement. The period also saw an upsurge in civil rights and labor organizing in the nation's Latino communities, exemplified by the struggle for farmworkers' rights led by Cesar Chavez. All of these struggles owed much to the example of the black civil rights movement, the first broad-based effort to challenge the racial and gender inequalities that characterized post–World War II America.

The New Deal reforms of the 1930s had addressed many of the most glaring inequalities and injustices of industrial America but had left much work to be done. The New Deal established the principle that all Americans had the right to share in the blessings of American prosperity, but persistent inequalities of race and gender had prevented many from sharing equally in those blessings. As had happened in previous periods of turmoil, the gap between American principles and American practice once again compelled Americans to demand change. "Why did millions of citizens become activists, take to the streets, and participate in the movement," asks historian Terry Anderson. "Activists felt that problems existing in the nation were inconsistent with the American ideal, with ideas expressed in the Declaration of Independence and the U.S. Constitution."[3] Though the 1960s was a harrowing decade for many who lived through it, Maurice Isserman and Michael Kazin remind us that "it is in just such eras of discord and conflict that Americans have shown themselves most likely to rediscover and live out the best traditions to be found in our national experience."[4]

---

3 Anderson, *The Movement and the Sixties*, xxi.

4 Maurice Isserman and Michael Kazin, *America Divided: The Civil War of the 1960s*, 2nd ed. (New York: Oxford University Press, 2004), 309.

POSITION #2—THE DESTRUCTIVE GENERATION OF THE 1960S

Over the generations, Americans have confronted many difficult challenges. For most of American history, however, the people of the United States have taken a patient and pragmatic approach toward social change. Americans have generally rejected utopian visions of social perfection and have understood that social progress comes gradually through hard work and sacrifice. In the 1960s, however, a new idea gained currency—that the world should conform, and conform immediately, to one's own desires and expectations. While most Americans held to traditional virtues of patience, pragmatism, and self-sacrifice, enough embraced this new utopian attitude to provoke a profound cultural crisis. While the social issues of the 1960s were real, it was the destructive response on the part of the so-called sixties generation (who were never more than a minority of post–World War II baby boomers) that made that decade one of crisis and upheaval. Blind to the ability of America's democratic institutions to change and adapt, these young rebels turned against those very institutions and the values that these institutions embodied.

Over time, some members of the "sixties generation" came to see the damage caused by their youthful excesses. Among the most prominent of these repentant radicals were Peter Collier and David Horowitz, a pair of former New Leftists who in 1984 shocked their former comrades by proclaiming their support for the re-election of President Ronald Reagan, a conservative Republican whose rise to prominence was fueled largely by widespread public revulsion toward hippies, protesters, black power militants, and women's liberationists. In a series of widely read essays and books (including the aptly titled *Destructive Generation*), Collier and Horowitz detailed, as only insiders could, the ways in which a childish anti-Americanism came to infect the social movements of the 1960s. As Collier and Horowitz wrote, the sixties was "a time when what began as American mischief matured into real destructiveness."[5]

As former radicals turned conservative activists, it is not surprising that Collier and Horowitz would take a dim view of the political and cultural rebellions of the 1960s. Their critique, however, has been shared by historians writing from a variety of ideological perspectives. Among the first scholarly accounts of the sixties came from Rutgers University professor William L. O'Neill, a self-identified liberal who lauded the great legislative

5 Peter Collier and David Horowitz, *Deconstructing the Left* (Lanham, MD: Second Thoughts Books, 1991), 8; Collier and Horowitz, *Destructive Generation: Second Thoughts about the Sixties* (New York: Summit Books, 1989).

accomplishments of the decade. Nevertheless, much of O'Neill's classic 1971 work *Coming Apart* chronicles the destructive outbursts of the late 1960s. Reflecting back years later, O'Neill condemned the cultural legacy of the era. "The pleasure principle," wrote O'Neill, "epitomized in the sixties in the odious mantra, 'Do your own thing,' has flourished beyond belief . . . In this respect selfishness is the principal bequest of the sixties." Writing from a different perspective, conservative historian Paul Johnson spoke of the sixties as a "decade of illusion" in which "normally circumspect men and women, who had once made a virtue out of prudence, and were to resume responsible behavior in due course, did foolish things."[6]

The naïve utopianism that defined the so-called "sixties generation" was a product of the times in which they lived. Coming of age in the postwar period, these young rebels had been spared the horrors of the Great Depression and World War II, the two great cataclysms of modern times. Their parents, having suffered intense deprivation and loss, had come to cherish both American freedoms (imperfect though they might be) and the opportunities that the postwar boom offered. Harsh personal experience had taught the depression-era generation to persevere through life's inevitable disappointments. Their children, by contrast, could take peace and prosperity for granted and lacked experience with the type of adversity that had shaped their parents' worldview. Shocked to discover the nation's flaws, the sheltered children of the postwar period insisted that America live up to their expectations of social perfection immediately. When the nation failed to comply with their unrealistic wishes, the sixties generation turned destructive.

Surely, the America of the sixties faced real problems, most especially the wrenching experience of a failed war in Vietnam and the challenge of providing women and minorities full participation in the blessings of American life. In every case, however, legitimate concerns regarding these genuine problems degenerated into destructive flights of fancy powered by moral self-righteousness and utopian dreams. Take, for instance, the issue of race. In the period after World War II, Americans increasingly came to understand that the second-class status of black people had to be ended, and practical steps were taken to achieve this goal. In 1948, President Harry S. Truman issued an executive order desegregating the United States Armed Forces. That same year, the Democratic Party (the historical party of white supremacy) endorsed a pro–civil rights plank in its national platform. The United States Supreme Court struck a significant blow against the South's Jim Crow system in its 1954 *Brown vs Board of Education* decision, which declared racially segregated schools to be in violation of the US Constitution. By the end of the 1950s, despite the massive resistance of arch segregationists, Jim Crow was on the defensive and on the path toward its ultimate demise. The emergence of a mass civil rights movement in the early 1960s struck the final blow. The Civil Rights Act of 1964 and Voting Rights Act of 1965, passed in response to the black freedom upsurge in the South, effectively outlawed Jim Crow and offered a set of tools to combat racial discrimination nationwide.

By the late 1960s, however, the civil rights movement had been eclipsed by "black power" militants whose impatience with the pace of progress led them to conclude that America was

6 William L. O'Neill, *Coming Apart: An Informal History of America in the 1960s* (Chicago: Ivan R. Dee, 2005), xviii; Paul Johnson, *Modern Times: The World from the Twenties to the Nineties*, revised edition (New York: HarperCollins, 1992), 613; Paul Johnson, *A History of the American People* (New York: HarperCollins, 1998), 845.

incapable of embracing meaningful change at all. Rejecting participation in a system they considered racist to the core, black power activists instead sought to either bring the system itself crashing down or to escape it via racial separatism. Ironically, it was this very system that had just produced the 1964 Civil Rights Act and the 1965 Voting Rights Act, two of the most powerfully anti-racist measures in American history. Rejecting Martin Luther King, Jr.'s call for inter-racial brotherhood, black power leaders propagated the illusion that African American people had the power to achieve liberation on their own, without outside support and assistance. Some black militants were openly anti-white, but even those who were not could barely contain their disdain for white America and all it stood for. And though black power activists denied responsibility for the wave of destructive urban riots that swept American cities in the latter half of the decade, their calls for "armed self-defense" and casual talk of "revolution" contributed to an atmosphere of violence in which ghetto residents came to see arson and looting as acceptable forms of protest. By the end of the decade, the country found itself trapped in a cycle of racial polarization and mutual recriminations. As historian William O'Neill writes, "Militance alienated the white allies Negroes needed if conditions were to improve. Things therefore worsened, making black militants even angrier."[7]

The women's movement followed a similar trajectory. Through the decades, the United States had made gradual progress in the direction of greater equality for women, a trend accelerated by the emergence of a revived women's rights movement in the mid-1960s. Like the civil rights movement from which they took inspiration, the feminists of the mid-1960s focused their energies on combatting specific forms of discrimination that prevented women from participating in the workplace and in public life on an equal basis. Inspired by authors like Betty Friedan, whose 1963 book *The Feminine Mystique* was a runaway bestseller, younger college-educated women increasingly chose to pursue careers in traditionally male-dominated professions like medicine and law. Over time, this gradual reformist approach was successful in opening up doors of opportunity in education and in the workplace that had long been closed.

By 1970, however, the pragmatism of Friedan and the other founders of modern feminism had been eclipsed by those who called for "women's liberation." Adherents of women's liberation, like the black power militants they mimicked, fashioned themselves as revolutionaries and set as their goal the destruction (rather than the reform) of the sexist systems that they saw pervading all aspects of women's lives. The Redstockings organization, a pioneering women's liberation group founded in 1969, declared the oppression of women to be "total" and maintained that men had stripped women of their very humanity. *All* men, they proclaimed, were oppressors.[8] Kate Millett, whose 1970 book *Sexual Politics*, became a foundational text of women's liberation, argued that women could only truly be free if the traditional family were dismantled. The extreme ideas of women's liberation alienated many, both male and female, who might otherwise have been supportive of the struggle for women's equality, and the penchant of feminist militants for engaging

---

7 William L. O'Neill, *Coming Apart: An Informal History of America in the 1960s* (New York: Random House, 1971), 175.

8 "Redstockings Manifesto," http://www.redstockings.org/index.php?option=com_content&view=article&id=76&Itemid=59

in outrageous and shocking forms of protest, such as the 1968 demonstrations at the Miss America pageant, only further undermined their cause.

While the excesses of women's liberation and black power had roots in legitimate racial and gender grievances, the same cannot be said of the romantic "revolutionaries" of the New Left and narcissistic dropouts of the counterculture. The New Left drew its greatest support from a privileged group—middle-class college students on elite campuses such as Columbia University, the University of Wisconsin–Madison, and the University of California–Berkeley. Products of sheltered upbringings, the student radicals of the 1960s were shocked to discover America's imperfections. Their response was to turn viciously against America and the institutions that were responsible for their own privilege. For the New Left, the escalation of the Vietnam War in 1965 was the key turning point. The early New Left was relatively small, optimistic in its outlook, and essentially harmless. With the escalation of the war, however, the student movement grew rapidly and became increasingly radical in its pronouncements and militant in its actions. The young radicals saw the war not merely as a mistake, but as evidence that America was a racist empire built upon the backs of non-white people both at home and abroad. By 1968, Students for a Democratic Society (SDS), the most influential of the New Left groups, was dominated by self-proclaimed revolutionaries whose goal was to undermine a wide range of American institutions, from the universities to the military.

The radicals of the New Left sought to subvert American institutions. The so-called hippies of the counterculture, by contrast, seemed content to merely mock them. From their outlandish dress and hairstyles, to their open advocacy of marijuana and psychedelic drugs, the hippies seemed determined, more than anything else, to shock and appall mainstream Americans. Psychedelic rock (their music of choice) was loud, brash, and completely inaccessible to those who were not among the initiates. Jefferson Airplane, a leading psychedelic rock band, summed up the hippie self-image on the 1969 album *Volunteers*:

> We are forces of chaos and anarchy,
> Everything they say we are we are,
> And we are very proud of ourselves.[9]

Hippies (or "freaks," as they sometimes preferred to be called) mocked mainstream America for its materialism, conformity, and soullessness. Of course, the economic prosperity that made the hippie lifestyle possible was a product of the very mainstream culture that they decried. In this sense, the counterculture epitomized the self-indulgence that characterized the political and cultural rebellions of the decade. And the proposition, advanced by the counterculture—that a better way of life could be built upon mind-altering drugs and rock music—typified the self-delusion and arrogance of the "sixties generation."

In explaining their break from their radical youth, conservative activists Collier and Horowitz declared that the time had finally arrived when they had to "learn to live with adulthood."[10] The issues of race and gender that helped to spark the movements of 1960s are, of course, still with us. We can only hope that the people of today confront these challenges with a wisdom and humility that was sorely lacking in the destructive generation of the 1960s.

---

9 Jefferson Airplane, "We Can Be Together," *Volunteers* (RCA Victor Records, 1969).

10 Collier and Horowitz, *Deconstructing the Left*, 24.

POSITION #3—THE DANGERS OF ILLUSION: THE UNRAVELLING OF THE POSTWAR CONSENSUS

Americans entered the 1960s with a sense of confidence and optimism that it is difficult for those who are products of today's cynical culture to fully comprehend. And yet to make sense of the sixties, it is necessary to set aside our own experience and imagine the world as it seemed to members of that confident and optimistic generation. In 1976, British journalist Godfrey Hodgson published *America in Our Time*, a book that remains among our most perceptive accounts of the 1960s and one that is particularly useful in helping us see through the eyes of the past. Hodgson spent much of the sixties covering the United States for British newspapers, and his experience gave him keen insights into the events of the decade. His 1976 book was aimed primarily at an American audience, and it was intended to help its readers come to terms with the troubling times they had just experienced. *America in Our Time* challenged its readers to confront their most deeply held political and cultural assumptions, for it was here that Hodgson believed lay the key to understanding the sixties. Most Americans, Hodgson argued, had entered the decade as adherents of what he terms "the ideology of the liberal consensus"—a set of interlocking ideas and beliefs that provided Americans with a profound faith in the basic soundness of the nation's economic and political institutions. "There was a sense at the beginning of the 1960s," he writes, "that the businessman and the unskilled laborer, the writer and the housewife, the Harvard University and the Strategic Air Command, International Business Machines and the labor movement, all had their parts to play in one harmonious political, intellectual, and economic system."[11] No social system, however, is fully harmonious nor is any nation without its flaws and dysfunctions. As Americans discovered this uncomfortable truth, the result was a crisis of faith that challenged the legitimacy of virtually every social institution.

Hodgson pointed out that the post–World War II period was a time of unusual consensus (broad-based agreement) in American politics and culture. Most Americans accepted the basic goodness of nation's free enterprise system, particularly as modified by the New Deal reforms of the 1930s. Gone was the unrestrained capitalism of the past with its barbaric working conditions, its vast gulf between rich and poor, and its painful cycles of

---

11 Godfrey Hodgson, *America in Our Time: From World War II to Nixon, What Happened and Why?* (Garden City, NY: Doubleday, 1976), 12.

boom and bust. In its place stood a modern, regulated economy in which enlightened government policy and powerful labor unions ensured that the benefits of economic growth were broadly shared and that economic catastrophes like the Great Depression would not be repeated. The postwar boom, it seemed, was eliminating misery and want. Rapid wage growth, the nation's leaders proclaimed, was bringing industrial workers into the great American middle class. The unprecedented productivity of the American economy, many assumed, made conflicts over wealth and resources obsolete as the relentless class struggles of the age of industrialization faded into historical memory. Thoughtful Americans did recognize a variety of social problems (from racial discrimination to "juvenile delinquency," as it was then termed) but were confident that the nation had the resources and expertise to meet these challenges. And few doubted that the booming economy could generate the resources needed to solve these problems without pitting one social group against another.

There were dissenters from this liberal consensus on both the left and right, but by the late 1950s such skeptics had been pushed to the margins of American politics and culture. Gone were the radical voices of earlier decades that called for the break-up of corporate monopolies and for the empowerment of the working classes. And the dead-end conservatives who continued to rail against the New Deal and the dangers of intrusive government were mostly ignored by the political mainstream. The leaders of both major political parties embraced and even celebrated the postwar domestic status quo and agreed that the greatest challenge facing the nation was the threat posed by the international communist movement and the Soviet Union, the great communist superpower. Indeed, the chief item of dispute in the 1960 presidential election was whether Democrat John F. Kennedy or Republican Richard M. Nixon would be better able to meet the communist threat.

By the early 1970s, this political and cultural consensus lay in tatters. In its place was a cacophony of bitter and frustrated voices railing against each other and against the nation's institutions. As it turned out, neither the New Deal reforms of the 1930s nor the booming postwar economy had resolved America's deep structural inequalities—inequalities that led the nation to fracture along racial, gender, and class lines in the 1960s. As Americans from a variety of backgrounds were forced to confront a series of challenges that defied easy solutions, the naïve optimism of the postwar consensus turned into bitterness and disillusionment. It was perhaps inevitable that illusions of the postwar consensus would be shattered; the nation's inequalities and submerged social divisions were simply too deep to ignore. Nevertheless, the very confidence that the postwar consensus promoted left Americans ill-prepared to face the difficult challenges of the 1960s and left many struggling to make sense of what had gone wrong.

The evolution of the black freedom movement typifies the progression from naïve optimism to embittered frustration. The civil rights movement of the early 1960s, while challenging inequalities of race, assumed the basic soundness of American institutions and saw its mission as that of opening up doors of opportunity so that African American people could share in the benefits of American capitalism. African American people, argued Martin Luther King, Jr., inhabited a "lonely island of economic insecurity in the midst of a vast ocean of material prosperity" confined there by a pattern of discrimination that denied them "normal education and normal social and economic opportunities."[12] Simply provide access to educational and economic opportunities, King believed, and black people could share in the bounty of the postwar boom. In truth, however, racial inequalities were deeply imbedded within the structure of American capitalism. As black activists discovered this fact, they simply flipped King's optimistic formula on its head. Rather than seeking access to social and economic institutions that they saw as irredeemably flawed, black power advocates sought to escape them by constructing racially defined institutions of their own. By the late 1960s, King himself had come to recognize the deep structural roots of racial inequality. This realization (along with the war in Vietnam) led him to a profound crisis of faith and a growing fear that if the nation did not undergo what he termed a "revolution of values" it faced the prospect of a "spiritual death."[13]

The New Left followed a similar pattern. Products of the optimistic postwar years, the young idealists who founded groups like Students for Democratic Society (SDS) believed deeply in American ideals. "When we were kids the United States was the wealthiest and strongest country in the world," proclaimed the 1962 Port Huron Statement, the founding document of SDS. "Freedom and equality for each individual, government of, by, and for the people—these American values we found good, principles by which we could live as men"[14] It was the gap between these ideals and that nation's practices that first compelled the student radicals to action. Yet, as they learned just how deeply America's inequalities reached, a profound sense of disillusionment set in. The War in Vietnam, the failures of President Lyndon Johnson's anti-poverty programs, the urban riots, and the violence to which both civil rights and anti-war protesters were subjected, all served to radicalize the New Left. Their optimistic image of America shattered, by the late 1960s student radicals had concluded that the American myth was, in fact, an outright lie, and they set out to subvert the institutions that had deceived them. Idealistic calls for social reform were replaced by calls for revolution and, in some cases, by an embrace of political violence. The New Left bequeathed this sense of outrage and betrayal to the women's liberation movement to which it helped give birth.

The 1960s counterculture was the most profound expression of this growing disillusionment. As with the New Left, the hippie lifestyle held its greatest appeal for middle-class youth to whom the "American Dream" was offered on the proverbial silver platter. Despite their unprecedented access to material prosperity and educational opportunities, a significant number of such youth felt let down by mainstream America, particularly in the context of the unpopular war in Vietnam. In response, they embraced a bohemian way of life that flouted conventional definitions of success. Although the numbers of youth who "dropped out" to join the countercultural colonies that developed in communities across the country was relatively small, the wider popularity of rock music, marijuana and psychedelic drugs

12 Martin Luther King, Jr., *Why We Can't Wait* (New York: Harper & Row, 1964), 23.

13 Martin Luther King, Jr., "Beyond Vietnam—Breaking Silence," *American Rhetoric Online Speech Bank*, http://www.americanrhetoric.com/speeches/mlkatimetobreaksilence.htm

14 "The Port Huron Statement of the Students for a Democratic Society, 1962," http://www.h-net.org/~hst306/documents/huron.html

like LSD, and alternative clothing and hairstyles reflected a broader sense of disillusionment with mainstream American culture and the opportunities that it offered.

Perhaps the greatest illusion of the postwar years was the widespread belief that the booming economy had dissolved the nation's class divisions, a belief shattered by the conservative backlash. While many blue collar white workers did enjoy relative prosperity during the postwar period, their membership in the "middle class" was precarious at best, as they faced financial and status insecurities that were largely alien to college-educated professionals. When they saw young affluent rebels spurn opportunities that they themselves lacked and attack elite universities that neither they nor their children had the privilege to attend, they seethed. When they saw hippies mock their cultural values, they fumed. And when they saw political leaders like President Lyndon Baines Johnson declare war on poverty and racism, they reflected on their own economic struggles and embraced politicians like President Richard Nixon and his vice president Spiro Agnew who sang the praises of the "silent majority" of Americans who endured life's hardships without complaint or protest. The backlash, originally aimed at the various cultural and political rebellions of the decade, was ultimately harnessed by conservative politicians like California's Ronald Reagan to challenge the very idea of an activist problem-solving government, an article of postwar liberal faith. This growing cynicism toward government activism helped pave the way for the election of Reagan to the presidency in 1980 on a platform that declared the government itself to be the problem, rather than a source of solutions.

The postwar liberal consensus, Hodgson writes, "equipped the United States with an elaborately interrelated structure of coherent and plausible working assumptions, all poised like an inverted pyramid on two fundamental assumptions, both of which happened to be diametrically wrong." The American free enterprise system had not produced a harmonious social order free from serious social conflict. Nor did the nation's greatest challenges lie abroad.[15] While the New Deal reforms of the 1930s had addressed many of the worst abuses of American capitalism and provided many working people with a degree of economic security that they had previously lacked, deeply rooted social inequalities persisted. The college-educated and the non-college-educated inhabited vastly different social worlds in the postwar United States, as did black and white, and these fissures were woven into the very fabric of American life. Unbeknownst to the nation and its leaders, it was these rifts rather than the threat of foreign communism that posed the country's greatest challenge.

The postwar consensus fostered a set of false expectations that ill-prepared Americans to confront the controversies of the 1960s. When optimistic illusions were shattered by the rush of events, the result was bitterness and disillusion. Americans lost faith in their institutions and their leaders, and they turned on each. Pre-existing racial and class divides ruptured, and the wounds of the battles that followed hang like shadows over the nation to this day. The crisis of the 1960s exposed America's persistent social divisions. So long as the depth of these divides goes unrecognized, the ghost of the sixties will remain.

---

15 Hodgson, *America in Our Time*, 97.

DEBATING THE QUESTION

ECONOMIC DATA FROM THE POSTWAR BOOM

The period after World War II was a time of rapid economic growth in which the benefits of the economic expansion were more broadly shared than in any other time in American history before or since. The unique economic circumstances of the postwar period can be examined through a variety of types of economic data.

GUIDING QUESTIONS:

- What do the statistics provided in each individual graph reveal about economic conditions in the United States after World War II?
- What, if anything, do the statistics in each individual graph reveal about the ways in which economic conditions in the period after World War II differed from the eras that came before and after?

REAL PER CAPITA INCOME

Per capita income measures the total income earned within a nation divided by the nation's population. "Real" per capita income takes into account the impact of inflation to provide a measure of how actual purchasing power per person in a nation changes over time. It is among the most common measures of a nation's economic well-being. One drawback of per capita income as a measure of well-being is that it does not provide any information regarding how income growth is distributed among people at different income levels. Nor does it measure elements of well-being that do not have a dollar value.

REAL MEDIAN FAMILY INCOME

Median family income represents the exact middle point in the distribution of family income—half of all families earn more than the median family income and half of all families earn less. Real median family income takes into account the impact of inflation. Median family income provides a measure of the economic well-being of the typical family.

REAL HOURLY WAGES AND COMPENSATION OF PRIVATE PRODUCTION AND NON-SUPERVISORY WORKERS

This graph shows the changes in the average earnings of private sector workers, taking into account the impact of inflation. "Wages" refers to the actual cash wages earned by

TABLE 1 REAL PER CAPITA INCOME, 1920–1980 (1996 DOLLARS)

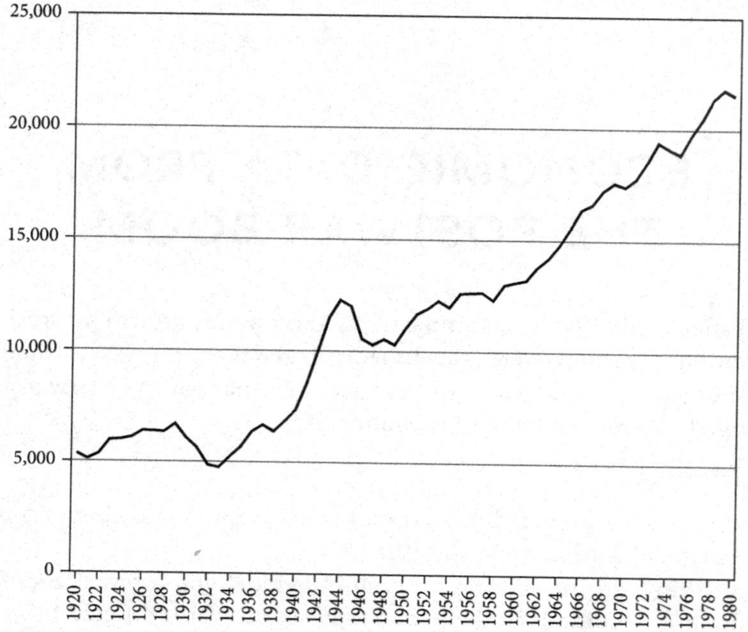

Data taken from *Historical Statistics of the United States*, millennial edition, Vol 3., *Economic Structure and Performance* (New York: Cambridge University Press, 2006), 3-25–3-26.

TABLE 2 REAL MEDIAN FAMILY INCOME, 1947–2010

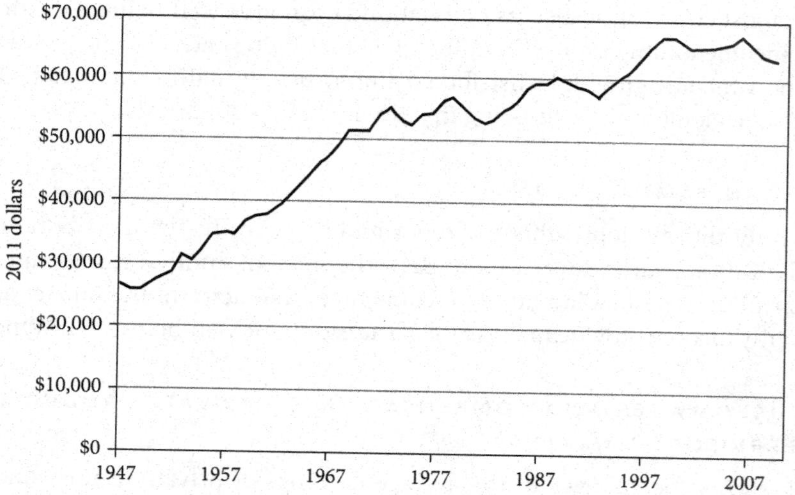

From Lawrence Mischel et al., *The State of Working America*, 12th ed. (Ithaca, NY: Cornell University Press, 2012), 41.

TABLE 3 REAL HOURLY WAGES AND COMPENSATION OF PRIVATE PRODUCTION AND NON-SUPERVISORY WORKERS, 1947–2011

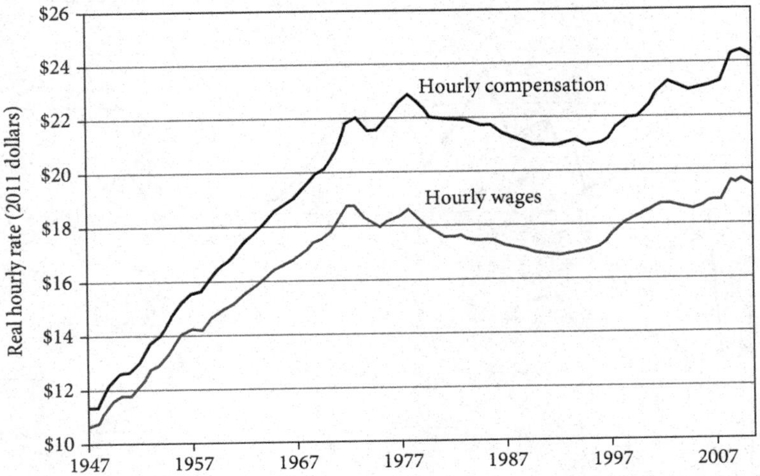

Production and non-supervisory workers excludes higher paid managers and supervisors. It comprises about 80% of all wage and salary workers. Hourly compensation includes the value of benefits plus the value of wages.

From Lawrence Mischel et al., *The State of Working America*, 12th ed. (Ithaca, NY: Cornell University Press, 2012), 185.

the average private sector worker. "Compensation" refers to cash wages plus the value of employment benefits provided by employers. Higher earning managers and supervisors are excluded from this measure.

REAL VALUE OF THE MINIMUM WAGE

This graph shows the actual purchasing power of the federal minimum wage, taking into account the impact of inflation. The jagged nature of the line is a result of periodic increases in the minimum wage followed by its gradual loss of purchasing power due to inflation.

UNEMPLOYMENT

The unemployment rate measures the percentage of the labor force that is out of work at any given time. The labor force is defined as all those who either have a job or who are actively seeking a job. Those who have given up looking for a job are not considered part of the labor force. The civilian labor force excludes those currently serving in the military.

UNION DENSITY

Union density measures the percentage of workers who are members of labor unions. Union density is the most common measure of the economic influence of labor unions.

TABLE 4 REAL VALUE OF THE MINIMUM WAGE, 1947–2009 (2009 DOLLARS)

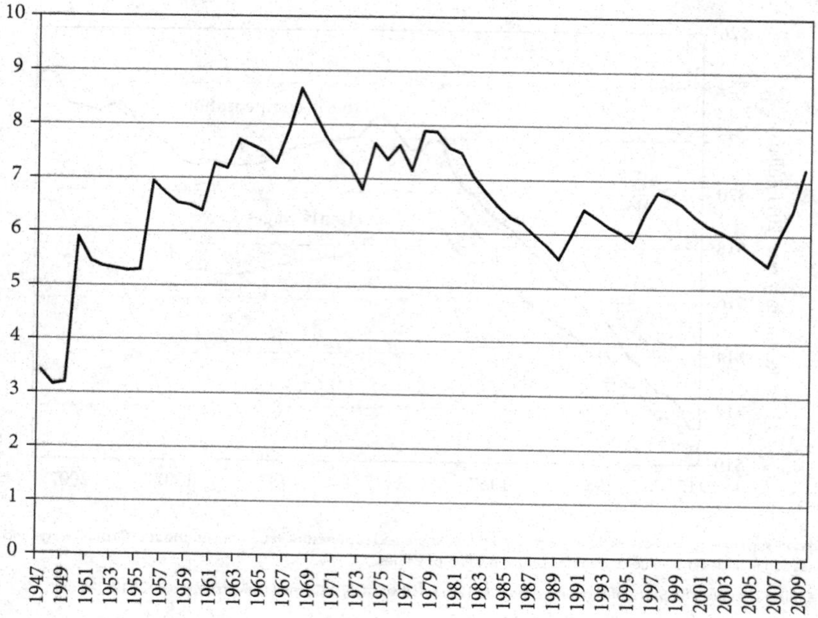

Data taken from Economic Policy Institute Analysis based on data from the US Department of Labor.

TABLE 5 UNEMPLOYMENT RATE, 1900–1990 (PERCENTAGE OF CIVILIAN LABOR FORCE)

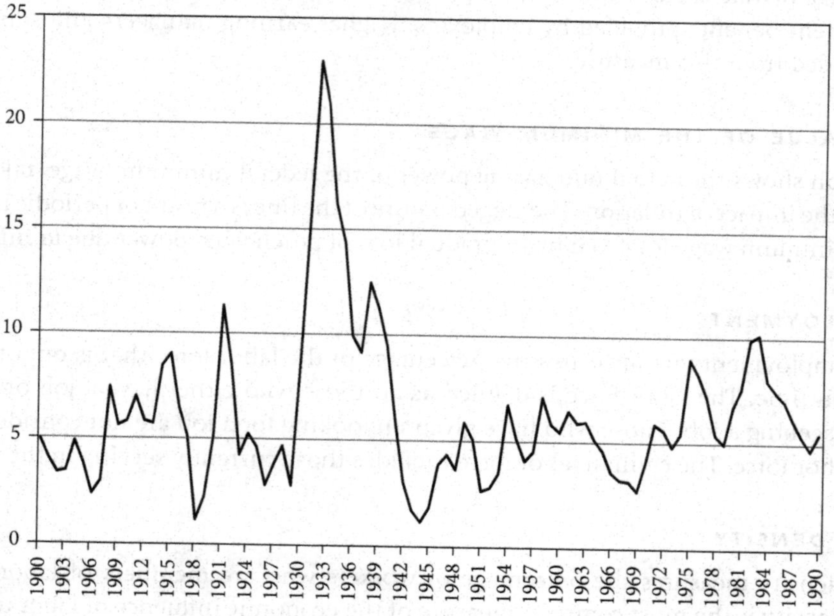

Data from *Historical Statistics of the United States*, millennial edition, Vol 2., *Work and Welfare* (New York: Cambridge University Press, 2006), 2-82–2-83.

TABLE 6 UNION DENSITY: UNION MEMBERSHIP AS A PERCENTAGE OF NONAGRICULTURAL EMPLOYMENT, 1880–1999

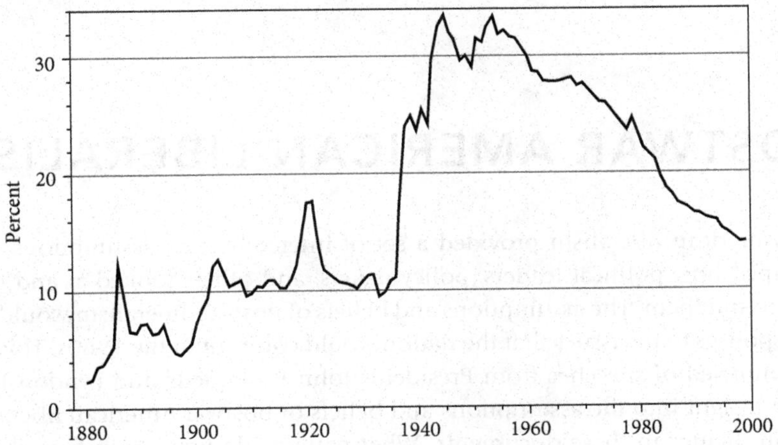

From *Historical Statistics of the United States*, millennial edition, Vol 2. *Work and Welfare* (New York: Cambridge University Press, 2006), 2-56.

DRAWING CONCLUSIONS:

- Taken together, what do these statistics reveal about economic conditions in the United States in the post–World War II period?
- How did economic conditions during the postwar period differ from the time period that came before and after?

POSTWAR AMERICAN LIBERALISM

Postwar American liberalism provided a set of interconnected assumptions and beliefs that shaped how political leaders, policymakers, and others looked at and understood the world around them. The assumptions and beliefs of postwar liberalism would also shape people's responses to the issues that the nation would confront in the 1960s. This set of documents, comprised of speeches from Presidents John F. Kennedy and Lyndon B. Johnson, can provide insight into the assumptions and beliefs of postwar American liberalism. Look for common themes in these documents. What patterns do you see in how these various leaders describe the problems and challenges facing the United States?

1.1 JOHN F. KENNEDY, "PRESIDENTIAL INAUGURAL ADDRESS" AND "MESSAGE TO CONGRESS" (1961)

John F. Kennedy emerged victorious from the 1960 presidential election and took office in January of 1961. In his inaugural address, Kennedy set forth an overall vision for his administration. Several months later, he sent a message to the Congress that included a request for funding that would allow America's space program to place a person on the moon by the end of the decade. Although the content of the two speeches is quite different, it is still possible to identify common themes and assumptions. By doing so, we can gain insights into the nature of postwar American liberalism.

GUIDING QUESTIONS:

- In his inauguration speech, what does JFK define as the central challenge facing the United States? Why does he say it is so important for the people of the United States to meet this challenge?
- In his message to Congress, why does JFK say it is essential for the United States to reach the moon by the end of the decade?
- How would you describe the tone of these two documents? Optimistic? Pessimistic? Angry? Cynical? Hopeful? Something else?

PRESIDENTIAL INAUGURAL ADDRESS

JOHN F. KENNEDY

JANUARY 20, 1961

We observe today not a victory of party, but a celebration of freedom—symbolizing an end, as well as a beginning—signifying renewal, as well as change. For I have sworn before you and Almighty God the same solemn oath our forebears prescribed nearly a century and three quarters ago.

The world is very different now. For man holds in his mortal hands the power to abolish all forms of human poverty and all forms of human life. And yet the same revolutionary beliefs for which our forebears fought are still at issue around the globe—the belief that the rights of man come not from the generosity of the state, but from the hand of God.

We dare not forget today that we are the heirs of that first revolution. Let the word go forth from this time and place, to friend and foe alike, that the torch has been passed to a new generation of Americans—born in this century, tempered by war, disciplined by a hard and bitter peace, proud of our ancient heritage—and unwilling to witness or permit the slow undoing of those human rights to which this Nation has always been committed, and to which we are committed today at home and around the world.

Let every nation know, whether it wishes us well or ill, that we shall pay any price, bear any burden, meet any hardship, support any friend, oppose any

From the John F. Kennedy Presidential Museum and Library, https://www.jfklibrary.org/archives/other-resources/john-f-kennedy-speeches/inaugural-address-19610120 foe, in order to assure the survival and the success of liberty.

This much we pledge—and more.

To those old allies whose cultural and spiritual origins we share, we pledge the loyalty of faithful friends. United, there is little we cannot do in a host of cooperative ventures. Divided, there is little we can do—for we dare not meet a powerful challenge at odds and split asunder.

To those new States whom we welcome to the ranks of the free, we pledge our word that one form of colonial control shall not have passed away merely to be replaced by a far more iron tyranny. We shall not always expect to find them supporting our view. But we shall always hope to find them strongly supporting their own freedom—and to remember that, in the past, those who foolishly sought power by riding the back of the tiger ended up inside.

To those peoples in the huts and villages across the globe struggling to break the bonds of mass misery, we pledge our best efforts to help them help themselves, for whatever period is required—not because the Communists may be doing it, not because we seek their votes, but because it is right. If a free society cannot help the many who are poor, it cannot save the few who are rich.

To our sister republics south of our border, we offer a special pledge—to convert our good words into good deeds—in a new alliance for progress—to assist free men and free governments in casting off the chains of poverty. But this peaceful revolution of hope cannot become the prey of hostile powers. Let all our neighbors know that we shall join with them to oppose aggression or subversion anywhere in the Americas. And let every other power know that this Hemisphere intends to remain the master of its own house.

To that world assembly of sovereign states, the United Nations, our last best hope in an age where the instruments of war have far outpaced the instruments of peace, we renew our pledge of support—to prevent it from becoming merely a forum for invective—to strengthen its shield of the new and the weak—and to enlarge the area in which its writ may run.

Finally, to those nations who would make themselves our adversary, we offer not a pledge but a request: that both sides begin anew the quest for peace, before the dark powers of destruction unleashed by science engulf all humanity in planned or accidental self-destruction.

We dare not tempt them with weakness. For only when our arms are sufficient beyond doubt can we be certain beyond doubt that they will never be employed.

But neither can two great and powerful groups of nations take comfort from our present course—both sides overburdened by the cost of modern weapons, both rightly alarmed by the steady spread of the deadly atom, yet both racing to alter that uncertain balance of terror that stays the hand of mankind's final war.

So let us begin anew—remembering on both sides that civility is not a sign of weakness, and sincerity is always subject to proof. Let us never negotiate out of fear. But let us never fear to negotiate.

Let both sides explore what problems unite us instead of belaboring those problems which divide us.

Let both sides, for the first time, formulate serious and precise proposals for the inspection and control of arms—and bring the absolute power to destroy other nations under the absolute control of all nations.

Let both sides seek to invoke the wonders of science instead of its terrors. Together let us explore the stars, conquer the deserts, eradicate disease, tap the ocean depths, and encourage the arts and commerce.

Let both sides unite to heed in all corners of the earth the command of Isaiah—to "undo the heavy burdens and to let the oppressed go free."

And if a beachhead of cooperation may push back the jungle of suspicion, let both sides join in creating a new endeavor, not a new balance of power, but a new world of law, where the strong are just and the weak secure and the peace preserved.

All this will not be finished in the first 100 days. Nor will it be finished in the first 1,000 days, nor in the life of this Administration, nor even perhaps in our lifetime on this planet. But let us begin.

In your hands, my fellow citizens, more than in mine, will rest the final success or failure of our course. Since this country was founded, each generation of Americans has been summoned to give testimony to its national loyalty. The graves of young

Americans who answered the call to service surround the globe.

Now the trumpet summons us again—not as a call to bear arms, though arms we need; not as a call to battle, though embattled we are—but a call to bear the burden of a long twilight struggle, year in and year out, "rejoicing in hope, patient in tribulation"—a struggle against the common enemies of man: tyranny, poverty, disease, and war itself.

Can we forge against these enemies a grand and global alliance, North and South, East and West, that can assure a more fruitful life for all mankind? Will you join in that historic effort?

In the long history of the world, only a few generations have been granted the role of defending freedom in its hour of maximum danger. I do not shrink from this responsibility—I welcome it. I do not believe that any of us would exchange places with any other people or any other generation. The energy, the faith, the devotion which we bring to this endeavor will light our country and all who serve it—and the glow from that fire can truly light the world.

And so, my fellow Americans: ask not what your country can do for you—ask what you can do for your country.

My fellow citizens of the world: ask not what America will do for you, but what together we can do for the freedom of man.

Finally, whether you are citizens of America or citizens of the world, ask of us the same high standards of strength and sacrifice which we ask of you. With a good conscience our only sure reward, with history the final judge of our deeds, let us go forth to lead the land we love, asking His blessing and His help, but knowing that here on earth God's work must truly be our own.

MESSAGE TO CONGRESS

JOHN F. KENNEDY, MAY 25, 1961

. . . Finally, if we are to win the battle that is now going on around the world between freedom and tyranny, the dramatic achievements in space which occurred in recent weeks should have made clear to us all, as did the Sputnik in 1957, the impact of this adventure on the minds of men everywhere, who are attempting to make a determination of which road they should take. Since early in my term, our efforts in space have been under review. With the advice of the Vice President, who is Chairman of the National Space Council, we have examined where we are strong and where we are not, where we may succeed and where we may not. Now it is time to take longer strides—time for a great new American enterprise—time for this nation to take a clearly leading role in space achievement, which in many ways may hold the key to our future on earth.

I believe we possess all the resources and talents necessary. But the facts of the matter are that we have never made the national decisions or marshalled the national resources required for such leadership. We have never specified long-range goals on an urgent time schedule, or managed our resources and our time so as to insure their fulfillment.

Recognizing the head start obtained by the Soviets with their large rocket engines, which gives them many months of lead-time, and recognizing the likelihood that they will exploit this lead for some time to come in still more impressive successes, we nevertheless are required to make new efforts on our own. For while we cannot guarantee that we shall one day be first, we can guarantee that any failure to make this effort will make us last. We take an additional risk by making it in full view of the world, but as shown by the feat of astronaut Shepard, this very risk enhances our stature when we are successful. But this is not merely a race. Space is open to us now; and our eagerness to share its meaning is not governed by the efforts of others. We go into space because whatever mankind must undertake, free men must fully share.

I therefore ask the Congress, above and beyond the increases I have earlier requested for space activities, to provide the funds which are needed to meet the following national goals:

From the National Aeronautics and Space Administration, https://www.nasa.gov/vision/space/features/jfk_speech_text.html

First, I believe that this nation should commit itself to achieving the goal, before this decade is out, of landing a man on the moon and returning him safely to the earth. No single space project in this period will be more impressive to mankind, or more important for the long-range exploration of space; and none will be so difficult or expensive to accomplish. We propose to accelerate the development of the appropriate lunar space craft. We propose to develop alternate liquid and solid fuel boosters, much larger than any now being developed, until certain which is superior. We propose additional funds for other engine development and for unmanned explorations—explorations which are particularly important for one purpose which this nation will never overlook: the survival of the man who first makes this daring flight. But in a very real sense, it will not be one man going to the moon—if we make this judgment affirmatively, it will be an entire nation. For all of us must work to put him there.

Secondly, an additional 23 million dollars, together with 7 million dollars already available, will accelerate development of the Rover nuclear rocket. This gives promise of some day providing a means for even more exciting and ambitious exploration of space, perhaps beyond the moon, perhaps to the very end of the solar system itself.

Third, an additional 50 million dollars will make the most of our present leadership, by accelerating the use of space satellites for world-wide communications.

Fourth, an additional 75 million dollars—of which 53 million dollars is for the Weather Bureau—will help give us at the earliest possible time a satellite system for world-wide weather observation.

Let it be clear—and this is a judgment which the Members of the Congress must finally make—let it be clear that I am asking the Congress and the country to accept a firm commitment to a new course of action, a course which will last for many years and carry very heavy costs: 531 million dollars in fiscal '62—an estimated seven to nine billion dollars additional over the next five years. If we are to go only half way, or reduce our sights in the face of difficulty, in my judgment it would be better not to go at all.

Now this is a choice which this country must make, and I am confident that under the leadership of the Space Committees of the Congress, and the Appropriating Committees, that you will consider the matter carefully.

It is a most important decision that we make as a nation. But all of you have lived through the last four years and have seen the significance of space and the adventures in space, and no one can predict with certainty what the ultimate meaning will be of mastery of space.

I believe we should go to the moon. But I think every citizen of this country as well as the Members of the Congress should consider the matter carefully in making their judgment, to which we have given attention over many weeks and months, because it is a heavy burden, and there is no sense in agreeing or desiring that the United States take an affirmative position in outer space, unless we are prepared to do the work and bear the burdens to make it successful. If we are not, we should decide today and this year.

This decision demands a major national commitment of scientific and technical manpower, materiel and facilities, and the possibility of their diversion from other important activities where they are already thinly spread. It means a degree of dedication, organization and discipline which have not always characterized our research and development efforts. It means we cannot afford undue work stoppages, inflated costs of material or talent, wasteful interagency rivalries, or a high turnover of key personnel.

New objectives and new money cannot solve these problems. They could in fact, aggravate them further—unless every scientist, every engineer, every serviceman, every technician, contractor, and civil servant gives his personal pledge that this nation will move forward, with the full speed of freedom, in the exciting adventure of space.

DRAWING CONCLUSIONS:

- What similarities do you see in the tone and content of the two Kennedy speeches?
- What can we learn from these speeches about the assumptions and beliefs of postwar American liberalism?

1.2 LYNDON B. JOHNSON, THE "GREAT SOCIETY" SPEECH (1964)

Vice President Lyndon Johnson assumed the office of president in November 1963 following the assassination of John F. Kennedy. The following year, Johnson sought re-election to a full term as president. As he campaigned for re-election, Johnson challenged the public to work with him to make the United States a "Great Society" free from racial inequality and poverty. After his landslide 1964 re-election victory, Johnson worked with the Congress to enact a series of new laws and new federal programs designed to achieve his vision of a Great Society. Johnson's Great Society initiative is often considered to be the high-point of postwar American liberalism.

Johnson announced his goal to make American a "Great Society" in a May 1964 speech at the University of Michigan.

GUIDING QUESTIONS:

- What does LBJ mean by the "Great Society"?
- What does he say must be done to make the United States a "Great Society"?
- Why does he believe the United States must become a "Great Society"?
- How would you describe the tone of the speech? Optimistic? Pessimistic? Angry? Cynical? Hopeful? Something else?

THE "GREAT SOCIETY" SPEECH

LYNDON BAINES JOHNSON

MAY 22, 1964

UNIVERSITY OF MICHIGAN; ANN ARBOR, MICHIGAN

I have come today from the turmoil of your Capital to the tranquility of your campus to speak about the future of your country.

The purpose of protecting the life of our Nation and preserving the liberty of our citizens is to pursue the happiness of our people. Our success in that pursuit is the test of our success as a Nation.

For a century we labored to settle and to subdue a continent. For half a century we called upon unbounded invention and untiring industry to create an order of plenty for all of our people.

The challenge of the next half century is whether we have the wisdom to use that wealth to enrich and elevate our national life, and to advance the quality of our American civilization.

Your imagination, your initiative, and your indignation will determine whether we build a society where progress is the servant of our needs, or a society where old values and new visions are buried under unbridled growth. For in your time we have the opportunity to move not only toward the rich society and the powerful society, but upward to the Great Society.

The Great Society rests on abundance and liberty for all. It demands an end to poverty and racial injustice, to which we are totally committed in our time. But that is just the beginning.

From *The Michigan Quarterly Review* 3 (Fall 1964): 230–232.

The Great Society is a place where every child can find knowledge to enrich his mind and to enlarge his talents. It is a place where leisure is a welcome chance to build and reflect, not a feared cause of boredom and restlessness. It is a place where the city of man serves not only the needs of the body and the demands of commerce but the desire for beauty and the hunger for community.

It is a place where man can renew contact with nature. It is a place which honors creation for its own sake and for what it adds to the understanding of the race. It is a place where men are more concerned with the quality of their goals than the quantity of their goods.

But most of all, the Great Society is not a safe harbor, a resting place, a final objective, a finished work. It is a challenge constantly renewed, beckoning us toward a destiny where the meaning of our lives matches the marvelous products of our labor.

So I want to talk to you today about three places where we begin to build the Great Society—in our cities, in our countryside, and in our classrooms.

Many of you will live to see the day, perhaps 50 years from now, when there will be 400 million Americans—four-fifths of them in urban areas. In the remainder of this century urban population will double, city land will double, and we will have to build homes, highways, and facilities equal to all those built since this country was first settled. So in the next 40 years we must re-build the entire urban United States.

Aristotle said: "Men come together in cities in order to live, but they remain together in order to live the good life." It is harder and harder to live the good life in American cities today.

The catalog of ills is long: there is the decay of the centers and the despoiling of the suburbs. There is not enough housing for our people or transportation for our traffic. Open land is vanishing and old landmarks are violated.

Worst of all expansion is eroding the precious and time honored values of community with neighbors and communion with nature.

The loss of these values breeds loneliness and boredom and indifference.

Our society will never be great until our cities are great. Today the frontier of imagination and innovation is inside those cities and not beyond their borders.

New experiments are already going on. It will be the task of your generation to make the American city a place where future generations will come, not only to live but to live the good life.

I understand that if I stayed here tonight I would see that Michigan students are really doing their best to live the good life.

This is the place where the Peace Corps was started. It is inspiring to see how all of you, while you are in this country, are trying so hard to live at the level of the people.

A second place where we begin to build the Great Society is in our countryside. We have always prided ourselves on being not only America the strong and America the free, but America the beautiful. Today that beauty is in danger. The water we drink, the food we eat, the very air that we breathe, are threatened with pollution. Our parks are overcrowded, our seashores overburdened. Green fields and dense forests are disappearing.

A few years ago we were greatly concerned about the "Ugly American." Today we must act to prevent an ugly America.

For once the battle is lost, once our natural splendor is destroyed, it can never be recaptured. And once man can no longer walk with beauty or wonder at nature his spirit will wither and his sustenance be wasted.

A third place to build the Great Society is in the classrooms of America. There your children's lives will be shaped. Our society will not be great until every young mind is set free to scan the farthest reaches of thought and imagination. We are still far from that goal.

Today, 8 million adult Americans, more than the entire population of Michigan, have not finished 5 years of school. Nearly 20 million have not finished 8 years of school. Nearly 54 million—more than one quarter of all America—have not even finished high school.

Each year more than 100,000 high school graduates, with proved ability, do not enter college because they cannot afford it. And if we cannot educate today's youth, what will we do in 1970 when elementary school enrollment will be 5 million greater than 1960? And high school enrollment will rise by 5 million. College enrollment will increase by more than 3 million.

In many places, classrooms are overcrowded and curricula are outdated. Most of our qualified teachers are underpaid, and many of our paid teachers are unqualified. So we must give every child a place to sit and a teacher to learn from. Poverty must not be a bar to learning, and learning must offer an escape from poverty.

But more classrooms and more teachers are not enough. We must seek an educational system which grows in excellence as it grows in size. This means better training for our teachers. It means preparing youth to enjoy their hours of leisure as well as their hours of labor. It means exploring new techniques of teaching, to find new ways to stimulate the love of learning and the capacity for creation.

These are three of the central issues of the Great Society. While our Government has many programs directed at those issues, I do not pretend that we have the full answer to those problems.

But I do promise this: We are going to assemble the best thought and the broadest knowledge from all over the world to find those answers for America. I intend to establish working groups to prepare a series of White House conferences and meetings—on the cities, on natural beauty, on the quality of education, and on other emerging challenges. And from these meetings and from this inspiration and from these studies we will begin to set our course toward the Great Society.

The solution to these problems does not rest on a massive program in Washington, nor can it rely solely on the strained resources of local authority. They require us to create new concepts of cooperation, a creative federalism, between the National Capital and the leaders of local communities.

Woodrow Wilson once wrote: "Every man sent out from his university should be a man of his Nation as well as a man of his time."

Within your lifetime powerful forces, already loosed, will take us toward a way of life beyond the realm of our experience, almost beyond the bounds of our imagination.

For better or for worse, your generation has been appointed by history to deal with those problems and to lead America toward a new age. You have the chance never before afforded to any people in any age. You can help build a society where the demands of morality, and the needs of the spirit, can be realized in the life of the Nation.

So, will you join in the battle to give every citizen the full equality which God enjoins and the law requires, whatever his belief, or race, or the color of his skin?

Will you join in the battle to give every citizen an escape from the crushing weight of poverty?

Will you join in the battle to make it possible for all nations to live in enduring peace—as neighbors and not as mortal enemies?

Will you join in the battle to build the Great Society, to prove that our material progress is only the foundation on which we will build a richer life of mind and spirit?

There are those timid souls who say this battle cannot be won; that we are condemned to a soulless wealth. I do not agree. We have the power to shape the civilization that we want. But we need your will, your labor, your hearts, if we are to build that kind of society.

Those who came to this land sought to build more than just a new country. They sought a new world. So I have come here today to your campus to say that you can make their vision our reality. So let us from this moment begin our work so that in the future men will look back and say: It was then, after a long and weary way, that man turned the exploits of his genius to the full enrichment of his life.

DRAWING CONCLUSIONS:

- What does Johnson's "Great Society" speech reveal about the assumptions and beliefs of postwar American liberalism?

THE RACIAL CRISIS OF THE 1960S

At the heart of the turmoil of the 1960s was a racial crisis that engulfed the entire country. While racial inequality and race-based oppression had characterized the United States since its founding, there have been periods in American history when issues of race gather such intensity that they became impossible to ignore. The 1960s was one such period. The racial crisis of the 1960s began with the southern civil rights movement that reached its peak mid-decade. In the late 1960s, however, the racial crisis gained intensity and spread to the entire country. To understand the turmoil that Americans experienced in the 1960s, the racial crisis of that decade must be explained.

2.1 RACIAL DISPARITIES IN POSTWAR AMERICA

While the incomes of virtually all Americans rose during the postwar period, long-standing disparities along lines of race persisted. These disparities were not limited to the southern states - they were in evidence nationwide. Economic data document these disparities.

GUIDING QUESTIONS:

- What do the statistics provided in each individual graph reveal about racial disparities in the United States during the post–World War II period?

TABLE 7 INCOME DISPARITIES BY RACE

Median Family Income, by Race and Ethnicity (2011 Dollars)			
Year	White	Black	Black Income as a Share of White Income
1947	$27,807	$14,216	51.1%
1969	$53,120	$32,537	61.3%
Families in Poverty			
Year	All Families	White	Black
1959	18.5%	15.2%	48.1%

Data from *The State of Working America*, http://stateofworkingamerica.org/chart/swa-income-table-2-5-median-family-income/ and *Historical Statistics of the United States: Earliest Times to the Present*, millennial edition, Vol. 2 (New York: Cambridge University Press, 2006), 2-675.

TABLE 8 UNEMPLOYMENT BY RACE, 1948–1970

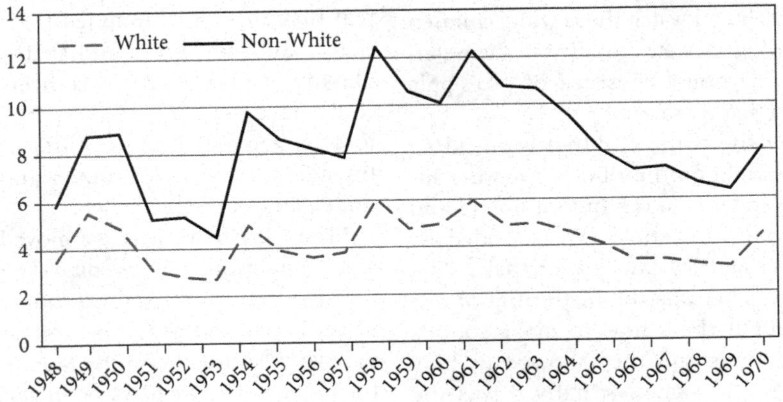

Note: Prior to 1970, most non-white members of the labor force were black.

Data from Thomas Kurian, ed., *Datapedia of the United States: American History in Numbers*, 3rd ed. (Lanham, MD: Bernan Press, 2004), 116.

DRAWING CONCLUSIONS:

- Taken together, what do these statistics reveal about racial disparities in the United States during the post–World War II period?

2.2 ANNE MOODY, EXCERPT FROM *COMING OF AGE IN MISSISSIPPI* (1968)

Anne Moody was born in rural Mississippi in the early 1940s. Her parents, like many African Americans in the rural South, were impoverished tenant farmers who tried to eke out a living on a white-owned plantation. Moody's acclaimed 1968 autobiography, *Coming of Age in Mississippi*, traces her life from early childhood, through high school and college, and to her experiences in the civil rights movement. Through her life story, she hopes to convey what it meant to grow up under the Jim Crow system. In this excerpt, she shares a memory of a formative child experience.

GUIDING QUESTIONS:

- Why did Anne Moody's mother react as she did when young Anne followed her friends into the "white" section of the movie theater?
- What impact did this incident have on young Anne Moody?

COMING OF AGE IN MISSISSIPPI (EXCERPTS)

ANNE MOODY

There was a wide trench running from the street alongside our house. It separated our house and the Johnsons' place from a big two-story house up on the hill. A big pecan tree grew on our side of the trench, and we made our playhouse under it so we could sit in the trench and watch those white children without their knowing we were actually out there staring at them. Our playhouse consisted of two apple crates and a tin can that we sat on.

One day when the white children were riding up and down the street on their bikes, we were sitting on the apple crates making Indian noises and beating the tin can with sticks. We sounded so much like Indians that they came over to ask if that was what we were. This was the beginning of our friendship. We taught them how to make sounds and dance like Indians and they showed us how to ride their bikes and skate. Actually, I was the only one who learned. Adline and Junior were too small and too scared, although they got a kick out of watching us. I was seven, Adline five, and Junior three, and this was the first time we had ever had other children to play with. Sometimes, they would take us over to their playhouse. Katie and Bill, the children of the whites that owned the furniture store, had a model playhouse at the side of their parents' house. That little house was just like the big house, painted snow white on the outside, with real furniture in it. I envied their playhouse more than I did their bikes and skates. Here they were playing in a house that was nicer than any house I could have dreamed of living in. They had all this to offer me and I had nothing to offer them but the field of clover in summer and the apple crates under the pecan tree.

The Christmas after we moved there, I thought sure Mama would get us some skates. But she didn't. We didn't get anything but a couple of apples and oranges. I cried a week for those skates, I remember.

Every Saturday evening Mama would take us to the movies. The Negroes sat upstairs in the balcony and the whites sat downstairs. One Saturday we arrived at the movies at the same time as the white children. When we saw each other, we ran and met. Katie walked straight into the downstairs lobby and Adline, Junior, and I followed. Mama was talking to one of the white women and didn't notice that we had walked into the white lobby. I think she thought we were at the side entrance we had always used which led to the balcony. We were standing in the white lobby with our friends, when Mama came in and saw us. "C'mon! C'mon!" she yelled, pushing Adline's face on into the door. "Essie Mae, um gonna try my best to kill you when I get you home. I told you 'bout running up in these stories and things like you own 'em!" she shouted, dragging me through the door. When we got outside, we stood there crying, and we could hear the white children crying inside the white lobby. After that, Mama didn't even let us stay at the movies. She carried us right home.

All the way back to our house, Mama kept telling us that we couldn't sit downstairs, we couldn't do this or that with white children. Up until that time I had never really thought about it. After all, we were playing together. I knew that we were going to separate schools and all, but I never knew why.

After the movie incident, the white children stopped playing in front of our house. For about two weeks we didn't see them at all. Then one day they were there again and we started playing. But things were not the same. I had never really thought of them as white before. Now all of a sudden they were white, and their whiteness made them better than me. I now realized that not only were they better than me because they were white, but everything they owned and everything connected with them was better than what was available to me. I hadn't realized before that downstairs in the movies was any better than upstairs. But now I saw that it was. Their whiteness provided them with a pass to downstairs in that nice section and my blackness sent me to the balcony.

Now that I was thinking about it, their schools, homes, and streets were better than mine. They had a large red brick school with nice sidewalks connecting the buildings. Their homes were large and beautiful with indoor toilets and every other convenience that I knew of at the time. Every house I had ever lived in was a one- or two-room shack with an outdoor toilet. It really bothered me that they had all these nice things and we had nothing. "There is a secret to it besides being white," I thought. Then my mind got all wrapped up in trying to uncover that secret.

One day when we were all playing in our playhouse in the ditch under the pecan tree, I got a crazy idea. I thought the secret was their "privates." I had seen everything they had but their privates and it wasn't any different than mine. So I made up a game called "The Doctor." I had never been to a doctor myself. However, Mama had told us that a doctor was the only person that could look at children's naked bodies besides their parents. Then I remembered the time my Grandma Winnie was sick. When I asked her what the doctor had done to her she said, "He examined me." Then I asked her about "examined" and she told me he looked at her teeth, in her ears, checked her heart, blood and privates. Now I was going to be the doctor. I had all of them, Katie, Bill, Sandra, and Paul plus Adline and Junior take off their clothes and stand in line as I sat on one of the apple crates and examined them. I looked in their mouths and ears, put my ear to their hearts to listen for their heartbeats. Then I had them lie down on the leaves and I looked at their privates. I examined each of them about three times, but I didn't see any differences. I still hadn't found that secret.

That night when I was taking my bath, soaping myself all over, I thought about it again. I remembered the day I had seen my two uncles Sam and Walter. They were just as white as Katie them. But Grandma Winnie was darker than Mama, so how could Sam and Walter be white? I must have been thinking about it for a long time because Mama finally called out, "'Essie Mae! Stop using up all that soap! And hurry up so Adline and Junior can bathe 'fore that water gits cold."

"Mama," I said. "why ain't Sam and Walter white?"

"'Cause they mama ain't white," she answered.

"But you say a long time ago they daddy is white."

"If the daddy is white and the mama is colored, then that don't make the children white."

"But they got the same hair and color like Bill and Katie them got," I said.

'"That still don't make them white! Now git out of that tub!" she snapped.

Every time I tried to talk to Mama about white people she got mad. Now l was more confused than before. If it wasn't the straight hair and the white skin that made you white, then what was it?

DRAWING CONCLUSIONS:

- How did Anne Moody learn what it meant to be black in Jim Crow Mississippi?
- What can we learn about the Jim Crow system of the American South from this episode in Anne Moody's life?

2.3 RECOLLECTIONS OF THE MONTGOMERY BUS BOYCOTT (1977)

The Montgomery Bus Boycott of 1955–1956 is usually considered the event that gave birth to the civil rights movement of the 1950s and 1960s. While the boycott was not the first time that black southerners had challenged the Jim Crow system, it did provide a model of successful non-violent collective action that helped inspire similar efforts around the South. A local ordinance in the city of Montgomery, Alabama, required segregated seating on city busses. (Similar laws existed in other southern cities.) Black patrons were required to sit in the back of the bus with the front of the bus reserved for white patrons. If the seats in front were filled, the furthest front row of black riders was required to give up their seats to white patrons. On December 5, 1955, a black bus rider named Rosa Parks was arrested for refusing to give up her seat to a white woman. The arrest of Parks was the catalyst for a year-long African American boycott of city buses that brought national attention to the issue of racial segregation in the South. These recollections of the Montgomery bus boycott provide insights into its beginnings and its impact. Rosa Parks reflects upon the events surrounding her arrest. Black community leader E. D. Nixon describes how the boycott was launched and how Martin Luther King, Jr. (a young minister recently arrived in Montgomery) was selected as the spokesperson for the boycott. Finally, civil rights leader John Lewis describes the impact that the boycott had on him as a teenager growing up in rural Alabama.

GUIDING QUESTIONS:

- What can we learn about the origins of the Montgomery Bus Boycott from the testimony of Rosa Parks and E. D. Nixon?
- What can we learn about the impact of the Montgomery Bus Boycott from the testimony of John Lewis?

ROSA L. PARKS

I had had problems with bus drivers over the years, because I didn't see fit to pay my money into the front and then go around to the back. Sometimes bus drivers wouldn't permit me to get on the bus, and I had been evicted from the bus. But as I say, there had been incidents over the years. One of the things that made this get so much publicity was the fact the police were called in and I was placed under arrest. See, if I had just been evicted from the bus and he hadn't placed me under arrest or had any charges brought against me, it probably could have been just another incident.

I had left my work at the men's alteration shop, a tailor shop in the Montgomery Fair department store, and as I left work, I crossed the street to a drugstore to pick up a few items instead of trying to go directly to the bus stop. And when I had finished this, I came across the street and looked for a Cleveland Avenue bus that apparently had some seats on it. At that time it was a little hard to get a seat on the bus. But when I did get to the entrance to the bus, I got in line with a number of other people who were getting on the same bus.

As I got up on the bus and walked to the seat I saw there was only one vacancy that was just back

From Howell Raines, *My Soul Is Rested: The Story of the Civil Rights Movement in the Deep South* (New York: G. P. Putnam's Sons, 1977), 40–51, 71–74.

of where it was considered the white section. So this was the seat that I took, next to the aisle, and a man was sitting next to me. Across the aisle there were two women, and there were a few seats at this point in the very front of the bus that was called the white section. I went on to one stop and I didn't particularly notice who was getting on the bus, didn't particularly notice the other people getting on. And on the third stop there were some people getting on, and at this point all of the front seats were taken. Now in the beginning, at the very first stop I had got on the bus, the back of the bus was filled up with people standing in the aisle and I don't know why this one vacancy that I took was left, because there were quite a few people already standing toward the back of the bus. The third stop is when all the front seats were taken, and this one man was standing and when the driver looked around and saw he was standing, he asked the four of us, the man in the seat with me and the two women across the aisle, to let him have those front seats.

At his first request, didn't any of us move. Then he spoke again and said, "You'd better make it light on yourselves and let me have those seats." At this point, of course, the passenger who would have taken the seat hadn't said anything. In fact, he never did speak to my knowledge. When the three people, the man who was in the seat with me and the two women, stood up and moved into the aisle, I remained where I was. When the driver saw that I was still sitting there, he asked if I was going to stand up. I told him, no, I wasn't. He said. "Well, if you don't stand up, I'm going to have you arrested." I told him to go on and have me arrested.

He got off the bus and came back shortly. A few minutes later two policemen got on the bus, and they approached me and asked if the driver had asked me to stand up, and I said yes, and they wanted to know why I didn't. I told them I didn't think I should have to stand up. After I had paid my fare and occupied a seat, I didn't think I should have to give it up. They placed me under arrest then and had me to get in the police car, and I was taken to jail and booked on suspicion, I believe. The questions were asked, the usual questions they ask a prisoner or somebody that's under arrest. They had to determine whether or not the driver wanted to press charges or swear out a warrant, which he did. Then they took me to jail, and I was placed in a cell. In a little while I was taken from the cell, and my picture was made and fingerprints taken. I went back to the cell then, and a few minutes later I was called back again, and when this happened I found out that Mr. E. D. Nixon and Attorney and Mrs. Clifford Durr had come to make bond for me.

In the meantime before this, of course . . . I was given permission to make a telephone call after my picture was taken and fingerprints taken. I called my home and spoke to my mother on the telephone and told her what had happened, that I was in jail. She was quite upset and asked me had the police beaten me. I told her, no, I hadn't been physically injured, but I was being held in jail, and I wanted my husband to come and get me out . . . He didn't have a car at that time, so he had to get someone to bring him down. At the time when he got down, Mr. Nixon and the Durrs had just made bond for me, so we all met at the jail and we went home . . .

E. D. NIXON

Then we went on up to the house and I said to Mrs. Parks, "Mrs. Parks"—her mother had some coffee made—I said, "Mrs. Parks, this is the case we've been looking for. We can break this situation on the bus with your case."

She said, "Well, I haven't thought of it just like that." So we talked to her mother and her husband, and finally they came 'round, said they'd go along with it.

She said, "All right." She said, "You know, Mr. Nixon, if you say so, I'll go along with it."

I said, "Okay, we can do it."

What was there about Mrs. Parks that made her the right litigant as opposed to these others?

Mrs. Parks was a married woman. She had worked for me for twelve years, and I knew her. She was morally clean, and she had a fairly good academic training. Now, she wasn't afraid and she didn't get excited about anything. If there ever was a person that we woulda been able to break the situation that existed on the Montgomery city line, Rosa L. Parks was the woman to use. And I knew that. I probably woulda examined a dozen more before I got there if Mrs. Parks hadn't come along before I found the right 'un. 'Cause, you see, it's hard for you to see it, it's hard for the average person—it's hard for the black people here in Montgomery to see. It's hard for a whole lot of people far away from here to see it. But when you have set 'cross the table and talked with black people in investigations as long as I have over a period of years, you just know it . . . Well, I spent years in it and I knew it . . . when I selected Mrs. Parks, that was the person.

E. D. Nixon and Rosa Parks first met when he was president of Montgomery's struggling NACCP chapter. Nixon: "Mrs. Parks came to a NAACP meetin'. When she joined the NAACP, she got to the place she never missed, and I selected her secretary. I ran her for secretary; she was elected. And one year, she didn't run, they elected somebody else, and then I hired her." As Nixon's employee, she ran the office from which he operated as state NAACP president and as a regional officer of the Brotherhood of Sleeping Car Porters. Nixon recalls that on one occasion, without consulting him, Mrs. Parks drafted a letter over his signature protesting an Alabama politician's statement that passage of a federal antilynching law would "destroy the peaceful relations between the two races."

Despite this background, Mrs. Parks has been inaccurately characterized in many accounts as a simple drudge who, though temporarily emboldened by the bus driver's abuse, had no concept of the larger struggle for racial justice. Such characterizations are based on her much-quoted remark that she refused to stand because "my feet hurt."

Actually, "I had almost a life history of being rebellious against being mistreated because of my color," and although no one could have predicted that moment on the bus, Rosa Parks' "life history" had prepared her for it. Only a few months before, in the summer of 1955, she had received through her work in the NAACP an invitation to visit Highlander Folk School, an integrated retreat in the Tennessee hills. . . . "That was the first time in my life I had lived in an atmosphere of complete equality with the members of the other race, and I did enjoy going up there, and I felt it could be done without the signs that said 'White' and 'Colored'—well, without any artificial barriers of racial segregation."

And so after we agreed, oh, I guess we spent a couple of hours discussing this thing. Then I went home and I took a sheet of paper and I drew right in the center of the paper. I used that for the square and then I used Hunter Station, Washington Park, Pickett Springs, all the different areas in Montgomery, and I used a slide rule to get an estimate. I discovered that nowhere in Montgomery at that time a man couldn't walk to work if he wanted to. I said, "We can beat this thing."

I told my wife about it and I said, "You know what?"

She said, "What?"

I said, "We're going to boycott the buses."

She said, "Cold as it is?"

I said, "Yeah."

She said, "I doubt it."

I said, "Well, I'll tell you one thing. If you keep 'em off when it cold, you won't have no trouble keeping 'em off when it get hot."

She shook her head. She said, "My husband! If headaches were selling for a dollar a dozen, my husband would be just the man to walk in the drugstore and say, 'Give me a dozen headaches.'" [Laughs]

So anyhow, I recorded quite a few names, starting off with Rev. Abernathy, Rev. Hubbard, Rev. King, and on down the line, and I called some of the people who represent peoples so that they could get the word out. The first man I called was Reverend Ralph Abernathy. He said, "Yes, Brother Nixon, I'll go along. I think it's a good thing."

The second person I called was the late Reverend H. H. Hubbard. He said, "Yes, I'll go along with you."

And I called Rev. King, was number three, and he said, "Brother Nixon, let me think about it awhile, and call me back."

When I called him back, he was number nineteen, and of course, he agreed to go along. I said, "I'm glad you agreed because I already set the meeting up to meet at your church." 'Course, he didn't even know Mrs. Parks at that time. I couldn't attend the meeting, and I asked another man, another minister, Methodist minister, to chair the meeting with the understanding that no permanent officers be elected until I come back, and there wasn't any elected.

Why did you make that stipulation?

I wanted to be shore the right people was in office, and I felt that I was, with my work in the community, better prepared to know who the right person would be than anybody else. So nobody was elected. They set up a temporary meeting for Monday evening. So I came back Sunday morning and my wife met me at the station. I got in about nine o'clock. She give me the morning paper. They had an article, a two-column spread wrote by Joe Azbell, on the front page of the Advertiser, talking about the bus boycott, a favorable article. The kind of article I'm almost sure that that's what got him fired. But anyhow, he wrote a good article, kept his promise.

Had you tipped him off?

Oh, yes, I knew him personally.

How did you handle that?

I just called him and told him I had a hot lead, a story. I said, "Now, if you promise me you would write a good story, I would fill you in on it. I'll be at the station at two o'clock." He met me down there and we talked about it and I made him promise he'd write a good story, and knowing him like I did, I felt he'd tell me the truth about it. He did write a good story. He wrote a heck of a good story . . .

The Advertiser ran its story as an exposé, quoting from a leaflet Nixon had circulated in the black neighborhoods: ". . . don't ride the bus to work, to town, to school, or anyplace, Monday, December 5. . . . Another Negro woman has been arrested and put in jail because she refused to give up her bus seat . . . Come to a mass meeting Monday at 7 P.M. at the Holt Street Baptist Church for further instructions." By reprinting the leaflet for the titillation of white Montgomery, the Advertiser—as Nixon had anticipated when he tipped off its reporter—had in effect distributed the leaflet to most of the black households in Montgomery.

Montgomery police, adopting the pattern of overreaction that Southern police were to follow for a decade, announced that there would be "two police behind every bus in the city" to prevent black "goon squads" from enforcing the boycott against those of either race who wished to ride. Of course, the police failed to consider what the presence of police escorts signified to black bus riders. "Monday morning, the black folks come out there and saw two police . . . behind every bus. They just went the other way, see. Ended up at eight o'clock that morning, the buses ain't hauled nobody, hadn't hauled nobody, didn't haul nobody else for the next 381 days."

Then Mrs. Parks was tried that morning and she was found guilty . . . I'd been in court off and on for twenty years, hearing different peoples, and very seldom, if ever, there was another black man unless he was being tried. But that particular morning, the morning of December the fifth, 1955, the black man was reborn again. I couldn't believe it when they found her guilty and I had to go through the vestibule down the hall to the clerk's office to sign her appeal bond . . . People came in that other door, and that door was about ten feet wide, and they was just that crowded in there, people wanting to know what happened. I said, "Well, they found her guilty. Now, I'm gon' have to make another bond for her. As soon as we can get her bond signed, we'll bring her right out." They said, "If you don't hurry and come out, we're coming in there and getchya." I couldn't believe it. When we got outside, police were standing outside with sawed-off shotguns, and the people all up and down the streets was from sidewalk to sidewalk out there. I looked around there, and I bet you there was over a thousand black people—black men—on the streets out there.

Did they understand that the guilty verdict was what you were after?

. . . No, they didn't understand that. I didn't tell anybody that. But I know if they'da found her not guilty, we'da had the same thing again. They really did the thing that was best for us when they found her guilty.

He sensed that Montgomery's segregationists had committed a historic tactical blunder. By prosecuting Mrs. Parks under a segregation ordinance rather than on some subterfuge such as disobeying an officer, they were inviting a federal court test of the Jim Crow laws upon which segregation throughout the Deep South depended. Within a few weeks four Montgomery women, spurred by Mrs. Parks' conviction, filed in federal district court in Montgomery what would prove to be a successful challenge of both city and state bus segregation laws.

However, he was more concerned with the immediate future of the boycott than with the long grind of litigation as he left City Hall that day, December 5, 1955. He fell into step with Rev. Abernathy and Rev. E. N. French, who had also attended the trial. From them, he learned that prior to the rally that night, there was to be a meeting of the city's ministers. In that preliminary meeting the ministers would decide on basic policies for the boycott and pick its leaders. He told Abernathy, "Well, what we need to do, me and you and Rev. French . . . right now, is agree on a recommendation, agree on a resolution and agree on a name." With such preparation, he sensed, they could dominate the meeting.

I had wrote three mild recommendations . . . I know one was "Seatin' on the bus, first come, first served," and "Negro bus drivers in predominant Negro neighborhoods." I forgot what the other one was. "More courtesy to Negro patrons," I believe. But anyhow, they agreed on it. Then he and Rev. French wrote the resolution and they read it and I agreed with them. Then we came up with a name for the organization, and I said, "What about the Citizens' Committee?" Rev. Abernathy said, "No, I don't want no Citizens' Committee. Too close to the white Citizens Council." They he came up and said, "What about the Montgomery Improvement Associate?" I said, "I'll go along with it," so we agreed on it.

And Abernathy was sittin' as close to me in here to you, and he leant over. He said, "Brother Nixon, now you gon' serve as president, ain'tchya?" I said, "Naw, not unless'n you all don't accept my man." He said, "Who is you man?" I said, "Martin Luther King." He said, "I'll go along with it." French said, "I'll go along with it." So then we had not only our recommendation, our resolution, our name, we had our president.

Why did you put your finger on King?

In August of 1955 he was the guest speaker for the NAACP, and a professor over at the State Teachers College and I were sitting in the back. His name was J. E. Pierce. When King got through talking, I said, "Pierce, you know that guy made a heck of a speech."

He said, "I agree with you. He sho' did."

I said, "I don't know how I'm going to do it yet, but someday I'm gon' hang him to the stars."

The next thing, he had not been here long enough for the city fathers to put their hand on him. Usually, you come to a town and you start wantin' to do this and do that, and the city fathers get their hand on you probably and give you a suit of clothes or somethin' of that kind, and it ends up you're on their side. He wasn't the kind ever to accept it, even if they'da tried it.

In that meetin', that evening, everybody was still—all the ministers was still afraid . . . and if you read Rev. King's book, *Stride Toward Freedom*, you'll see my quotation in there. They would talk about tryin' to do it so the white people wouldn't know about it, and one of 'em said, ". . . well, we'll mimeograph some little pamphlets. Everybody come in the meetin' that night we'll pass 'em one, and nobody will know how it happened."

Well, I was sitting there boiling over, so made I didn't know what to do, so I jumped up, and I forgot about we was up in the balcony of the church. I said, "What the hell you people talkin' 'bout?" Just like that, see, and I cussed. I said, "How you gonna have a mass meeting, gonna boybott a city bus line without the white folks knowing it?" [Voice rising] I said, "You guys have went around here and lived off these poor wash-women all your lives and ain't never done nothing for 'em. And now you got a chance to do something for 'em, you talkin' about you don't want the white folks to know it."

I said, "Unless'n this program is accepted and brought into the church like a decent, respectable organization, . . . I'll take the microphone and tell 'em the reason we don't have a program is 'cause you all are too scared to stand on your meet and be counted. You oughta make up your mind right now that you gon' either admit you are a grown man or concede to the fact that you are a bunch of scared boys." And King hollered that he wasn't no coward, that nobody called him a coward.

Once prodded into defending his courage, King, who was then twenty-six years old, had no choice but to accept the presidency of the Montgomery Improvement Associate and to make the main address at the MIA's first rally that night. "I said, 'When he's through, I'm gon' come behind him.'"

Rev. King made a *masterpiece* that evenin'. So when he did, then I came behind him, and I never shall forget, I said, "Good evenin', my friends." I said, "I'm so happy to see all of you out here tonight, but I wanna tell you somethin'. If you're scared, you better get your hat and coat and go home. It's gon' be a long drawn-out affair and before it's over with somebody gon' die." I said, "May be me, I don't know . . . The only request I have is if I'm the one that dies, don't let me die in vain. For twenty-some-odd years I been fighting and saying to myself that I didn't want the children to come along and have to suffer all the insults that I've suffered. Well, hell, I changed my mind tonight." Just like that. "I decided that I want to enjoy some of this freedom myself." And everybody hollered when I said that.

And anyhow then we took up a collection after that. I served as treasurer for the first three years. We took up a collection, took up $785 there that night. And I ribbed . . . the commissioner of police that night. He was in the meetin', with two or three police and everything, two of the black police were there. I had my car there and went by there and I told him at the door, I said, "Say, I cain't go home with all this money in the street myself. You got to send me home in the police car." And he turned around and told a policeman named Worthy . . ." You all take Nixon home." He carried me home, 'cause nobody thought the thing gon' last over a week or ten days, then everybody be back on the bus. He carried me home; my wife had to drive my car home by herself. [Laughs]

I'm called an Uncle Tom now because I can deal with the power structure. For instance, I don't mind telling you, I had an appointment with Governor Wallace day before yesterday evenin'. All the mayor, the commissioners, I can deal with 'em . . .

You see, I figure now if I'm what you call an Uncle Tom . . . you need ten thousand of 'em here . . .

I figure it was the best thing that ever happened in Montgomery, and I'm proud that I was part of it, even though . . . so many people got famous out of it and I was still left here. And I'm still here servin' the people and the rest of 'em gone. So I'm gettin' more joy out of it now than I imagine them guys did you got in it for a name. And I haven't ever looked for a name . . .

What do you think the history books ought to say about your role and Mrs. Parks' role?

I certainly think history books ought to, if you're gonna talk about the boycott, they oughta start from the day Rosa L. Parks was arrested and not just December the fifth when Rev. King was elected president . . .

I haven't seen anybody yet that wanted to believe anything about the Movement except something what the Reverend King said. I ain't see nobody yet. Now I've had peoples interviewed me. I betcha I've had a thousand people interview me. Everybody, they'll set and listen at me talk, then they go away and write. Even in the foreign country, they want to start off with December the fifth. Well, we was doing things before Rev. King had ever finished school, come out of school. We's doing things in this town here. The Movement didn't spring up overnight. It came up that particular night because we found the right person.

'Course, even today, people don't wanna hear the truth about MIA. If you gonna say somethin' that Rev. King didn't do, you're almost spittin' in folks' face. I was on an airplane coming down from New York some time ago, sittin' beside a lady, and she asked me who I was and I hold her. She said, "Oh, you're down in Montgomery, Alabama." She said, "Lord, I don't know what'ud happened to the black people if Rev. King hadn't went to town."

I said, "If Mrs. Parks had got up and given that white man her seat, you'd never aheard of Rev. King."

When I said that, man, I as well as spit in her face.

JOHN LEWIS

AN ALABAMA BOYHOOD

He was born at Dunn's Chapel, a black sharecropper community about forty miles west of Montgomery.

My parents rented land. They tended land that was owned by a very, very wealthy white landowner, who for many years had provided land for my mother's brothers, my mother's father, and other relatives to farm. So I was born on a piece of that land in 1940. In 1944 when I was four years old, my father bought a hundred and ten acres of land for three hundred dollars. I guess the man that he bought it from almost, in my estimation, gave it to him.

In this whole area it was really a black-and-white world. It was just rural Alabama; the land was not that rich; we planted cotton, corn, peanuts—but it was two separate worlds, one black and one white. From time to time when growing up, we would complete our work, and then we would go and work by the day, work in the cotton field pickin' cotton by the pound, particularly to get money for books or clothing for school in August or September.

I guess as a young child, I saw the dual system of segregation and racial discrimination. The grade school that I attended was a little one-room school, from the first through the sixth grade, and it was just a shack really . . . From the seventh through the twelfth grade, we were bused through Pike County to the Pike County Training School. In many parts of Alabama, the high schools for blacks were considered "training schools," and the county high schools for whites were just called "the county high school." We had the worst buses. We never had a new bus. The white children had new buses. Our school was a run-down school, and all that had an impact on me . . .

We didn't have electric lights, we didn't have indoor plumbing, anything like that, until very, very later. I was a teenager, getting ready to go to college, matter of fact, before we got even the highway. We had unpaved roads, and for many years the county refused to pave the major road. They paved it up to where the black section of the county started . . . Our house was on a hill, a red-clay hill . . . and the road, this highway, came right through our property. And when it would rain—it was a steep hill—people would get stuck in the mud and the ditches and that type of thing. The same thing would happen to the school bus . . . The bus may get stuck; you may be late getting' to school. Or coming back from school in the evening, the same thing would happen . . . That area was very, very poor, very, very poor . . .

Do you remember discussing it much among yourselves?

Not—not really, not really. [A long pause] Not really . . . see . . . we didn't have a subscription to a newspaper. But my grandfather had a subscription to the Montgomery Advertiser, and we would get the paper maybe two or three days later—sometimjes it would be a week later—and we kept up with what was happening in Montgomery or in Alabama or the South by reading the newspaper after he had read it. But we really didn't discuss the whole question of segregation. It was something that existed and that we saw when we went to the town, into Troy, to the dimestore. We saw the sign saying White Only or Colored. When you went to go to the water fountain, you knew not to drink out of that fountain that said White Only, that you were directed to drink out of the one saying Colored. You couldn't go to the soda fountain and get a Coke. Somehow we grew up knowing that you couldn't cross that line, but there was not that much discussing it within my family, not at all. It was a sense of fear, I guess, on the part of my parents, that we must stay in our place. There was a certain point where then you couldn't—you knew not to go any further.

In 1954, when the school desegregation decision came down, you would have been about fourteen . . .

I was fourteen and I remember that. I do remember the Supreme Court decision of 1954 . . . As I recall, we rejoiced. It was like a day of jubilee . . . that segregation would be ended in the public school system. We thought that we would go to a better school . . . get better transportation, better buses, and that type of thing. But that didn't happen, so I never attended a desegregated public school. Then, a year later was the Montgomery Bus Boycott in 1955, and I think perhaps that incident, what happened in Montgomery, had the greatest impact on me, more than anything else . . . I grew up with this whole idea of wanting to be a minister. I don't know where it came from . . . I recall, when I was four years old, I remember baptizing a chicken, and the chicken drowned. I kept it under the water too long, I would preach to the chicken and baptize a particular chicken . . . Then one of my uncles, my mother's brother, had Santa Claus to bring a Bible. So I went through this whole idea, even going through grade school, of becoming a minister, and though grade school and high school, people referred to me as Preacher . . .

But coming back to 1955, I think the Montgomery Bus Boycott did more than anything else. We didn't have television, but I kept up with what was going on, on radio, in newspaper, everything. In the papers that we got in the public school system in the library, I read everything about what was happening there, and it was really one of the most exciting, one of the most moving things to me to see just a few miles away the black folks of Montgomery stickin' together, refusing to ride segregated buses, walking the streets. It was a moving movement.

And I'd head Dr. King even before the Montgomery Bus Boycott. There's a local radio station in Montgomery . . . a soul station . . . and Dr. King had a sermon. It was called "Paul's Letter to the American Christians," and some of the things that he said sorta stuck with me. As you well know, his message was sort of social-political oriented. It was sort of the social gospel, making religion something real and using the emotionalism within religion to make it do something else for people, and that had an impact.

Do you recall hearing him more or less by chance?

Yeah, that's right, but chance, because I didn't know anything about him. I'd never heard anything about him. Now this was before—before the Montgomery Bus Boycott—when he first came to Montgomery and they would have different ministers preaching. And then when he emerged during the buy boycott, I took some particular note.

How is that you happen to remember the name of that sermon?

Well, I knew one thing, there was no such thing in the New Testament. You know, how can Paul be writing to the American Church? So what he did, he took Paul's letters, . . . Paul's message to the church at Corinth, which is a place in the Bible, and so I remembered that. 'Cause he was saying that certain things that had been happening in America just shouldn't be happening. It stuck with me.

DRAWING CONCLUSIONS:

- What insights do the testimonies of Parks, Nixon, and Lewis provide into the reasons for the emergence of a mass civil rights movement in the American South in the 1950s and 1960s?

2.4 RESIDENTIAL SEGREGATION IN CHICAGO (1950)

By the late 1960s, racial unrest had spread beyond the South to black communities in the urban centers of America's North and West, such as Detroit, Chicago, Oakland, and Los Angeles. These communities were a product of the so-called Great Migration of African American people out the South, a migration that began in the early twentieth century and that gathered steam in the 1940s and 1950s. Prior to 1910, the vast majority of the country's black population remained in the former slave states of the American South. By 1960, by contrast, nearly four in ten African American people lived outside the southern states. The Great Migration was spurred by the search for better job opportunities and a desire to escape the harsh conditions of life in the Jim Crow South. Migrants to northern and western cities did find new opportunities, but they were also confronted by widespread racial discrimination, most notably in the housing and labor markets. One result was a pattern of racially segregated neighborhoods that was even more intense than in the Jim Crow South. The city of Chicago, which by the 1950s was home to the nation's largest African American community, typified this pattern, as demonstrated in this 1950 map of Chicago neighborhoods.

GUIDING QUESTIONS:

- What does this map tell us about patterns of racial segregation in Chicago neighborhoods in the post–World War II period?

DRAWING CONCLUSIONS:

- What do the patterns of racial segregation in 1950s Chicago contribute to our understanding of issues of race in post–World War II America?

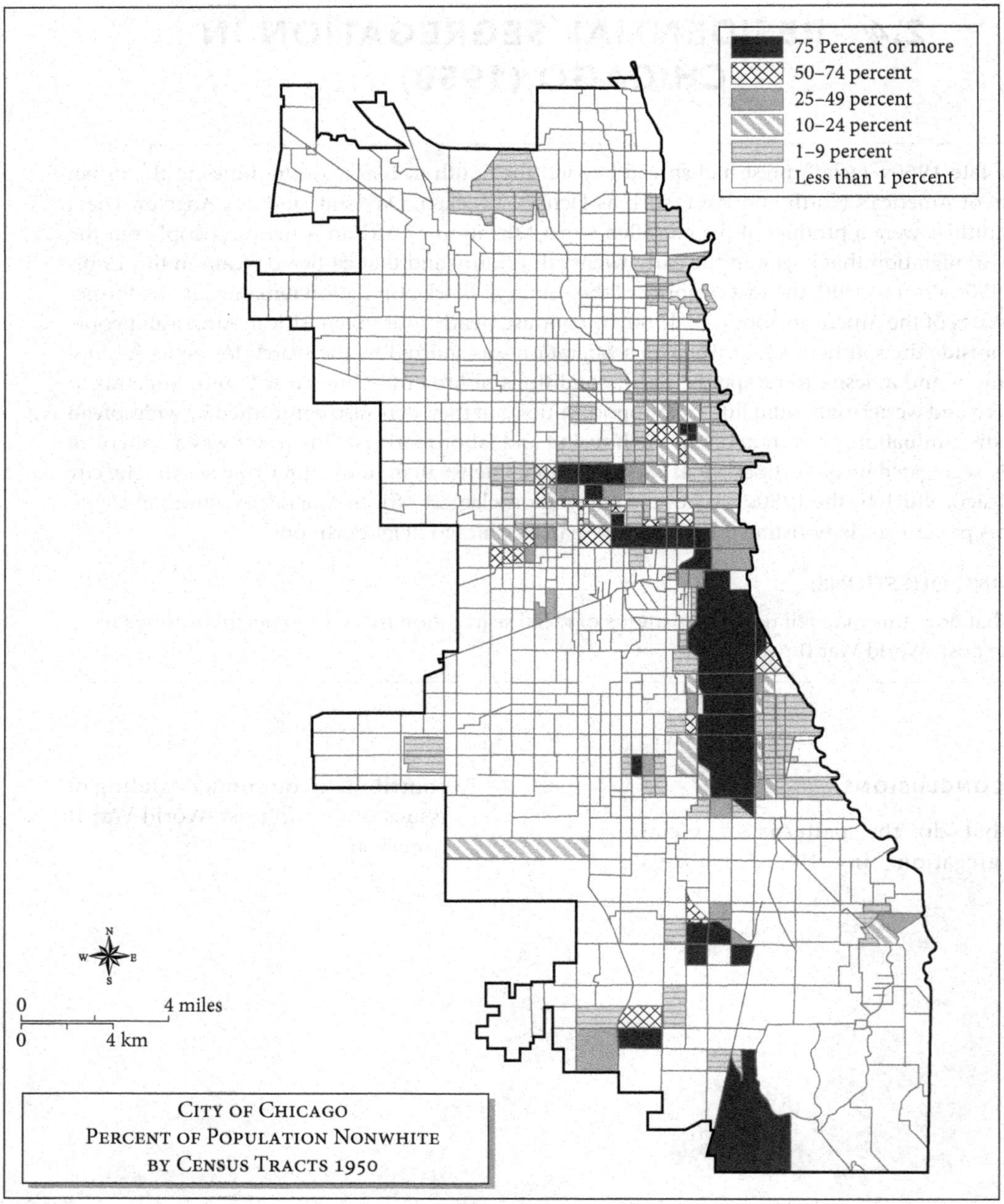

MAP 1 Residential Segregation in Chicago, 1950

2.5 THE BLACK PANTHER PARTY, "WHAT WE WANT, WHAT WE BELIEVE" (1966)

In October 1966, a pair of black power activists in Oakland, California, named Huey Newton and Bobby Seale founded the Black Panther Party for Self Defense. In founding the Black Panthers, Newton and Seale's goal was to build an explicitly revolutionary organization that would link the cause of black liberation to the overthrow of capitalism and imperialism. The Black Panthers initially gained renown for engaging in armed patrols (perfectly legal under California's gun laws) in Oakland's African American neighborhoods to monitor incidents of police brutality. By 1969, the party had chapters in cities across the country and had become a significant force within many black communities. At the party's founding meeting, Newton and Seale drafted a ten-point program ("What We Want, What We Believe") that would serve as a rallying point for the Black Panthers as the organization grew into one of the most influential black power organizations of the late 1960s.

GUIDING QUESTIONS:

- What are the specific demands of the Black Panther Party?
- What common themes tie together the specific demands of the Black Panther Party?
- What justifications do the Black Panthers give for their demands?

"WHAT WE WANT, WHAT WE BELIEVE"

OCTOBER 1966

1. We want freedom. We want power to determine the destiny of our Black Community.

   We believe that black people will not be free until we are able to determine our destiny.
2. We want full employment for our people.
   We believe that the federal government is responsible and obligated to give every man employment or a guaranteed income. We believe that if the white American businessmen will not give full employment, then the means of production should be taken from the businessmen and placed in the community so that the people of the community can organize and employ all of its people and give a high standard of living.
3. We want an end to the robbery by the CAPITALIST of our Black Community.
   We believe that this racist government has robbed us and now we are demanding the overdue debt of forty acres and two mules. Forty acres and two mules was promised 100 years ago as restitution for slave labor and mass murder of black people. We will accept the payment in currency which will be distributed to our many communities. The Germans are now aiding the Jews in Israel for the genocide of the Jewish people. The Germans murdered six million Jews, The American racist has taken part in the slaughter of over fifty million black people; therefore, we feel that this is a modest demand that we make.
4. We want decent housing, fit for shelter of human beings.
   We believe that if the white landlords will not give decent housing to our black community, then the housing and the land should be made into cooperatives so that our community, with government aid, can build and make decent housing for its people.
5. We want education for our people that exposes the true nature of this decadent American society. We want education that teaches us our true history and our role in the present-day society.

From Alexander Bloom and Wini Breines, eds., *"Takin' It to the Streets: A Sixties Reader* (New York: Oxford University Press, 1995), 164–167.

We believe in an educational system that will give to our people a knowledge of self. If a man does not have knowledge of himself and his position in society and the world, then he has little chance to relate to anything else.

6. We want all black men to be exempt from military service.
   We believe that black people should not be forced to fight in the military service to defend a racist government that does not protect us. We will not fight and kill other people of color in the world who, like black people, are being victimized by the white racist government of America. We will protect ourselves from the forces and violence of the racist police and the racist military, by whatever means necessary.
7. We want an immediate end to POLICE BRUTALITY and MURDER of black people.
   We believe we can end police brutality in our black community by organizing black self-defense groups that are dedicated to defending our black community from racist police oppression and brutality. The Second Amendment to the Constitution of the United States gives a right to bear arms. We therefore believe that all black people should arm themselves for self-defense.
8. We want freedom for all black men held in federal, state, county and city prisons and jails.
   We believe that all black people should be released from the many jails and prisons because they have not received a fair and impartial trial.
9. We want all black people when brought to trial to be tried in court by a jury of their peer group or people from their black communities, as defined by the Constitution of the United States.
   We believe that the courts should follow the United States Constitution so that black people will receive fair trials. The Fourteenth Amendment of the U.S. Constitution gives a man a right to be tried by his peer group. A peer is a person from similar economic, social, religious, geographical, environmental, historical, and racial background. To do this the court will be forced to select a jury from the black community from which the black defendant came. We have been and are being tried by all-white juries that have no understanding of the "average reasoning man" of the black community.
10. We want land, bread, housing, education, clothing, justice, and peace. And as our major political objective, a United Nations–supervised plebiscite to be held throughout the black colony in which only the black colonial subjects will be allowed to participate, for the purpose of determining the will of black people as to their national destiny.

When, in the course of human events, it becomes necessary for one people to dissolve the political bands which have connected them with another, and to assume, among the powers of the earth, the separate and equal station to which the laws of nature and nature's God entitle, a decent respect to the opinions of mankind requires that they should declare the causes which impel them to the separation.

We hold these truths to be self-evident, that all men are created equal; that they are endowed by their Creator with certain unalienable rights; that among these are life, liberty and the pursuit of happiness. That, to secure these rights, governments are instituted among men, deriving their just powers from the consent of the governed; that, whenever any form of government becomes destructive of these ends, it is the right of the people to alter such principles, and organizing its powers in such a form, as to them shall seem most likely to effect their safety and happiness. Prudence, indeed, will dictate that governments long established should not be changed for light and transient causes; and, accordingly, all experience hath shown, that mankind are more disposed to suffer, while evils are sufferable, than to right themselves by abolishing the forms to which they are accustomed. But, when a long train of abuses and usurpations, pursuing invariably the same object, evinces a design to reduce them under absolute despotism, it is their right, it is their duty, to throw off such government, and to provide new guards for their future security.

DRAWING CONCLUSIONS:

- What can we learn about the ideas of black power from the Black Panthers' ten-point program?

2.6 HUEY P. NEWTON, EXCERPTS FROM *REVOLUTIONARY SUICIDE* (1973)

Along with Bobby Seale, Huey P. Newton was one of the founders of the Black Panther Party. Newton was born in Louisiana and moved to Oakland, California, with his family while still young. After graduating high school, Newton attended college on and off. He participated in a number of campus black power groups, but soon grew frustrated by what he saw as their reluctance to engage in meaningful action to achieve black liberation. Newton conceived of the idea of the Black Panther Party while attending night law school. In the first part of his 1973 autobiography, *Revolutionary Suicide,* Newton recounts the formative experiences that primed him to become a black revolutionary.

GUIDING QUESTIONS:

- What were Hampton's most important formative experiences?
- How did these experiences prime him to become a black revolutionary?

1

Many migrants like us were driven and pursued, in the manner of characters in a Greek play, down the paths of defeat; but luck must have been with us, for we somehow survived. . . .

Richard Wright, Preface to *Black Metropolis*

STARTING OUT

Life does not always begin at birth. My life was forged in the lives of my parents before I was born, and even earlier in the history of all Black people. It is all of a piece.

I have little knowledge of my grandparents or those who went before. Racism destroyed our family history. My father's father was a white rapist.

Both of my parents were born in the Deep South, my father in Alabama, my mother in Louisiana. In the mid-thirties, their families migrated to Arkansas, where my parents met and married. They were very young, in their mid-teens—some said too young to marry—but my father, Walter Newton, is a very good talker, and when he decided he wanted Amelia Johnson for his bride, she found him hard to resist. He has always known how to be charming; even today I love to see his eyes light up with that special glow when he gets ready to work his magic. They were married in Parkdale, Arkansas, and lived there for seven years before moving to Louisiana to take advantage of better employment prospects.

My father was not typical of southern Black men in the thirties and forties. Because of his strong belief in the family, my mother never worked at an outside job, despite seven children and considerable economic hardship. Walter Newton is rightly proud of his role as family protector. To this day, my mother has never left her home to earn money.

My father believed in work. He worked constantly, in a variety of jobs, usually holding several at one time to provide for us. During those years in Louisiana he worked in a gravel pit, a carbon plant, in sugar-cane mills, and sawmills. He eventually became a railroad brakeman for the Union Saw Mill Company. This pattern did not change when we moved to Oakland. As a youngster, I well remember my father leaving one job in the afternoon, coming home for a while, then going to the other. In spite of this, he always found time for his family. It was always high-quality time when he was home.

In addition, my father was a minister. He pastored the Bethel Baptist Church in Monroe, Louisiana, and later assisted in several of the Oakland churches. His preaching was powerful, if a little unusual. The Reverend Newton planned his sermons in advance and announced the topic a week early, but he never seemed able to preach the sermon he had chosen. Eventually, he adopted the practice of stepping right into the pulpit and letting the spirit move him to deliver whatever message was appropriate. As a child I swelled up proud to see him up there leading church services, moving the congregation with his messages. All of us shared the dignity and respect he commanded. Walter Newton is not a particularly tall man, but when he stepped into that pulpit, he was the biggest man in the world to me.

My mother likes to say that she married young and finished growing up with her children, and this is true. Only seventeen years separate her from Lee Edward, the oldest child in the family. When my older brothers and sisters were growing up in Louisiana, Mother was one of their best playmates. She played ball, jackrocks, and hide-and-go-seek. Sometimes my father joined in, rolling tires and shooting marbles and keeping the rules straight. This sense of family fun and participation has helped to keep us close. My parents are more than the word usually implies; they are also our friends and companions.

My mother's sense of humor affected all of us. It was pervasive, an attitude toward life that led us to insight, affection, humor, and understanding with each other. She helped us to see the light side in even the most difficult situations. This lightness and balance have carried me through some difficult days. Often, when others expect to find me depressed by difficult circumstances, and especially by the extreme condition of prison, they see that I look at things in another way. Not that I am happy with the suffering; I simply refuse to be defeated by it.

I was born in Monroe, Louisiana, on February 17, 1942, last of seven children. Like other Black people of that time and place, I was born at home. They tell me that my mother was quite sick while she carried me, but Mother says only that I was a fine and pretty baby. My brothers and sisters must have agreed because they often teased me when I was young, telling me I was too pretty to be a boy, that I should have been a girl. This baby-faced appearance dogged me for a long time, and it was one of the reasons I fought so often in school. I looked younger than I actually was, and soft, which encouraged schoolmates to test me. I had to show them. When I went to jail in 1968, I still had the baby face. Until then I rarely shaved.

My parents named me after Huey Pierce Long, the former Governor of Louisiana, assassinated seven years before I came along. Even though he could not vote, my father had a keen interest in politics and followed the campaigns carefully. Governor Long had impressed him by his ability to talk one philosophy while carrying out programs that moved Louisiana in exactly the opposite direction. My father says he was up front, "looking right into his mouth," when Huey P. Long made a speech about how Black men in the hospitals, "out of their minds and half naked," had to be cared for by white nurses. This was, of course, unacceptable to southern whites, and therefore a number of Black nurses were recruited to work in Louisiana hospitals. This was a major breakthrough in employment opportunities for Black professionals. Huey Long used this tactic to bring other beneficial programs to Blacks: free books in the schools, free commodities for the poor, public road- and bridge-construction projects that gave Blacks employment. While most whites were blinded by Long's outwardly racist philosophy, many Blacks found their lives significantly improved. My father believed that Huey P. Long had been a great man, and he wanted to name a son after him.

In our family there was a tradition that each older child had particular responsibility for a younger one, looking after him at play, feeding him, taking him to school. This was called "giving" the newborn to an older brother or sister. The older child had the privilege of first taking the new baby outdoors. I was "given" to my brother Walter, Jr. A few days after I was born he took me outside, hauled me up onto the back of a horse, and circled the house while the rest of the family followed. This ritual is undoubtedly a surviving "Africanism" from the age-old matriarchal-communal tradition. I do not remember that or anything else of our life in Louisiana. Everything I know about that time I learned from the family. In 1945, we followed my father to Oakland when he came West to look for work in the wartime industries. I was three years old.

The great exodus of poor people out of the South during World War II sprang from the hope for a better life in the big cities of the North and West. In search of freedom, they left behind centuries of southern cruelty and repression. The futility of that search is now history. The Black communities of Bedford-Stuyvesant, Newark, Brownsville, Watts, Detroit, and many others stand as testament that racism is as oppressive in the North as in the South.

Oakland is no different. The Chamber of Commerce boasts about Oakland's busy seaport, its museum, professional baseball and football teams, and the beautiful sports coliseum. The politicians speak of an efficient city government and the well-administered poverty program. The poor know better, and they will tell you a different story.

Oakland has one of the highest unemployment rates in the country, and for the Black population it is even higher. This was not always the case. After World War I, there was a hectic period of industrial expansion, and again during World War II, when government recruiters went into the South and encourages thousands of Blacks to come to Oakland to work in the shipyards and wartime industries. They came—and stayed after the war, although there were few jobs and they were no longer wanted. Because of the lack of employment opportunities in Oakland today, the number of families on welfare is the second-highest in California, even though the city is the fifth largest in the state. The police department has a long history of brutality and hatred of Blacks. Twenty-five years ago official crime became so bad that the California state legislature investigated the Oakland force and found corruption so pervasive that the police chief was forced to resign and one policeman was tried and sentenced to jail. The Oakland "system" has not changed since then. Police brutality continues and corruption persists. Not everyone in Oakland will admit this, particularly the power structure and the privileged white middle class. But, then, none of them actually lives in Oakland.

Oakland spreads from the northern border of Berkeley, dominated by the University of California with its liberal to radical lifestyle, south to the Port of Oakland and Jack London Square, a complex of mediocre motels, novelty shops, and restaurants with second-rate food. To the west, eight miles across the bay, spanned by the San Francisco-Oakland Bay Bridge, is a metropolitan San Francisco; to the east is a lily-white bedroom city called San Leandro.

There are two very distinct geographic Oaklands, the "flatlands" and the hills. In the hills, and the rich area known as Piedmont, the upper-middle and upper class—the bosses of Oakland—live, among them former United States Senator William Knowland, the owner of the ultraconservative *Oakland Tribune*, Oakland's only newspaper. His neighbors include the mayor, the district attorney, and other wealthy white folks, who live in big houses surrounded by green trees and high fences.

The other Oakland—the flatlands—consists of substandard-income families that make up about 50 per cent of the population of nearly 450,000. They live in either rundown, crowded West Oakland or dilapidated East Oakland, hemmed in block after block, in ancient, decaying structures, now cut up into multiple dwellings. Here the majority of Blacks, Chicanos, and Chinese people struggle to survive. The landscape of East and West Oakland is depressing; it resembles a crumbling ghost town, but a ghost town with inhabitants, among them more than 200,000 Blacks, nearly half the city's population. There is a dreary, grey monotony about Oakland's flatlands, broken only by a few large and impressive buildings in the downtown section, among them (significantly) the Alameda County Court House (which includes a jail) and the Oakland police headquarters building, a ten-story streamlined fortress for which no expense was spared in its construction. Oakland is a ghost town in the sense that many American cities are. Its white middle class has fled to the hills, and their indifference to the plight of the city's poor is everywhere evident.

Like countless other Black families in the forties and fifties, we fell victim to this indifference and corruption when we moved to Oakland. It was as difficult then as it is now to find decent homes for large families, and we moved around quite bit in my early years in search of a house that would suit our needs. The first house I remember was on the corner of Fifth and Brush streets in a rundown section of Oakland. It was a two-bedroom basement apartment, and much too small to hold all of us comfortably. The floor was either dirt or cement, I cannot remember exactly; it did not seem to be the kind of floor that "regular" people had in their homes. My parents slept in one bedroom and my sisters, brothers, and I in the other. Later, when we moved to a two-room apartment at Castro and Eighteenth streets, there were fewer of us. Myrtle and Leola had married, and Walter had been drafted into the Army. On Castro Street, I slept in the kitchen. That memory returns often. Whenever I think of people crowded into a small living space, I always see a child sleeping in the kitchen and feeling upset about it; everybody knows that the kitchen is not supposed to be a bedroom. That is all we had, however. I still burn with the sense of unfairness I felt every night as I crawled into the cot near the icebox.

We were very poor, but I had no idea what that meant. They were happy times for me. Even though we were discriminated against and segregated into a poor community with substandard living conditions, I never felt deprived when I was small. I had a close, strong family and many playmates, including my brother Melvin, who was four years older than me; nothing else was needed. We just lived and played, enjoying everything to the fullest, particularly the glorious California weather, which is kind to the poor.

Unlike many others I knew, we never went hungry, although our food was the food of the poor, Cush was standard fare. Cush is made out of day-old corn bread mixed with other leftovers, such as gravy and onions, spiced very heavily and fried in a skillet. Sometimes we ate cush twice a day, because that was all we had. It was one of my favorite dishes, and I looked forward to it. Now I see that cush was not very nutritious and was downright bad for you if you ate it often; it is just bread—corn bread.

Life grew even sweeter when I was big enough—six or seven years old—to play outdoors with Melvin. Our games were filled with the joy and exuberance of innocent children, but even they reflected our economic circumstances. We rarely had store-bought toys. We improvised with the materials at hand. Rats were close at hand, and we hated rats because they infested our homes; one had almost bitten off my nephew's toe. Partly because of the hate and partly for the game of it, we caught rats and put them in a large can and poured coal oil into the can, then lighted it. The whole can would go up in flames while we watched the rats scoot around inside, trying to escape the fire, their tails sticking straight up like smoking grey toothpicks. Usually they died from the smoke before the flames consumed them.

We also despised cats, because we were told that cats killed little babies by sucking the breath out of them. We tested the tale about cats always landing on their feet. When we caught cats and took them to the top of the stairs and hurled them down, they would land on their feet—most of the time.

Dirt was a favorite toy. We used it to play at being builders. The roof of the house was our building site. We would climb up there and pull up the dirt-filled buckets behind us with rope, hand over hand, to the top of the house, and then dump the dirt down on the other side. There were no swimming pools near us, but when we got a little older we began to wander down to the bay with the other kids and go swimming off the pier in the dirty water. Dirt, rats, cats: these are the games and toys of the poor, as old and cruel as economic reality.

My parents insisted that we learn to get along with each other. When there was a dispute, my father never took sides. He was always an impartial judge, listening to both parties and getting to the bottom of things before making a decision. He was a fair and careful judge about all disputes, and later, when we had trouble in school, my father went every time to the teacher or the principal to learn what had happened. When we were right, he stood up for us, but he never tolerated wrongdoing.

We were not taught to fight by our parents, although my father insisted that we stand our ground when attacked. He told us never to start a fight, but once in it to stand fast until the end.

This was how we grew up—in a close family with a proud, strong, protective father and a loving, joyful mother. No wonder we came to feel that all our needs—from religion to friendship to entertainment—were met within the family circle. There was no felt need for outside friends; we were such good friends with each other.*

In this way the days of our childhood slipped past. We shared the dreams of other American children. In our innocence we planned to be doctors, lawyers, pilots, boxers, and builders. How could we know then that we were not going anywhere? Nothing in our experience had shown us yet that the American dream was not for us. We, too, had great expectations. And then we went to school.

2

The clash of cultures in the classroom is essentially a class war, socio-economic and racial warfare being waged on the battleground of our schools, with middle-class aspiring teachers provided with a powerful arsenal of half-truths, prejudices, and rationalizations, arrayed against hopelessly outclassed working-class youngsters. This is an uneven balance, particularity since, like most battles, it comes under the guise of righteousness.

Kenneth Clark, Dark Ghetto

LOSING

Because we moved around a lot when I was growing up, I attended almost every grammar and junior high school in the city of Oakland and had wide experience with the kind of education Oakland offers its poor people.

At the time, I did not understand the size or seriousness of the school system's assault on Black people. I knew only that I constantly felt uncomfortable and ashamed of being Black. This feeling followed me everywhere, without letup. It was a result of the implicit understanding in the system that whites were "smart" and Blacks were "stupid." Anything presented as "good" was always white, even the stories teachers gave us to read in the early grades. Little Black Sambo, Little Red Riding Hood, and Snow White and the Seven Dwarfs told us what we were.

I remember my reaction to Little Black Sambo. Sambo was, first of all, a coward. When confronted by the tigers, he gave up the presents from his father without a struggle—first the umbrella, then the beautiful crimson, felt-lined shoes, everything, until he had nothing left. And afterward, Sambo wanted only to eat pancakes. He was totally unlike the courageous white knight who rescued Sleeping Beauty. The knight was our symbol of purity, while Sambo stood for humiliation and gluttony. Time after time, we heard the story of Little Black Sambo. We did not want to laugh, but finally we did, to hide our shame, accepting Sambo as a symbol of what Blackness was all about.

As I suffered through Sambo and the Black Tar Baby story in Brer Rabbit in the early grades, a great weight began to settle on me. It was the weight of ignorance and inferiority imposed by the system. I found myself wanting to identify with the white heroes in the primers and in the movies I saw, and in time I cringed at the mention of Black. This created a gulf of hostility between the teachers and me, a lot of it repressed, but still there, like the strange mixture of hate and admiration we Blacks felt toward whites generally.

We simply did not feel capable of learning what the white kids could learn. From the beginning, everyone—including us—judged smart Blacks in terms of how they compared with whites, whether they could read or do arithmetic as well as the white kids. Whites were the standard of comparison in all things, even personal attractiveness. Bushy African hair was bad; straight hair was good; light was better than dark. Our image of ourselves was defined for us by textbooks and teachers. We not only accepted ourselves as inferior; we accepted the inferiority as inevitable and inescapable.

By the third or fourth grade, when we began to do simple mathematics, I had learned to maneuver my way around the teachers. It was a simple matter

*Even today my entire family lives in the San Francisco Bay area, close to our parents. Any disagreements among us are still taken to our parents for arbitration. When one member of the family entertains, most of the guests are other family members. Outsiders are rarely included in such gatherings.

to put pressure on the white kids to do my arithmetic and spelling assignments. The feeling that we could not learn this material was a general attitude among Black children in every public school I ever attended. Predictably, this sense of despair and futility led us into rebellious attitudes. Rebellion was the only way we knew to cope with the suffocating, repressive atmosphere that undermined our confidence.

Of all the unpleasant things that happened to me in elementary school, I remember two in particular. I had disciplinary problems from the beginning, plenty of them, but often they were not my fault. For instance, in the fifth grade at Lafayette Elementary School (I was eleven) I had an old white lady for a teacher. I have forgotten her name, but not her stern, disapproving face. Thinking once that I was not paying attention, she called me to the front of the room and pointedly told the class that I was misbehaving because I was stupid. She would show them just how stupid I was. Handing me a piece of chalk, she told me to write the word "business" on the blackboard. Now, I knew how to spell the word; I had written it many times before, and I knew I was not stupid. However, when I walked to the board and tried to write, I froze, unable to form even the first letter. Inside I knew she was wrong, but how could I prove it to her? I resolved the situation by walking out of the room without a word.

This happened to me time and again, growing worse with repetition. When I was asked to read aloud in class or spell a word, my mind went black and cold. Everybody thought I was dumb, I suppose, but I knew it was the lock inside my head. I had lost the key. Even now, when I read to a group of people, I am likely to stumble.

The other incident also happened at Lafayette. The school had a rule that you could dump the sand out of your shoes after recess, just before you sat down. One day I was sitting on the floor, dumping the sand from each shoe. I had quite a bit of sand, and dumping it took time, too much for the teacher, who came up behind me and slapped me across the ear with a book, accusing me of deliberately delaying the class. Without thinking, I threw the shoe at her. She headed for the door at a good clip and made it through just in front of my other one.

Of course I was sent to the principal, but I received a great deal of respect from the other children for that act; they backed me for resisting unjust authority. In our working- and lower class community we valued the person who successfully bucked authority. Group prestige and acceptance were won through defiance and physical strength, and both of them led to racial and class conflict between the authorities and the students.

The only teacher with whom I never had trouble was Mrs. McLaren, who taught me sixth grade at Santa Fe Elementary School. She had also taught my brother Melvin several years earlier, and since he was a model student, Mrs. McLaren expected a lot of me. I felt, in turn, a responsibility to live up to Melvin's reputation. Mrs. McLaren never raised her voice. She was a tranquil person, at ease and peaceful, no matter what was happening. Nobody wanted to start a fight with her. She was the exception to the rule.

By then, however—even in the sixth grade—I had such a tough reputation in school there was no need to start fights with the instructors. They were waiting for me and often provoked trouble, thinking I would pull something anyway, even when I was going along with the program. I went through a series of conversions and lapses. Each suspension brought a strong lecture from my parents, followed by a week or so of heavy soul searching and a decision to co-operate with the teachers and give my best effort. Mother and Father argued that the instructors had something I needed and that I could not expect to go into the class as an equal. I would return to school full of firm and good intentions; then, invariably, the instructors would provoke me, thinking I was there to continue the struggle. Sharp words, a fight, expulsion, and another semester down the drain. It often seemed that they simply wanted me out of the classroom.

During those long years in the Oakland public schools, I did not have one teacher who taught me anything relevant to my own life or experience. Not one instructor even awoke in me a desire to learn more or question or explore the worlds of literature, science, and history. All they did was try to rob me of the sense of my own uniqueness and worth, and in the process they nearly killed my urge to inquire.

3

He who would be free must strike the first blow.

Frederick Douglass, My Bondage and My Freedom

GROWING

. . .

My years in junior high were a repeat of elementary school. The teachers attempted to embarrass and humiliate me, and I countered defiantly to protect my dignity. While I did not see it at the time, fierce pride was at the bottom of my resistance. These struggles had the same result: I continued to be suspended from school. My parents, the principal, and the counselor lectured me for hours, and I would again make up my mind to knuckle under and go along. As soon as I hit the classroom, however, there would be another provocation, another visit with the principal, and back on the streets again. It was a kind of revolving door: each week things were the same.

The one class I took in junior high school that was not painful was a cooking class taught by the only Black teacher I had in all my years at school—Miss Cook. There was a reason for my taking this class. Most of the white kids had money to buy their lunch, but my family could not afford that. Since I was too proud to bring my lunch in a brown paper bag, and be ridiculed by my friends, I took cooking—and eating. It was either that, or gambling, or stealing from the white kids.

Crawford and I were in the same class, and we were always getting kicked out together. I remember clearly one of the teachers at Woodrow Wilson—Mrs. Gross. We had her three periods every day in what was called the dumb class; only Blacks were in it. We spent each day gambling and poking each other and generally raising hell. Crawford would shoot a rubber band at me, or I would slap him on the head, and then we would fight, and Mrs. Gross would kick us out. Sometimes she sent us to the principal's office, and sometimes she told us to stand in the hall. When you were booted from one of her classes, you were out for the whole day. It was a form of liberation—liberation from the dumb class.

Her class was particularly bad during reading sessions. We hated being there to begin with, because we were not interested in what Mrs. Gross was saying. When the reading-aloud sessions came, we were frantic to get out. We could not read, and we did not want the rest of the class to know it. The funny thing is that most of the others could not read, either. Still, you did not want them to know it.

At that time, and earlier, I associated reading with being an adult: when I became an adult, I would automatically be able to read, too. It was a skill that people naturally acquired in the process of maturation. Anyhow, why should I want to read when all they gave us were irrelevant and racist stories? Refusing to learn became a matter of defiance, a way of preserving whatever dignity I could hold onto in an oppressive system.

Therefore, when it was time for Crawford or me to read, we made a conscious effort to get kicked out of class, and were usually successful. Then we would sneak out of the school and steal a bottle of wine or ride our bikes to one of our partners' houses and while away the day playing cards. Later, after school let out in the afternoon, we often sneaked into the movies with other kids or went to David's house and listened to records and danced with the girls.

This is pretty much the way things went all during junior high. On the surface, my record was dismal. Yet those years were not significantly different from the adolescence of many Blacks. We went to school and got kicked out. We drifted into patterns of petty delinquency. We were not necessarily criminally inclined, but we were angry. We did not feel that stealing a bottle of wine or "cracking" parking meters was wrong. We were getting back at the people who made us feel small and insignificant at a time when we needed to feel important and hopeful. We struck out at those who trampled our dreams.

James Crawford had his dreams. He dreamed of becoming a great singer. There were days when Melvin and I sat listening for hours while James sang in his beautiful tenor voice. He was also a good cook and dreamed of opening a restaurant. James Crawford was talented, but the educational system and his psychological scars held him back. He never learned to read. To this day he cannot read. His fear of failure was reinforced rather than helped by those charged with his education, and his dreams slipped away. As he became more fearful and frustrated with each passing year, James was finally expelled from school as an "undesirable." Gradually, he sank into alcoholism and has been in and out of state mental hospitals since our school years. His face is scarred where the police beat him.

That is the story of my friend James Crawford; another dream blown to hell.

4

The glory of my boyhood years was my father . . . there was no hint of servility in my father's make-up. Just as in youth he had refused to remain a slave, so in all the years of his manhood he disdained to be an Uncle Tom. From him we learned, and never doubted it, that the Negro was in every way equal to the white man. And we fiercely resolved to prove it.

Paul Robeson, Here I Stand

CHANGING

. . .

When I look back on my early years, I see how lucky I was. Strong and positive influences in my life helped me escape the hopelessness that afflicts so many of my contemporaries. First, there was my father, who gave me a strong sense of pride and self-respect. Second, my brother Melvin awakened in me the desire to learn, and third, because of him, I began to read. What I discovered in books led me to think, to question, to explore, and finally to re-direct my life. Numerous other factors influenced me—my mother and the rest of my family, my experiences on the street, my friends, and even religion in a peculiar way. But these three—and most of all my father—helped me to develop and change.

When I say that my father was unusual, I mean that he had a dignity and pride seldom seen in southern Black men. Although many other Black men in the South had a similar strength, they never let it show around whites. To do so was to take your life in your hands. My father never kept his strength from anybody.

Traditionally, southern Black women have always had to be careful about how they bring up their sons. Through generations, Black mothers have tried to curb the natural masculine aggressiveness in their young male children, lest this quality bring swift reprisal, or even death, from the white community. My father was never subjected to this pressure, or, if he was, he chose to ignore it. He somehow managed to grow up with all his pride and dignity intact. As an adult he never let a white man humiliate him or any member of his family; he kept his wife at home, even though whites in Monroe, Louisiana, felt she should be working in their kitchens, and made that plain to him. He never yielded, always maintaining his stand as a strong protector, and he never hesitated to speak up to a white man. When we children were small, my father entertained us with stories of his encounters with whites. He has not been well for the past few years, but even now, as he tells these stories, the old strength surges through him again. None of us realized it then but those old stories were more than simple entertainment; he was teaching us how to be men.

One time in Louisiana he got into an argument with a young white man for whom he was working. The disagreement had to do with some detail about the job, and the white man became angry when my father stood his ground. He told my father that when a colored man disputed his word, he whipped him. My father replied just as firmly that no man whipped him unless he was a better man, and he doubted that the white man qualified. This shocked the white man, and confused him, so that he backed down by calling my father crazy. The story spread quickly around town; my father became known as a "crazy man" because he would not give in to the harassment of whites. Strangely, this "crazy" reputation meant that whites were less likely to bother him. That is often the way of the oppressor. He cannot understand the simple fact that people want to be free. So, when a man resists oppression, they pass it off by calling him "crazy" or "insane." My father was called "crazy" for his refusal to let a white man call him "nigger" or to play the Uncle Tom or allow whites to bother his family. "Crazy" to them, he was a hero to us.

He even stood up to white men when they were armed. One evening, as he rode home from work with some other Black men, for some reason they stopped their car in front of a white man's house and began to talk and laugh. They did not see the white woman on the front porch, but pretty soon a white man came out of the house with an ax and yelled at them for laughing at his sister. The driver panicked and drove off. When they reached the corner, my father made him stop. He climbed out and walked back alone. The white man was advancing down the road with the ax. My father asked him why he had come out with that ax and what he had in mind to do with it. The white man passed off the incident lightly by saying something about "you know how these southern women can be," and how he had to make a show to satisfy his sister. My father realized that in the etiquette of southern race relations this was an apology. He accepted it, but not before he made it clear to the white man that he would be threatened.

He never hesitated to make his view known to anyone who would listen. Once, when he felt cheated by a white man, he let all the town know what had happened. The man heard the stories and came to our house to see my father. This white man carried a gun in the glove compartment of his car. My father knew that, but he nevertheless went outside unarmed to talk. He maneuvered around to the right side of the car, and sat on the running board with the white man in front of him so that he could not get to the gun. Then he told the white man what he thought of him and said, "If you hit me a lick, the other folks will have to hunt me down because you'll be lying here in the road dead." The white man drove off, and my father heard no more about it.

Another time some whites invited him to go hunting. To this day I do not know why they asked him. They all took their shotguns. Knowing my father was a preacher, they tried to goad him into a discussion about the Bible and the origin of man. Adam and Eve were surely white, they said, so where did Black people come from? Their convenient interpretation was that Blacks must have spring from the union of Adam and a gorilla. My father countered by saying that Adam must have been a low-life white man to have had sex with a gorilla. At this, the situation grew fairly tense, but nothing came of it.

His protection extended to every member of his family. At the age of fifteen, my oldest brother, Lee Edward, went to work with my father in a sugar-cane mill. The first step in the sugar-cane process was to feed stalks into a gasoline-powered grinder. The grinder never stopped, and it had to be kept fully or it would burn out. This was Lee Edward's job. They had cut the engine down some in the hope that Lee Edward could run it, but he got tired his first day in the mill, and about eleven o'clock, after four hours on the job, he could not keep the machine full. It ran down and burned out. When the owner saw this, he began yelling at Lee Edward, but before he could say much, my father was right there. This white man was over six feet tall and weighed 200 pounds, but my father got right in the middle of it. He shut off the motor and told the owner it took a grownup to keep cane in the mill. My father took Lee Edward off the job after that. He wanted us to be good workers, just as he was, but he also wanted us to grow up proud.

I heard these stories and others like them over and over again until in a way his experiences became my own. Anyone who tried to bother us, Black or white, had to contend with my father. It made no difference that the South did not tolerate such behavior from Blacks. My father stood up to the white South until the day he left for California. He has never returned.

The fact that my father survived despite these encounters may do deeper than a simple white defense mechanism. His blood was, after all, half white, and that same blood flowed in the veins of other local people—in his father, his cousins, aunts, and uncles. While local whites were willing enough to shed the blood of Black people, it may be that they were afraid of being haunted by the murder of another "white." Statistics bear this out. The history of lynching in the South shows that Blacks of mixed blood had a much higher chance of surviving racial oppression than their all-Black brothers.

In any case, my father's pride meant that the threat of death was always there; yet it did not destroy his desire to be a man, to be free. Now I understand that because he was a man he was also free, and he was able to pass this freedom on to his children. No matter how much society tried to steal our self-esteem, we survived on what we got from him. It was the greatest possible gift. All else stems from that.

This strong sense of self-worth created a sense of closeness among us and a sense of responsibility for each other. Since I was the youngest in the family, all the other children had a deep influence on me, but particularly my three brothers. Of the three, it was Melvin who opened up most decisively the possibilities for intellectual growth and a special kind of self-realization.

Melvin is only four years older than I am, and during childhood we were constant playmates. Melvin planned to become a doctor, and I dreamed of being a dentist so that we could open an office together in the community. Somewhere along the way these desires were lost, probably in school, where my scholarly ambitions died early. Although Melvin did not go to medical school, he was always a good student. Now he teaches sociology at Merritt College in Oakland.

I always admired Melvin's intellectual activities; it was he who helped me to overcome my reading difficulties. When he began college, I used to follow him around and listen to him discuss books and courses with his friends. I think this later influenced me to go to college, even though I had not learned anything in high school. Melvin also taught me poetry by playing recordings of poems or reading to me. He was studying literature in school, and I suppose teaching me poems was a way of learning them himself. We often discussed their meanings. Sometimes Melvin explained the poems to me, but after a while I found that I could understand them along, and I began to explain them to him.

I seem to remember poetry without effort, and by the time I had entered high school, my memory held a lot of poetry I had heard read aloud. As Melvin studied for his literature class at Oakland City College, I learned Edgar Allan Poe's "The Bells" and "The Raven," "The Love Song of J. Alfred Prufrock" by T. S. Eliot, Shelley's "Ozymandias" and "Adonais." I also liked Shakespeare, particularly Macbeth's despairing speech that begins "Tomorrow, and tomorrow, and tomorrow / Creeps in this petty pace from day to day. . . ." Shakespeare was speaking of the human condition. He was also speaking to me, for my life sometimes crept aimlessly from day to day. I was often like the player fretting and strutting my brief hour upon the stage. Soon, like a brief candle, my life would go out. I was learning a lesson, however, that contradicted Macbeth's despair. While life will always be filled with sound and fury, it can be more than a tale signifying nothing.

"Adonais," too, had a special impact on me. The poem tells the story of a man whose friend dies or is killed. One of the best things in the poem is the sense that with the passing of years the poet's feelings alter and he begins to see things differently. He tells how he feels, how his attitude toward his friend changes as time goes on. This was an experience I began to have near the end of high school as my friends drifted into the service, or got married, or tried to become part of the very system that had humiliated us all the way through school. As time passed, I began to see the futility of the lives toward which they were headed. Marriage, family, and debt; in a sense, another kind of slavery.

"Ozymandias" impressed me because I felt there were different levels of meaning in it. It is a rich and complex poem:

I met a traveler from an antique land
Who said: Two vast and trunkless legs of stone
Stand in the desert. Near them, on the sand,
Half sunk, a shattered visage lies, whose frown,
And wrinkled lip, and sneer of cold command,
Tell that its sculptor well those passions read
Which yet survive, stamped on these lifeless
    things,
The hand that mocked them and the heart that fed:
And on the pedestal these words appear:
"My name is Ozymandias, king of kings;
Look on my works, ye Mighty, and despair!"
Nothing beside remains. Round the decay
Of that colossal wreck, boundless and bare
The lone and level sands stretch far away.

The poem could mean that a man's life is like the myth of Sisyphus. Each time you push the rock up the mountain, it rolls back down on you. Men build mighty works, and yet they are all destroyed. This king foolishly thought that his works would last forever, but not even works of stone survive. The king's great monument was destroyed, victim of the inevitable changes that come with time. On the other hand, it could be that the king was so wise that he wanted people to take their minds off their achievements and look with despair because they, too, would reach that edge of time, where everything around will be leveled.

Often it is impossible to understand at any specific period in your life just what is happening to you, since changes take place in imperceptible ways. This was true of my own adolescence. My admiration for Melvin led to a love of poetry and later to my interest in literature and philosophy. When my brother and I analyzed and interpreted poetry, we were dealing in concepts. Even though I could not read, I was becoming familiar with conceptual abstractions and the analysis of ideas and beginning to develop the questioning attitude that later allowed me to analyze my experiences. That led in turn to the desire to read, and the books I read eventually changed my life profoundly.

6

We love our country, dearly love her, but she does not love us—she despises us.

Martin Delany, 1852

HIGH SCHOOL

Throughout high school I constantly did battle with the instructors. The clashes I had steadily intensified and finally led to my transfer out of the Oakland system for a while. In the tenth grade I was attending Oakland Technical High School on Broadway and Forty-first. One day the teacher sent me to the principal's office for a minor offense I had committed the day before. The principal and teacher agreed that I could come back if I said nothing in class for the rest of the semester. I had already decided that I wanted out of school entirely, but I tried to sit mutely in class and not violate any of the rules, such as chewing gum, or eating sunflower seeds. One day I forgot the agreement and raised my hand to ask a question. "Put your hand down," he said. "I don't want to hear any more from you this whole term!" I stood up and told him it was impossible to learn anything if I was forbidden to ask questions. Then I walked out of the class.

Leaving school then meant I was short of classes and would be unable to go on to the eleventh grade and graduate. So I went to live in Berkeley with my oldest sister, Myrtle, and transferred to Berkeley High School.

Although Oakland was known in the East Bay Area as a rough community, it was not until I transferred to Berkeley High School that real trouble started with the police. One Sunday, while walking over to a girl's house, I met four or five girls I knew. They asked me to go with them to a party. Although I did not take up their offer, we walked along together, since we were going the same way. Pretty soon a car pulled up carrying a guy named Mervin Carter (he's dead now) and some others. They jumped out and began hassling me about messing around with their girl friends. I recognized Merv Carter; in fact, I had hung around Berkeley High with him and a couple of his friends. Like everybody else, they were turf-conscious and hated to see an outsider making time with their girls. I reminded him that we knew each other, that I was not interfering with the girls, and was on my way somewhere else. "Anyway," I said, "we hang around together in school." He told me we were friends inside school but not outside. I could not understand why he said that, whether he meant it or was just trying to impress his buddies.

By that time they had dropped a half circle on me. I realized they were going to jump me, so I hit Merv in the mouth, and then they all came at me. They beat me up pretty badly, but I refused to fall down. The girls were yelling at me to run, but I would not. No matter how many guys Merv had with him, I meant to stand my ground. As long as I could, I was going to look them in the eye and keep going forward.

Somebody called the police, but by the time they arrived Carter and the others had gone, and I was there along, bleeding, and missing several teeth. Although the police tried to find out who did it, I would not tell them anything. I did not want to be an informer because this was a problem between the brothers; the outside racist authorities had nothing to do with it. I have always believed that to inform on someone to the teacher, to the principal, or to the police is wrong. These people represent another world, another racial group. To be white is to have power and authority, and for a Black to say anything to them is a betrayal. So I did not inform, and they escaped the police; but they could not escape me.

The next day I went to school carrying a carpenter's hammer and an old pistol I had swiped from my father. The pistol did not work—it lacked a firing pin—but I had no intention of shooting anybody anyway. At lunchtime I "cold-trailed" Merv and about six of his buddies downtown. Catching up with them finally, I started to swing on him with the hammer. I hit him several times, wanting to hurt him, but he rolled with most of the blows and was not hurt too badly. Meanwhile, I forgot I had the gun. When the others began picking up rocks and sticks, I remembered the gun and used it to keep them at bay. This was the only way I could defend myself, because I had no friends at Berkeley High School to help me. I could not let them get away with what they had done, particularly since they had falsely accused me of messing with their girl friends. Somebody called the police again, and when I heard the sirens, I ran further downtown, where I was arrested. I was only about fourteen then, so they took me to Juvenile Hall, where I stayed for a month while they investigated my family background. Then I was released to the custody of my parents.

This was the first time into anything that could be called "criminal," even though I had raided fruit trees, cracked parking meters, and helped myself to stuff in the neighborhood stores. I never looked upon that as stealing or doing anything illegal, however. To me, that was not taking things that did not belong to us but getting something really ours, something owed us. That "stealing" was merely retribution.

When I was released from Juvenile Hall, Berkeley High School refused to admit me again because my parents lived in Oakland. I went back to Oakland Tech. My friends there and others who knew me praised what I had done in Berkeley. What I had done was an accepted action under the circumstances. If I had not retaliated, I would have been less respected.

Things went along well at Oakland Tech for a change. I was able to handle my differences with the teachers a little better because of my satisfaction with life outside of the classroom. My reputation as a fighter kept the wolves away. I was also known as a hipster like my brother Sonny Man, and I liked that, too. Some of the kids even called me "crazy," but that never bothered me because they used to call my father that too. To me, "crazy" was a positive identity.

. . .

Somehow I managed to stay in Oakland Tech until I graduated, despite my continued defiance of the authorities. They tried to down me for many years, but I knew inside that I was a good person, and the only way I could hold on to any self-esteem was to resist and defy them.

Everything they opposed I supported. That was how I first became a supporter of Fidel Castro and the Cuban Revolution. Earlier, when I heard teachers criticizing Paul Robeson, I defended him and believed in him, even though I knew very little about his life. When they started putting down Castro and the revolution of the Cuban people, I knew it must be good, too. I became an advocate of the Cuban Revolution.

My high school diploma was a farce. When my friends and I graduated, we were ill-equipped to function in society, except at the bottom, even though the system said we were educated. Maybe they knew what they were doing, preparing us for the trash heap of society, where we would have to work long hours for low wages. They never realized how much they had actually educated me by teaching the necessity of resistance and the dignity of defiance. I was on my way to becoming a revolutionary.

DRAWING CONCLUSIONS:

- What does Newton's memoir reveal about the factors that contributed to the rise of black power in the late 1960s?

2.7 "STRIKE DEMANDS OF THE BLACK STUDENT UNION AND THIRD WORLD LIBERATION FRONT," SAN FRANCISCO STATE COLLEGE (1969)

In the late 1960s, colleges and universities became centers of black power organizing. San Francisco State College in San Francisco, California, was such campus. San Francisco State was an urban campus that had traditionally served a largely commuter, non-traditional, and working-class student population. In 1967, African American students at San Francisco State began to advocate for curricular changes, including the creation of a Black Studies department. Tensions between black students and the campus administration escalated in 1969 when George Mason Murray, a prominent figure in the Black Panther Party, was fired from his job as a part-time English instructor on campus. On November 6, 1969, the campus Black Student Union called for a student strike in support of a list of ten "non-negotiable" demands. A few days later, the Third World Liberation Front (an alliance of Latino and Asian American student groups) joined the strike and issued its own set of demands. The student strike threw the campus into four months of turmoil, marked by scuffles between students and San Francisco city police, class cancellations, and intermittent closure of the campus. The strike ended in March 1969 when the campus administration agreed to the creation of a College of Ethnic Studies that included a Department of Black Studies.

GUIDING QUESTIONS:

- What are the specific demands of the Black Student Union and the Third World Liberation Front at San Francisco State College?
- What common themes do you see in these demands?

STRIKE DEMANDS OF THE BLACK STUDENT UNION AND THIRD WORLD LIBERATION FRONT

SAN FRANCISCO STATE UNIVERSITY—NOVEMBER 1969

Following is a list of the 15 strike demands as put forth by the Black Student Union and The Third World Liberation Front.

THE TEN BSU DEMANDS

1. That all Black Studies courses being taught through various other departments be immediately made part of the Black Studies Department, and that all the instructors in this department receive full-time pay.
2. That Dr. Nathan Hare, Chairman of the Black Studies Department, receive a full professorship and a comparable salary according to his qualifications.
3. That there be a Department of Black Studies which will grant a Bachelor's Degree in Black Studies; that the Black Studies Department, the chairman, faculty and staff have the sole power to hire faculty and control and determine the destiny of its department.
4. That all unused slots for Black students from Fall, 1968 under the Special Admissions Program be filled in Spring, 1969.

From Alexander Bloom and Wini Breines, eds., *"Takin' It to the Streets": A Sixties Reader* (New York: Oxford University Press, 1995), 391–392.

5. That all Black students wishing so be admitted in Fall, 1969.
6. That twenty (20) full-time teaching positions be allocated to the Department of Black Studies.
7. That Dr. Helen Bedesem be replaced from the position of Financial Aids Officer, and that a Black person be hired to direct it, that Third World people have the power to determine how it will be administered.
8. That no disciplinary action will be administered in any way to any students, workers, teachers, or administrators during and after the strike as a consequence of their participation in the strike.
9. That the California State College Trustees not be allowed to dissolve the Black programs on or off the San Francisco State College campus.
10. That George Murray maintain his teaching position on campus for the 1968–69 academic year.

THE FIVE TWLF DEMANDS

1. That a school of Ethnic Studies for the ethnic groups involved in the Third World be set up with the students in each particular ethnic organization having the authority and control of the hiring and retention of any faculty member, director and administrator, as well as the curriculum in a specific area study.
2. That fifty (50) faculty positions be appropriated to the School of Ethnic Studies, 20 of which would be for the Black Studies Program.
3. That in the Spring Semester, the college fulfill its commitment to the non-white students in admitting those that apply.
4. That in the Fall of 1969, all applications of non-white students be accepted.
5. That George Murray, and any other faculty person chosen by non-white people as their teacher, be retained in their position.

DRAWING CONCLUSIONS:

- What do the demands of the BSU and TWLF at San Francisco reveal about the ideas and goals of those involved with black power politics?

2.8 EXCERPTS FROM THE *REPORT OF THE NATIONAL ADVISORY COMMISSION ON CIVIL DISORDERS* (1968)

Between 1965 and 1968, the United States experienced the most destructive wave of urban unrest in the nation's history. During that four-year period, there were three hundred riots and disturbances in African American neighborhoods in virtually all corners of the country. Most were relatively minor, but a number involved widespread arson and looting that, in some cases, lasted for several days. The major riots were met by massive police and National Guard responses that left well over one hundred people dead. The first major riot took place in the Watts neighborhood of Los Angeles, California, in August 1965. The wave of unrest reached its climax in the summer of 1967 with major riots in Newark, New Jersey, and Detroit, Michigan, and smaller disturbances in dozens of other communities. Following the disturbances of 1967, President Lyndon Baines Johnson appointed a special presidential commission to study the causes of the disorder and to recommend steps that could be taken to prevent more such riots in the future. The commission is best remembered for its central conclusion: that the United States was "moving toward two societies, one black, one white—separate and unequal." The report, however, also contained hundreds of pages of information and analysis that provided important insights into the nature of the riots and their causes. The chapter entitled "Patterns of Disorder" addresses such questions as the severity of the disturbances, the characteristics of those who participated, and the conditions in the cities and neighborhoods in which they took place.

GUIDING QUESTIONS:

- What did the Commission identify as the underlying grievances that led to the riots of 1967?
- What did the commission identify as precipitating events that sparked the riots of 1967?
- What did the commission determine were the characteristics of those who participated in the riots of 1967?
- What did the commission identify as the characteristics of the communities in which riots took place in 1967?

FROM *REPORT OF THE NATIONAL ADVISORY COMMISSION ON CIVIL DISORDERS* (1968)

SUMMARY OF REPORT

INTRODUCTION

The summer of 1967 again brought racial disorders to American cities, and with them shock, fear and bewilderment to the nation.

The worst came during a two-week period in July, first in Newark and then in Detroit. Each set off a chain reaction in neighboring communities.

On July 28, 1967, the President of the United States established this Commission and directed us to answer three basic questions:

What happened? Why did it happen? What can be done to prevent it from happening again?

From *Report of the National Advisory Commission on Civil Disorders* (Washington, DC: US Government Printing Office, 1968).

To respond to these questions, we have undertaken a broad range of studies and investigations. We have visited the riot cities; we have heard many witnesses; we have sought the counsel of experts across the country.

This is our basic conclusion: Our nation is moving toward two societies, one black, one white—separate and unequal.

Reaction to last summer's disorders has quickened the movement and deepened the division. Discrimination and segregation have long permeated much of American life; they now threaten the future of every American.

This deepening racial division is not inevitable. The movement apart can be reversed. Choice is still possible. Our principal task is to define that choice and to press for a national resolution.

To pursue our present course will involve the continuing polarization of the American community and, ultimately, the destruction of basic democratic values.

The alternative is not blind repression or capitulation to lawlessness. It is the realization of common opportunities for all within a single society.

This alternative will require a commitment to national action—compassionate, massive and sustained, backed by the resources of the most powerful and the richest nation on this earth. From every American it will require new attitudes, new understanding, and, above all, new will.

The vital needs of the nation must be met; hard choices must be made, and, if necessary, new taxes enacted.

Violence cannot build a better society. Disruption and disorder nourish repression, not justice. They strike at the freedom of every citizen. The community cannot—it will not—tolerate coercion and mob rule.

Violence and destruction must be ended—in the streets of the ghetto and in the lives of people.

Segregation and poverty have created in the racial ghetto a destructive environment totally unknown to most white Americans.

What white Americans have never fully understood—but what the Negro can never forget—is that white society is deeply implicated in the ghetto. White institutions created it, white institutions maintain, and white society condones it.

It is time now to turn with all the purpose at our command to the major unfinished business of this nation. It is time to adopt strategies for action that will produce quick and visible progress. It is time to make good the promises of American democracy to all citizens—urban and rural, white and black, Spanish-surname, American Indian, and every minority group.

Our recommendations embrace three basic principles:

To mount programs on a scale equal to the dimension of the problems;

To aim these programs for high impact in the immediate future in order to close the gap between promise and performance;

To undertake new initiatives and experiments that can change the system of failure and frustration that now dominates the ghetto and weakens our society.

These programs will require unprecedented levels of funding and performance, but they neither probe deeper nor demand more than the problems which called them forth. There can be no higher priority for national action and no higher claim on the nation's conscience. . . .

PART I—WHAT HAPPENED?

Chapter 1 —Profiles of Disorder

The report contains profiles of a selection of the disorders that took place during the summer of 1967. These profiles are designed to indicate how the disorders happened, who participated in them, and how local officials, police forces, and the National Guard responded. Illustrative excerpts follow:

NEWARK

. . . On Saturday, July 15, Spina received a report of snipers in a housing project. When he arrived he saw approximately 100 National Guardsmen and police officers crouching behind vehicles, hiding in corners and lying on the ground around the edge of the courtyard.

Since everything appeared quiet and it was broad daylight, Spina walked directly down the middle of the street. Nothing happened. As he came to the last building of the complex, he heard a shot. All around him the troopers jumped, believing themselves to be under sniper fire. A moment later a young Guardsman ran from behind a building.

The Director of Police went over and asked him if he had fired the shot. The soldier said yes, he had fired to scare a man away from a window; that his orders were to keep everyone away from windows.

Spina said he told the soldier: "Do you know what you just did? You have now created a state of hysteria. Every Guardsman up and down this street and every state policeman and every city policeman that is present thinks that somebody just fired a shot and that it is probably a sniper."

A short time later more "gunshots" were heard. Investigating, Spina came upon a Puerto Rican sitting on a wall. In reply to a question as to whether he knew "where the firing is coming from?" the man said:

"That's no firing. That's fireworks. If you look up to the fourth floor, you will see the people who are throwing down these cherry bombs."

By this time four truckloads of National Guardsmen had arrived and troopers and policemen were again crouched everywhere looking for a sniper. The Director of Police remained at the scene for three hours, and the only shot fired was the one by the Guardsmen.

Nevertheless, at six o'clock that evening two columns of National Guardsmen and state troopers were directing mass fire at the Hayes Housing Project in response to what they believed were snipers. . . .

DETROIT

. . . A spirit of carefree nihilism was taking hold. To riot and destroy appeared more and more to become ends in themselves. Late Sunday afternoon it appeared to one observer that the young people were "dancing amidst the flames."

A Negro plainclothes officer was standing at an intersection when a man threw a Molotov cocktail into a business establishment at the corner. In the heat of the afternoon, fanned by the 20 to 25 m.p.h. winds of both Sunday and Monday, the fire reached the home next door within minutes. As residents uselessly sprayed the flames with garden hoses, the fire jumped from roof to roof of adjacent two- and three-story buildings. Within the hour the entire block was in flames. The ninth house in the burning row belonged to the arsonist who had thrown the Molotov cocktail. . . .

* * *

. . . Employed as a private guard, 55-year-old Julius L. Dorsey, a Negro, was standing in front of a market when accosted by two Negro men and a woman. They demanded he permit them to loot the market. He ignored their demands. They began to berate him. He asked a neighbor to call the police. As the argument grew more heated, Dorsey fired three shots from his pistol into the air.

The police radio reported: "Looters, they have rifles." A patrol car driven by a police officer and carrying three National Guardsmen arrived. As the looters fled, the law enforcement personnel opened fire. When the firing ceased, one person lay dead.

He was Julius L. Dorsey . . .

* * *

. . . As the riot alternatively waxed and waned, one area of the ghetto remained insulated. On the northeast side the residents of some 150 square blocks inhabited by 21,000 persons had, in 1966, banded together in the Positive Neighborhood Action Committee (PNAC). With professional help from the Institute of Urban Dynamics, they had organized block clubs and made plans for the improvement of the neighborhood. . . .

When the riot broke out, the residents, through the block clubs, were able to organize quickly. Youngsters, agreeing to stay in the neighborhood, participated in detouring traffic. While many persons reportedly sympathized with the idea of a rebellion against the "system," only two small fires were set—one in an empty building.

* * *

. . . According to Lt. Gen. Throckmorton and Col. Bolling, the city, at this time, was saturated with fear. The National Guardsmen were afraid, the residents were afraid, and the police were afraid. Numerous persons, the majority of them Negroes, were being injured by gunshots of undetermined origin. The general and his staff felt that the major task of the troops was to reduce the fear and restore an air of normalcy.

In order to accomplish this, every effort was made to establish contact and rapport between the troops and the residents. The soldiers—20 percent of whom were Negro—began helping to clean up the streets, collect garbage, and trace persons who had disappeared in the confusion. Residents in the neighborhoods responded with soup and sandwiches for the troops. In areas where the National Guard tried to establish rapport with the citizens, there was a smaller response.

NEW BRUNSWICK

. . . A short time later, elements of the crowd—an older and rougher one than the night before—appeared in front of the police station. The participants wanted to see the mayor.

Mayor [Patricia] Sheehan went out onto the steps of the station. Using a bullhorn, she talked to the people and asked that she be given an opportunity to correct conditions. The crowd was boisterous. Some persons challenged the mayor. But, finally, the opinion, "She's new! Give her a chance!" prevailed.

A demand was issued by people in the crowd that all persons arrested the previous night be released. Told that this already had been done, the people were suspicious. They asked to be allowed to inspect the jail cells.

It was agreed to permit representatives of the people to look in the cells to satisfy themselves that everyone had been released.

The crowd dispersed. The New Brunswick riot had failed to materialize.

Chapter 2—Patterns of Disorder

The "typical" riot did not take place. The disorders of 1967 were unusual, irregular, complex and unpredictable social processes. Like most human events, they did not unfold in an orderly sequence. However, an analysis of our survey information leads to some conclusions about the riot process.

In general:

The civil disorders of 1967 involved Negroes acting against local symbols of white American society, authority and property in Negro neighborhoods—rather than against white persons.

Of 164 disorders reported during the first nine months of 1967, eight (5 percent) were major in terms of violence and damage; 33 (20 percent) were serious but not major; 123 (75 percent) were minor and undoubtedly would not have received national attention as "riots" had the nation not been sensitized by the more serious outbreaks.

In the 75 disorders studied by a Senate subcommittee, 83 deaths were reported. Eighty-two percent of the deaths and more than half the injuries occurred in Newark and Detroit. About 10 percent of the dead and 38 percent of the injured were public employees, primarily law officers and firemen. The overwhelming majority of the persons killed or injured in all the disorders were Negro civilians.

Initial damage estimates were greatly exaggerated. In Detroit, newspaper damage estimates at first ranged from $200 million to $500 million; the highest recent estimate is $45 million. In Newark, early estimates ranged from $15 to $25 million. A month later damage was estimated at $10.2 million, over 80 percent in inventory losses.

In the 24 disorders in 23 cities which we surveyed:

The final incident before the outbreak of disorder, and the initial violence itself, generally took place in the evening or at night at a place in which it was normal for many people to be on the streets.

Violence usually occurred almost immediately following the occurrence of the final precipitating incident, and then escalated rapidly. With but few exceptions, violence subsided during the day, and flared rapidly again at night. The night-day cycles continued through the early period of the major disorders.

Disorder generally began with rock and bottle throwing and window breaking. Once store windows were broken, looting usually followed.

Disorder did not erupt as a result of a single "triggering" or "precipitating" incident. Instead, it was generated out of an increasingly disturbed social atmosphere, in which typically a series of tension-heightening incidents over a period of weeks or months became linked in the minds of many in the Negro community with a reservoir of underlying grievances. At some point in the mounting tension, a further incident—in itself often routine or trivial—became the breaking point and the tension spilled over into violence.

"Prior" incidents, which increased tensions and ultimately led to violence, were police actions in almost half the cases; police actions were "final" incidents before the outbreak of violence in 12 of the 24 surveyed disorders.

No particular control tactic was successful in every situation. The varied effectiveness of control techniques emphasizes the need for advance training, planning, adequate intelligence systems, and knowledge of the ghetto community.

Negotiations between Negroes—including your militants as well as older Negro leaders—and white officials concerning "terms of peace" occurred during virtually all the disorders surveyed. In many cases, these negotiations involved discussion of underlying grievances as well as the handling of the disorder by control authorities.

The typical rioter was a teenager or young adult, a lifelong resident of the city in which he rioted, a high school dropout; he was, nevertheless, somewhat better educated than his nonrioting Negro neighbor, and was usually underemployed or employed in a menial job. He was proud of his race, extremely hostile to both whites and middle-class Negroes and, although informed about politics, highly distrustful of the political system.

A Detroit survey revealed that approximately 11 percent of the total residents of two riot areas admitted participation in the rioting, 20 to 25 percent identified themselves as "bystanders," over 16 percent identified themselves as "counter-rioters" who urged rioters to "cool it," and the remaining 48 to 53 percent said they were at home or elsewhere and did not participate. In a survey of Negro males between the ages of 15 and 35 residing in the disturbance area in Newark, about 45 percent identified themselves as rioters, and about 55 percent as "noninvolved."

Most rioters were young Negro males. Nearly 53 percent of arrestees were between 15 and 24 years of age; nearly 81 percent between 15 and 35.

In Detroit and Newark about 74 percent of the rioters were brought up in the North. In contrast, of the noninvolved, 36 percent in Detroit and 52 percent in Newark were brought up in the North.

What the rioters appeared to be seeking was fuller participation in the social order and the material benefits enjoyed by the majority of American citizens. Rather than rejecting the American system, they were anxious to obtain a place for themselves in it.

Numerous Negro counter-rioters walked the streets urging rioters to "cool it." The typical counter-rioter was better educated and had higher income than either the rioter or the noninvolved.

The proportion of Negroes in local government was substantially smaller than the Negro proportion of population. Only three of the 20 cities studied had more than one Negro legislator; none had ever had a Negro mayor or city manager. In only four cities did Negroes hold other important policy-making positions or serve as heads of municipal departments.

Although almost all cities had some sort of formal grievance mechanism for handling citizen complaints, this typically was regarded by Negroes as ineffective and was generally ignored.

Although specific grievances varied from city to city, at least 12 deeply held grievances can be identified and ranked into three levels of relative intensity:

First Level of Intensity

1. Police practices
2. Unemployment and underemployment
3. Inadequate housing

Second Level of Intensity

4. Inadequate education
5. Poor recreation facilities and programs
6. Ineffectiveness of the political structure and grievance mechanisms

Third Level of Intensity

7. Disrespectful white attitudes
8. Discriminatory administration of justice
9. Inadequacy of federal programs
10. Inadequacy of municipal services
11. Discriminatory consumer and credit practices
12. Inadequate welfare programs

The results of a three-city survey of various federal programs—manpower, education, housing, welfare and community action—indicate that, despite substantial expenditures, the number of persons assisted constituted only a fraction of those in need.

The background of disorder is often as complex and difficult to analyze as the disorder itself. But we find that certain general conclusions can be drawn:

Social and economic conditions in the riot cities constituted a clear pattern of severe disadvantage for Negroes compared with whites, whether the Negroes lived in the area where the riot took place or outside it. Negroes had completed fewer years of education and fewer had attended high school. Negroes were twice as likely to be unemployed and three times as likely to be in unskilled and service jobs. Negroes averaged 70 percent of the income earned by whites and were more than twice as likely to be living in poverty. Although housing cost Negroes relatively more, they had worse housing—three times as likely to be overcrowded and substandard. When compared to white suburbs, the relative disadvantage is even more pronounced.

A study of the aftermath of disorder leads to disturbing conclusions. We find that, despite the institution of some post-riot programs:

- Little basic change in the conditions underlying the outbreak of disorder has taken place. Actions to ameliorate Negro grievances have been limited and sporadic; with but few exceptions, they have not significantly reduced tensions.
- In several cities, the principal official response has been to train and equip the police with more sophisticated weapons.
- In several cities, increasing polarization is evident, with continuing breakdown of inter-racial communication, and growth of white segregationist or black separatist groups. . . .

PART II—WHY DID IT HAPPEN?

Chapter 4—The Basic Causes

In addressing the question "Why did it happen?" we shift our focus from the local to the national scene, from the particular events of the summer of 1967 to the factors within the society at large that created a mood of violence among many urban Negroes.

These factors are complex and interacting; they vary significantly in their effect from city to city and from year to year; and the consequences of one disorder, generating new grievances and new demands, become the causes of the next. Thus was created the "thicket of tension, conflicting evidence and extreme opinions" cited by the President.

Despite these complexities, certain fundamental matters are clear. Of these, the most fundamental is the racial attitude and behavior of white Americans toward black Americans.

Race prejudice has shaped our history decisively; it now threatens to affect our future.

White racism is essentially responsible for the explosive mixture which has been accumulating in our cities since the end of World War II. Among the ingredients of this mixture are:

Pervasive discrimination and segregation in employment, education and housing, which have resulted in the continuing exclusion of great numbers of Negroes from the benefits of economic progress.

Black in-migration and white exodus, which have produced the massive and growing concentrations of impoverished Negroes in our major cities, creating a growing crisis of deteriorating facilities and services and unmet human needs.

The black ghettos where segregation and poverty converge on the young to destroy opportunity and enforce failure. Crime, drug addiction, dependency on welfare, and bitterness and resentment against society in general and white society in particular are the result.

At the same time, most whites and some Negroes outside the ghetto have prospered to a degree unparalleled in the history of civilization. Through television and other media, this affluence has been flaunted before the eyes of the Negro poor and the jobless ghetto youth.

Yet these facts alone cannot be said to have caused the disorders. Recently, other powerful ingredients have begun to catalyze the mixture:

Frustrated hopes are the residue of the unfulfilled expectations aroused by the great judicial and legislative victories of the Civil Rights Movement and the dramatic struggle for equal rights in the South.

A climate that tends toward approval and encouragement of violence as a form of protest has been created by white terrorism directed against nonviolent protest; by the open defiance of law and federal authority by state and local officials resisting desegregation; and by some protest groups engaging in civil disobedience who turn their backs on nonviolence, go beyond the constitutionally protected rights of petition and free assembly, and resort to violence to attempt to compel alteration of laws and policies with which they disagree.

The frustrations of powerlessness have led some Negroes to the conviction that there is no effective alternative to violence as a means of achieving redress of grievances, and of "moving the system." These frustrations are reflected in alienation and hostility toward the institutions of law and government and the white society which controls them, and in the reach toward racial consciousness and solidarity reflected in the slogan "Black Power."

A new mood has sprung up among Negroes, particularly among the young, in which self-esteem and enhanced racial pride are replacing apathy and submission to "the system."

The police are not merely a "spark" factor. To some Negroes police have come to symbolize white power, white racism and white repression. And the fact is that many police do reflect and express these white attitudes. The atmosphere of hostility and cynicism is reinforced by a widespread belief among Negroes in the existence of police brutality and in a "double standard" of justice and protection—one for Negroes and one for whites.

To this point, we have attempted to identify the prime components of the "explosive mixture." In the chapters that follow we seek to analyze them in the perspective of history. Their meaning, however, is clear:

In the summer of 1967, we have seen in our cities a chain reaction of racial violence. If we are heedless, none of us shall escape the consequences.

DRAWING CONCLUSIONS:

- What can we learn from about the causes of the urban disturbances of the late 1960s from the information gathered by the National Advisory Commission on Civil Disorders?

THE YOUTH REBELLION

Given the realities of racial inequality and race-based oppression, the unrest within African American communities in the 1960s can be easily understood. By contrast, the rebellion that swept portions of the country's white middle-class youth in the latter portion of the decade is somewhat more mysterious. This so-called youth rebellion took two primary forms: (1) movements for radical social change, concentrated largely on college campuses, that came to be known as the "New Left"; and (2) a countercultural movement (the so-called hippies) that adopted ways of living that were at odds with mainstream culture. While the numbers of young people at the heart of the New Left and the counterculture were relatively small, these two movements ultimately touched the lives of millions of young people and sent shock waves through the country. Why, in the midst of the greatest economic boom in American history, would so many young people from relatively comfortable circumstances embrace forms of political and cultural rebellion?

3.1 STATEMENTS FROM THE NEW LEFT (1962-1969)

The early 1960s saw the emergence of social change movements among students on a number of college and university campuses. These movements focused on such issues as black civil rights and nuclear disarmament. Participants in these movements began to refer to themselves as the "New Left" to indicate their support for making racial changes in American society and culture and to distinguish themselves from older social change movements, such as the racial labor movements of the 1930s. (The term "left" has been used historically to refer to advocates of radical societal changes aimed at reducing or eliminating social inequalities.) Following the escalation of the Vietnam War in 1965, the participation in the New Left grew dramatically. So too did the movement's degree of militancy. By 1968 and 1969 the New Left had developed into a mass movement committed to militant action aimed at ending what participants perceived as the injustices of American society. The movement's size and commitment to confrontational protest tactics led to turmoil and upheaval on a variety of college and university campuses.

Founded in 1962, Students for a Democratic Society (SDS) was the leading organization of the New Left, and its growth and development parallel that of the movement as a whole. The evolution of the New Left can be traced by examining the following documents from SDS:

- The Port Huron Statement (1962)—a political manifesto adopted by SDS at its founding 1962 convention.
- Paul Potter, "The Incredible War" (1965)—a speech delivered by SDS President Paul Potter to the first major national protest against the Vietnam War organized by SDS in April 1965.
- Statement of the Columbia Strike Coordinating Committee (1968)—in April 1968, the SDS chapter at New York City's Columbia University (one of the country's most prestigious universities) called a student strike and occupied a number of campus buildings in support of a set of demands aimed at the severing University's connections to the US military and ending what SDS considered Columbia's racist practices toward the nearby African American community of Harlem. After New York City riot police ended the building occupations (arresting 712 individuals and injuring 148), the protests on campus escalated to the point that the spring semester had to be cancelled. This document is a statement issued by the SDS-led strike committee explaining the reasons for the student strike.

GUIDING QUESTIONS:

- How would you describe the tone of each of the SDS documents? Optimistic? Frustrated? Angry? Hopeful? Disappointed? Something else?
- What do the authors of each document say are the central problems facing the United States?
- What sorts of solutions does each document offer to these problems?
- How did the tone and content of the documents change over time?

THE PORT HURON STATEMENT OF THE STUDENTS FOR A DEMOCRATIC SOCIETY JUNE 1962

(EXCERPTS)

INTRODUCTION: AGENDA FOR A GENERATION

We are people of this generation, bred in at least modest comfort, housed now in universities, looking uncomfortably to the world we inherit.

When we were kids the United States was the wealthiest and strongest country in the world: the only one with the atom bomb, the least scarred by modern war, an initiator of the United Nations that we thought would distribute Western influence throughout the world. Freedom and equality for each individual, government of, by, and for the people—these American values we found good, principles by which we could live as men. Many of us began maturing in complacency.

As we grew, however, our comfort was penetrated by events too troubling to dismiss. First, the permeating and victimizing fact of human degradation, symbolized by the Southern struggle against racial bigotry, compelled most of us from silence to activism. Second, the enclosing fact of the Cold War, symbolized by the presence of the Bomb, brought awareness that we ourselves, and our friends, and millions of abstract "others" we knew more directly because of our common peril, might die at any time. We might deliberately ignore, or avoid, or fail to feel all other human problems, but not these two, for these were too immediate and crushing in their impact, too challenging in the demand that we as individuals take the responsibility for encounter and resolution.

While these and other problems either directly oppressed us or rankled our consciences and became our own subjective concerns, we began to see complicated and disturbing paradoxes in our surrounding America. The declaration "all men are created equal . . . rang hollow before the facts of Negro life in the South and the big cities of the North. The proclaimed peaceful intentions of the United States contradicted its economic and military investments in the Cold War status quo.

We witnessed, and continue to witness, other paradoxes. With nuclear energy whole cities can easily be powered, yet the dominant nation states seem more likely to unleash destruction greater than that incurred in all wars of human history. Although our own technology is destroying old and creating new forms of social organization, men still tolerate meaningless work and idleness. While two-thirds of mankind suffers undernourishment, our own upper classes revel amidst superfluous abundance. Although world population is expected to double in forty years, the nations still tolerate anarchy as a major principle of international conduct and uncontrolled exploitation governs the sapping of the earth's physical resources. Although mankind desperately needs revolutionary leadership, America rests in national stalemate, its goals ambiguous and tradition-bound instead of informed and clear, its democratic system apathetic and manipulated rather than "of, by, and for the people."

Not only did tarnish appear on our image of American virtue, not only did disillusion occur when the hypocrisy of American ideals was discovered, but we began to sense that what we had originally seen as the American Golden Age was actually the decline of an era. The worldwide outbreak of revolution against colonialism and imperialism, the entrenchment of totalitarian states, the menace of war, overpopulation, international disorder, supertechnology—these trends were testing the tenacity of our own commitment to democracy and freedom and our abilities to visualize their application to a world in upheaval.

Our work is guided by the sense that we may be the last generation in the experiment with living. But we are a minority—the vast majority of our people regard the temporary equilibriums of our society and world as eternally-functional parts. In this is perhaps the outstanding paradox: we ourselves are imbued with urgency, yet the message of our society is that there is

---

Port Huron Statement, in *"Takin' It to the Streets: A Sixties Reader*, ed. Alexander Bloom and Wini Breines (New York: Oxford University Press, 1995), 59–64.

no viable alternative to the present. Beneath the reassuring tones of the politicians, beneath the common opinion that America will "muddle through," beneath the stagnation of those who have closed their minds to the future, is the pervading feeling that there simply are no alternatives, that our times have witnessed the exhaustion not only of Utopias, but of any new departures as well. Feeling the press of complexity upon the emptiness of life, people are fearful of the thought that at any moment things might thrust out of control. They fear change itself, since change might smash whatever invisible framework seems to hold back chaos for them now. For most Americans, all crusades are suspect, threatening. The fact that each individual sees apathy in his fellows perpetuates the common reluctance to organize for change. The dominant institutions are complex enough to blunt the minds of their potential critics, and entrenched enough to swiftly dissipate or entirely repel the energies of protest and reform, thus limiting human expectancies. Then, too, we are a materially improved society, and by our own improvements we seem to have weakened the case for further change.

Some would have us believe that Americans feel contentment amidst prosperity—but might it not better be called a glaze above deeply felt anxieties about their role in the new world? And if these anxieties produce a developed indifference to human affairs, do they not as well produce a yearning to believe there is an alternative to the present, that something can be done to change circumstances in the school, the workplaces, the bureaucracies, the government? It is to this latter yearning, at once the spark and engine of change, that we direct our present appeal. The search for truly democratic alternatives to the present, and a commitment to social experimentation with them, is a worthy and fulfilling human enterprise, one which moves us and, we hope, others today. On such a basis do we offer this document of our convictions and analysis: as an effort in understanding and changing the conditions of humanity in the late twentieth century, an effort rooted in the ancient, still unfulfilled conception of man attaining determining influence over his circumstances of life . . .

THE INCREDIBLE WAR: SPEECH AT THE WASHINGTON ANTIWAR MARCH

(EXCERPTS)

PAUL POTTER

APRIL 17, 1965

Most of us grew up thinking that the United States was a strong but humble nation, that involved itself in world affairs only reluctantly, that respected the integrity of other nations and other systems, and that engaged in wars only as a last resort. This was a nation with no large standing army, with no design for external conquest, that sought primarily the opportunity to develop its own resources and its own mode of living. If at some point we began to hear vague and disturbing things about what this country had done in Latin America, China, Spain and other places, we somehow remained confident about the basic integrity of this nation's foreign policy. The Cold War with all of its neat categories and black and white descriptions did much to assure us that what we had been taught to believe was true.

But in recent years, the withdrawal from the hysteria of the Cold War era and the development of a more aggressive, activist foreign policy have done much to force many of us to rethink attitudes that were deep and basic sentiments about our country. The incredible war in Vietnam has provided the razor, the terrifying sharp cutting edge that has finally severed the last vestige of illusion that morality and democracy are the guiding principles of American foreign policy. The saccharine self-righteous moralism that promises the Vietnamese a billion dollars of economic aid at the very moment we are delivering billions for economic and social destruction and political repression is rapidly losing what power it might ever have had to reassure us about the

From *The Incredible War*, Massimo Teodori, ed., *The New Left: A Documentary History* (New York: Bobbs-Merrill, 1968), 246–248.

decency of our foreign policy. The further we explore the reality of what this country is doing and planning in Vietnam the more we are driven toward the conclusion of Senator Morse that the United States may well be the greatest threat to peace in the world today. That is a terrible and bitter insight for people who grew up as we did—and our revulsion at that insight, our refusal to accept it as inevitable or necessary, is one of the reasons that so many people have come here today . . .

. . . In many ways this is an unusual march because the large majority of people here are not involved in a peace movement as their primary basis of concern. What is exciting about the participants in this march is that so many of us view ourselves consciously as participants as well in a movement to build a more decent society. There are students here who have been involved in protests over the quality and kind of education they are receiving in growingly bureaucratized, depersonalized institutions called universities; there are Negroes from Mississippi and Alabama who are struggling against the tyranny and repression of those states; there are poor people here—Negro and white—from Northern urban areas who are attempting to build movements that abolish poverty and secure democracy; there are faculty who are beginning to question the relevance of their institutions to the critical problems facing the society. Where will these people and the movements they are a part of be if the President is allowed to expand the war in Asia? What happens to the hopeful beginnings of expressed discontent that are trying to shift American attention to long-neglected internal priorities of shared abundance, democracy and decency at home when those priorities have to compete with the all-consuming priorities and psychology of a war against an enemy thousands of miles away? . . .

. . . But the war goes on; the freedom to conduct that war depends on the dehumanization not only of Vietnamese people but of Americans as well; it depends on the construction of a system of premises and thinking that insulates the President and his advisors thoroughly and completely from the human consequences of the decisions they make. I do not believe that the President or Mr. Rusk or Mr. McNamara or even McGeorge Bundy are particularly evil men. If asked to throw napalm on the back of a ten-year-old child they would shrink in horror—but their decisions have led to mutilation and death of thousands and thousands of people.

What kind of system is it that allows good men to make those kinds of decisions? What kind of system is it that justifies the United States or any country seizing the destinies of the Vietnamese people and using them callously for its own purpose? What kind of system is it that disenfranchises people in the South, leaves millions upon millions of people throughout the country impoverished and excluded from the mainstream and promise of American society, that creates faceless and terrible bureaucracies and makes those the place where people spend their lives and do their work, that consistently puts material values before human values—and still persists in calling itself free and still persists in finding itself fit to police the world? What place is there for ordinary men in that system and how are they to control it, make it bend itself to their wills rather than bending them to its?

We must name that system. We must name it, describe it, analyze it, understand it and change it. For it is only when that system is changed and brought under control that there can be any hope for stopping the forces that create a war in Vietnam today or a murder in the South tomorrow or all the incalculable, innumerable more subtle atrocities that are worked on people all over—all the time. . .

STATEMENT OF COLUMBIA STRIKE COORDINATING COMMITTEE

APRIL 1968

The most important fact about the Columbia strike is that Columbia exists within American society. This statement may appear to be a truism, yet it is a

Statement of the Columbia Strike Committee - Alexander Bloom and Wini Breines, eds., *Takin' It to the Streets: A Sixties Reader* (New York: Oxford University Press, 1995), 387–390.

fact too often forgotten by some observers, reporters, administrators, faculty members, and even some students. These people attempt to explain the "disturbances" as reaction to an unresponsive and archaic administrative structure, youthful outbursts of unrest much like panty raids, the product of a conspiracy of communist agents in national SDS or a handful of hard-core nihilists ("destroyers") on the campus, or just general student unrest due to the war in Vietnam.

But in reality, striking students are responding to the totality of the conditions of our society, not just one small part of it, the university. We are disgusted with the war, with racism, with being a part of a system over which we have no control, a system which demands gross inequalities of wealth and power, a system which denies personal and social freedom and potential, a system which has to manipulate and repress us in order to exist. The university can only be seen as a cog in this machine; or, more accurately, a factory whose product is knowledge and personnel (us) useful to the functioning of the system. The specific problems of university life, its boredom and meaninglessness, help prepare us for boring and meaningless work in the "real" world. And the policies of the university—expansion into the community, exploitation of blacks and Puerto Ricans, support for imperialist wars—also serve the interests of banks, corporations, government, and military represented on the Columbia Board of Trustees and the ruling class of our society. In every way, the university is "society's child." Our attack upon the university is really an attack upon this society and its effects upon us. We have never said otherwise.

The development of the New Left at Columbia represents an organized political response to the society. We see our task, first as identifying for ourselves and for others the nature of our society—who controls it and for what ends—and secondly, developing ways in which to transform it. We understand that only through struggle can we create a free, human society, since the present one is dominated by a small ruling class which exploits, manipulates, and distorts for its own ends—and has shown in countless ways its determination to maintain its position. The Movement at Columbia began years ago agitating and organizing students around issues such as students' power in the university (Action), support of the civil rights movement (CORE), the war in Vietnam (the Independent Committee on Vietnam). Finally, Columbia chapter Students for a Democratic Society initiated actions against many of the above issues as they manifest themselves on campus. Politically speaking, SDS, from its inception on campus in November, 1966, sought to unite issues, "to draw connections," to view this society as a totality. SDS united the two main themes of the movement—opposition to racial oppression and to the imperialist war in Vietnam—with our own sense of frustration, disappointment, and oppression at the quality of our lives in capitalist society.

One of the most important questions raised by the strike was who controls Columbia, and for what ends? SDS pointed to the Board of Trustees as the intersection of various corporate, financial, real estate, and government interests outside the university which need the products of the university—personnel and knowledge—in order to exist. It is this power which we are fighting when we fight particular policies of the university such as expansion at the expense of poor people or institutional ties to the war-machine. We can hope for and possibly win certain reforms within the university, but the ultimate reforms we need—the elimination of war and exploitation—can only be gained after we overthrow the control of our country by the class of people on Columbia's Board of Trustees. In a sense, Columbia is the place where we received our education—our revolutionary education. . . .

But why do students, predominantly of the "middle-class," in effect, reject the university designed to integrate them into the system and instead identify with the most oppressed of this country and the world? Why did the gymnasium in Morningside Park become an issue over which Columbia was shut down for seven weeks? Why pictures of Che Guevara, Malcolm X, and red flags in liberated buildings?

Basically, the sit-ins and strike of April and May gave us a chance to express the extreme dissatisfaction we feel at being *caught in this "system."* We rejected the gap between potential and realization in this society. We rejected our present lives in the university and our future lives in business, government, or other universities like this one. In a word, we saw ourselves as oppressed, and began to understand the forces at work which make for our oppression. In turn, we saw those same forces responsible for the oppression and colonization of blacks and Puerto Ricans in ghettos, and Vietnamese and the people of the third world. By initiating a struggle in support of black and third world liberation, we create the conditions for our own freedom—by building a movement which will someday take power over our society, we will free ourselves.

As the strike and the struggle for our demands progressed, we learned more about the nature of our enemy and his unwillingness to grant any of our demands or concede any of his power. Illusions disappeared; the moral authority of the educator gave way to police violence, the faculty appeared in all its impotent glory. On the other hand, tremendous support came in from community residents, black and white alike, from university employees, from high school students, from people across the country and around the world. Inevitably, we began to reevaluate our goals and strategy. Chief among the lessons were (1) We cannot possibly win our demands alone: we must unite with other groups in the population; (2) The 6 demands cannot possibly be our ultimate ends: even winning all of them certainly would not go far enough toward the basic reforms we need to live as human beings in this society; (3) "Restructuring" the university, the goal of faculty groups, various "moderate" students, and even the trustees, cannot possibly create a "free" or "democratic" university out of this institution. (First, how can anyone expect any meaningful reforms when even our initial demands have not been met?) Secondly, we realize that the University is entirely synchronized with this society: how can you have a "free," human university in a society such as this? Hence the SDS slogan: "A free university in a free society." The converse is equally true.

The basic problem in understanding our strike—our demands, tactics, and history—consists of keeping in mind the social context of the university and of our movement. If you understand that we are the political response to an oppressive and exploitative social and economic system, you will have no difficulty putting together the pieces. . . .

3.2 MARK RUDD, EXCERPTS FROM *UNDERGROUND: MY LIFE WITH SDS AND THE WEATHERMEN* (2009)

Mark Rudd was an undergraduate student at Columbia University who became among the most prominent leaders of the New Left. As a first-year student, Rudd joined the campus chapter of Students for Democratic Society. Two years later he was elected chair of the Columbia SDS, and in that position he helped to organize the 1968 campus uprising that brought the spring semester screeching to a halt. The Columbia student uprising came to serve as a model for young radicals on other campuses, and Rudd found himself acting as a national spokesperson for SDS. In 1969, Rudd joined the Weatherman faction of SDS (which advocated armed political violence) and spent the next seven years living underground as a fugitive from the law. Today, Rudd works as a mathematics instructor at a community college in Arizona. In recent years, he has expressed regret for the violent tactics employed by the Weathermen, though he maintains that their critique of US imperialism and opposition to the war in Vietnam were justified. In 2009, he published an autobiography entitled *Underground: My Life with SDS and the Weathermen*. Although Rudd's experience is in many ways unusual (very few of those involved in the New Left, for instance, embraced terrorist violence or lived underground), his story offers a window into the factors that inspired many young college students to embrace the radical campus politics of the 1960s.

GUIDING QUESTIONS:

- What motivated Mark Rudd to become involved in the New Left?
- What explains Rudd's increasing political radicalization and embrace of increasingly militant political action?

UNDERGROUND: MY LIFE WITH SDS AND THE WEATHERMEN (EXCERPTS)

MARK RUDD

. . .

One night during the second semester of my freshman year, I was reading the eighteenth-century social philosopher John Locke in my eighth-floor dorm room, depressed as usual and struggling to stay awake. On the wall in front of my desk was a print that I had bought at the Museum of Modern Art of a Joan Miró painting, *Inverted Personages*. I thought its spontaneous lines and bold colors signified my intellectual avant-gardism. I answered the door, and in walked David Gilbert, the chairman of Columbia's Independent Committee on Vietnam (ICV). I had seen Dave, a senior sociology major, standing by the ICV literature table, near the Sundial at the center of campus, debating supporters of the war. He always seemed to demolish them. I had also read his articles arguing against the war in Vietnam in the *Daily Spectator*, the Columbia College paper. Dave introduced himself and said he

From Mark Rudd, *Underground: My Life with SDS and the Weathermen* (New York: HarperCollins, 2009), 9–12, 14–15, 17–24, 27–30, 35–37.

was canvassing the dorms to find people interested in antiwar work on campus.

"What do you think about the war in Vietnam?" He asked.

"I'm pretty sure it's wrong, but I don't know too much about it," I replied.

Dave was direct and honest, also genuinely friendly. Quick to smile, he had a broad, open face, heavy eyebrows, and short, dark, curly hair. Over the course of the next few hours, we sat and talked. He didn't harangue me or make me feel stupid. He just quietly told me about himself and what the others were doing. He came from a suburban Boston Jewish family, a background very much like my own. He'd been an Eagle Scout, and I had also been a Scout, though not attaining that level. Like me, Dave hadn't come from a left-wing background, but he had been inspired by the black college students who conducted the lunch-counter sit-ins in Greensboro, North Carolina. He described seeing Martin Luther King on television and thinking, "This is what it's like to be human, to be moral, to care about other people."

As a freshman at Columbia, in 1962, he had joined the campus chapter of CORE, the Congress of Racial Equality, one of the most militant civil-rights organizations. He had also, like me, gone into Harlem with the Citizenship council program, tutoring a black kid in his home. His conclusion from that experience was very different from mine. "The goal," he said, "isn't to make black people more like you and me. It's that they take control of their own lives and their community. That's the radical position. The liberal position of superiority is condescending."

Dave told me that he'd had a breakthrough moment just a year before. While taking the train to Harlem, he'd read in the paper that the United States had just begun the sustained bombing of Vietnam. He became extremely upset, and it must have shown on his face when he got to the house of the kid he tutored. The child's mother asked him if he was okay.

He replied, "I can't believe it. Our government is bombing people on the other side of the globe for no good reason."

"Bombing people for no good reason, huh?" she said. "Must be colored people who live there."

"That was a complete revelation to me," he said. "She had never heard of Vietnam, but she naturally made the connection that I had failed to make, even though I'd been working on both fronts, peace and civil rights, for almost four years. I was blinded by calling our system a democracy with some faults, while she understood it as being in essence a racist and violent system."

"Have you read *The Autobiography of Malcolm X* yet?" he asked me.

"No, I've been too busy with all the reading for freshman CC and Humanities." Contemporary Civilization and Humanities were both required courses.

"Well, you'll learn a lot more about contemporary civilization from Malcolm than you will from reading Plato," he said. "When Malcolm made the connection between Third World peoples' struggles abroad to free themselves from U.S. imperialism and the black struggle at home, the CIA signed his death warrant."

I did know that Malcolm had been shot and killed at the Audubon Ballroom on Broadway in upper Manhattan just a year before. I made a mental note to read the book.

"I heard him speak at Barnard three days before he was shot," Dave went on, "probably the most formative experience of my life. He said that the division in the world isn't between black and white, it's been the oppressed—who are mainly people of color—and the oppressors—who are mainly white. He also said that white people can play a positive role by organizing within their own communities."

Dave seemed to be knowledgeable on these things in a way that I wasn't, but even so, I recognized a lot of myself in him. He struck a chord in me when he said, "Our country unjustly attacked Vietnam. I can't stand by and allow this to happen, like a good German." Any Jew alive at the time would have known he was referring to the great mass of Germans who, in their ignorance, in their denial, and especially in their silence, allowed the Nazis to do their work. "We didn't know," was their phony cry when asked after the war about the destruction of the Jews.

I didn't want to be a good German either.

"Assuming what you say is true," I said, "and the war is morally wrong, so what? What can anyone do about it?"

"Well," he said, "we're part of a larger movement that will eventually end the war. People are working in different ways all over the country.

"We do what we can. In May, right before the summer vacation, we held an antiwar protest at the Naval ROTC graduation ceremony," he informed me, referring to the Reserve Officer Training Corps.

"Twenty-five of us were there. We actually caused the ceremony to be canceled. The university called the city cops, and they got real nasty with us. They grabbed me and a few others and beat us with billy clubs." He paused. "You know what I learned?"

"No, what?"

"Don't even wear a tie to a demonstration. That fucking cop chocked me with my own tie," he told me, laughing.

There was something so charming, so smart and warm about this guy, that I told him I'd be at the next ICV meeting.

. . .

After the ICV meetings, people would go to hang out at the West End Bar on Broadway or to an upperclassman's apartment. Over bears or a joint, I'd listen to discussions about China's Cultural Revolution, then just starting, and to Cuba's seven-year-old revolution. It was thrilling to be with these people who were tapping into something so much bigger than ourselves—something so grand, so historic: remaking the world.

There was this one guy, a freshman like me, named John Jacobs, or JJ, who got my attention because he was an animated madman. He talked in breathless whole paragraphs about Lenin and Mao and Marx in the nasal "dese" and "dose" accent of a working-class kid. Actually, JJ had been sent to an expensive prep school in Vermont by his wealthy Ridgefield, Connecticut, parents. He was almost my height, about five foot eleven, blond, thin but with very strong shoulders. His most prominent feature might have been his piercing blue eyes, which I later heard Barnard girls describe as "bedroom eyes."

JJ told me he had joined the anti-imperialist May 2 Movement right out of high school. M2M, as he called it, was "a mass front organization" for the Maoist Progressive Labor Party (PLP or PL). The party had let it run for less than two years, in which time it had grown by calling for militant resistance to the blockade of Cuba and urging men to resist the draft. JJ wasn't a member of PL himself, he told me, but he understood them.

In high-volume monologues that often shifted to yelling, JJ would hold forth while guzzling a beer and smoking a skinny joint. "In order to abolish colonialism and imperialism, we need to abolish capitalism, the root cause of war, domination, class and race exploitation. When that happens, we can substitute a humane, rational economic system, socialism. The majority of the people of the world will benefit, war will be eradicated, and history can then begin, as Marx himself said somewhere. An end to exploitation! Human beings will be liberated from servitude and toil for the first time in human history. What a wonderful era we're in!"

JJ was among the large number of my new antiwar activist friends who came from left-wing—that is, socialist or Communist families. It was from these "red-diaper babies" that I learned about "the struggle" that had been going on for generations. I felt lucky to be among them, because they seemed to embody an idealism that had passed my family by. My immigrant grandparents on both sides were not political, nor were my parents. They were pragmatists, too busy making a living to become involved in dreams of a better world. My father had seen friends he grew up with in Elizabeth become Communists in the thirties, then lose their jobs as teachers or engineers when the McCarthy repression was unleashed in the early fifties. He had often told me that his strategy for survival was to keep his head down.

The Great Depression of the thirties was the defining event in both my parents' lives. They came of age when there were no jobs to be had, and no money. My father earned two pensions by the time he was fifty, first as a lieutenant colonel in the U.S. Army Reserves and later as a civilian working for the Army & Air Force Exchange Service, the PXs. He and my mom then built a business of owning and managing apartment houses. Their lifelong goal, which they successfully reached, was the American dream of financial security. All these red-diaper babies talking about socialism challenged me to want something loftier: a utopia of freedom and justice and peace.

One other thrilling aspect of all this talk was that it gave us, the students with our brilliant ideas, a role to play. By agitating on campuses, we could have a hand in building the mass movement that would eventually change this country and the world.

Plus, having served my sentence as a loner, a bookworm, a nerd in high school, I had finally found my gang.

. . .

At the end of my first year at Columbia, in the spring of 1966, the Independent Committee on Vietnam voted to convert itself into a chapter of Students for a Democratic Society, SDS, a national organization. I vaguely understood that the change had something to do with creating a radical student organization at Columbia that would address more issues than just the war. It would unite such issues as racism, control over our own lives at the university, and imperialism as the underlying cause of warm. "Radical," I quickly picked up, meant getting at the root of things.

John Fuerst, skinny, long-faced, and hyper-intense, became chairman of the new SDS chapter—David Gilbert was graduating and going downtown to study sociology at the New School. John gave me a copy of its founding document, the Port Huron Statement, which had been written in 1962 by a small group of activist students lead by Tom Hayden. It was more than fifty pages long, and it challenged basic status quo assumptions about the country and the world.

I was astonished by Hayden and the other authors' intellectual breadth: In a single tour de force, they addressed politics, economics, the Cold War and anti-Communism, the nuclear arms race, decolonization around the world, and the civil-rights movement at home. They asked fundamental and important questions: How could poverty exist in the midst of such plenty? Why did the war system persist when we had the possibility of making peace? Ambitious and imaginative at the same time, the young writers proposed the realignment of U.S. political parties into true conservative and liberal, the revitalization of the public economic sector, the elimination of poverty and the spreading of civil rights, disarmament, and an end to the Cold War.

I was attracted to their intelligence, yes, but it was the idealism of the writers of the Port Huron Statement that pulled me in: "We would replace power rooted in possession, privilege, or circumstance by power and uniqueness rooted in love, reflectiveness, reason, and creativity." The "participatory democracy" they proposed would allow each individual citizen to make the decisions affecting his or her life. Plus, the Port Huron Statement gave students an important role in the development of a "New Left" in this country, as the visionaries and activists signed up for the new society.

Sign me up!

A few days later, I paid John my five-dollar dues. On the spot he filled out my membership card, which had LET THE PEOPLE DECIDE! printed at the top. I was now a card-carrying member of SDS. I also began wearing a little lapel button, about the size of a dime, white with the simple brown logo sds in lowercase. Sometimes the button would appear on my blue blazer. More often I'd substitute jeans, work shirt, and work boots, my comfortable new radical getup. By the end of that year, my preppy clothes were hanging permanently in the closet.

Many of the drafters of the Port Huron Statement were young white people like Tom Hayden, its principal author, fresh from the civil-rights battle lines in the South, where they had worked with the Student Nonviolent Coordinating Committee, SNCC. In the intervening four years, they had ambitiously sought to build something similar in the North, an "interracial movement of the poor," by organizing in working-class neighborhoods in northern industrial cities like Chicago, Cleveland, and Newark around jobs and income and housing conditions and welfare. SDS was often seen as a sister organization to SNCC: Both organizations considered participatory democracy a method as well as a goal. The first generation of SDS leaders had picked up the concept from SNCC in the South.

But the U.S. government had been gradually escalating the war in Vietnam during these years: At the end of 1964, there were 23,300 "advisers" stationed there. That number multiplied to 184,300 at the end of 1965, the year I turned eighteen and went down to my draft board to register, as U.S. ground forces went into direct combat, something three presidents had vowed would never happen. By the end of 1966, we had almost 385,000 GIs stationed in Vietnam, plus many thousands more in support positions around the world. Twenty-five thousand young men per month were drafted. Had I not been in school, I would have been drafted and sent to Vietnam.

As this escalation continued, SDS gradually shifted its focus from community organizing around economic issues toward Vietnam. The organization had called the first national antiwar demonstration in Washington on April 17, 1965. The marines had just landed at Da Nang, and their air force had begun its years-long Operation Rolling Thunder in Northern Vietnam to, as one general put it, "bomb Vietnam back to the Stone Age." Ten thousand people were expected; twenty-five thousand showed up.

A year and a half later, I picked up an SDS pamphlet that contained the transcript of SDS president Paul Potter's historic speech ending the first antiwar rally in front of the Washington Monument. As I read, I realized that he had captured my own growing hurt and sadness about the war:

> The incredible war in Vietnam has provided the razor, the terrifying sharp cutting edge that has finally severed the last vestige of illusion that morality and democracy are the guiding principles of American foreign policy. . . . That is a terrible and bitter insight for people who grew up as we did—and our revulsion at the insight, our refusal to accept it as inevitable or necessary, is one of the reasons that so many people have come here today.

By "people who grew up as we did," Potter was referring to me, the son of a World War II vet, who had spent my whole childhood believing that my country was a force for good in the world.

Potter then described the destruction and dictatorship our government was perpetrating on Vietnam. The U.S. goal was obviously not self-determination and freedom. At a midpoint he asked the question that made the speech famous:

> What kind of system is it that justifies the United States or any country seizing the destinies of the Vietnamese people and using them callously for its own purpose? What kind of system is it that disenfranchises people in the South, leaves millions upon millions of people throughout the country impoverished and excluded from the mainstream and promise of American society . . .?
>
> We must name that system. We must name it, describe it, analyze it, understand it, and change it.

At this point people in the crowd were screaming in response, "CAPITALISM!" and "IMPERIALISM!" Potter later wrote that he declined to use the word "capitalism" not out of opportunism but because it had become "for me and my generation an inadequate description of the evils of America—a hollow, dead word tied to the thirties."

Prophetic, Potter ended his speech by describing the movement we must build to end the war:

> . . . a movement that understands Vietnam in all its horror as but a symptom of a deeper malaise, . . . a movement that will build on the new and creative forms of protest that are beginning to emerge, such as the teach-in, and extend their efforts and intensify them; that we will build a movement that will find ways to support the increasing numbers of young men who are unwilling to and will not fight in Vietnam; a movement that will not tolerate the escalation or prolongation of this war but will, if necessary, respond to the administration war effort with massive civil disobedience all over the country, that will wrench the country into a confrontation with the issues of the war . . .

At the time—and still today—the moral and intellectual clarity of this speech sends shivers up my spine. It reminds me why it was such a thrill to be a member of SDS.

In my classes at Columbia, I was learning about the glories of Western civilization—the philosophers and literature that produced the Enlightenment, the rise of democracy, the idea of individual liberty. A few professors taught radical philosophy, such as the teachings of Hegel, Marx, and the contemporary Herbert Marcuse, but it was an abstract radicalism, unrelated to the current world. It seemed to me that most members of the faculty, even the renowned ones with leftists reputations, were not at all concerned with what the Left could accomplish today.

At SDS meetings I would listen to passionate debates by upperclassmen and graduate students about China's Cultural Revolution, the Cuban revolution, the nature of American class society, this country's role in blocking national liberation movements, including those of minorities such as blacks inside this country. They all agreed on one solution, Marxist revolution. I wanted to be like all these brilliant and burning young men—Michael Josefowicz, Harvey Blume, Howie Machtinger, David Gilbert, John Fuerst, Michael Klare—to understand the world as they did. I never once heard Vietnam mentioned in class, while outside of class Vietnam was everything.

Along with others in SDS, I was reading works of Australian journalism Wilfred Burchett, who described how the United States had assumed France's colonial role; how we had placed a handpicked dictator, Diem, in power and kept him there with massive bombing from the air and an enormous repressive puppet army. I also learned from Burchett, as well as from two publications, the scholarly *Viet Report* and the radical weekly *National Guardian*, that the Vietcong were a popular insurgency, guerrillas surviving among the people "like fish in the sea." The American strategy was to dry up the ocean—that is, remove the peasants from the countryside. The U.S. military used a host of brutal tactics, ranging from herding people into guarded concentration camps called "strategic hamlets" to destroying peasants' crops with herbicides like Agent Orange to simply murdering them and destroying all their villages with B-52 carpet bombing or artillery fire. As a result of our terror attack on the countryside of Vietnam, we generated 15 million refugees, most of whom went to the cities seeking safety and work.

I learned that the American military was an occupying army in Vietnam, and as part of such, no American soldier could ever feel secure. A kid carrying a cigarette pack filled with explosives could kill you as easily as could an armed guerrilla with a rifle. In this environment the rules of warfare made little sense, and all Vietnamese became the enemy. In 1969 the country would hear about the massacre at My Lai, which was not at all an isolated incident, but as early as 1966 I was reading about murder and torture by American troops in Vietnam. Given the nature of the war as a military occupation of a civilian population that did not want our soldiers there in the first place, such brutality was inevitable.

And what was the war for? An SDS pamphlet by David Gilbert, entitled U.S. Imperialism, explained that throughout the Third World, people were attempting to throw off the yoke of American and European control. That accounted for the dozens of U.S. military "interventions" around the world in the twentieth century. Revolts in such places as Cuba, Guatemala, Iran, Algeria, China, and Vietnam were "national liberation struggles"; there were the natural enemy of imperialism.

For me, only the radical analysis explained what was happening in the world. I wanted to place myself on the side of freedom, not empire.

Vietnam touched a wound inside me. The Holocaust had been a fact of my entire childhood, though I was born two years after World War II ended. In my home, as in millions of Jewish homes, "Hitler" was the name for Absolute Evil. As a kid I listened to two of my father's cousins describe how they had survived the concentration campus, and the whole while I was sneaking glances at the numbers tattooed on their arms. The suffering in their voices and their eyes told just part of the story; the rest I could only imagine. I was terrified, appalled, spellbound, reading the diary of Anne Frank or looking at *Life* magazine's images of Jewish families being rounded up, as well as the pictures taken when the camps were finally liberated.

With the solipsism of a child, I saw myself among the dead. Over and over I pondered what would have happened to me and my family if my father hadn't emigrated in 1917, or if my mother's family hadn't come to this country in 1911? Why was I allowed to be born while so many millions of other Jewish kids perished?

The Holocaust brought me to the knowledge that evil exists and that it is associated with racism; that's what Nazi anti-Semitism was. Growing up watching the civil-rights movement in this country and then learning about Vietnam, I saw evil again. Only this time it wasn't the sick, repressed Germans with their little brush-mustached dictator. It was us, the Americans, the most democratic, the most productive, the most egalitarian people ever to have graced the earth. We were responsible for these horrible atrocities.

Here I was, stuck with the knowledge of the evil of the American empire, the racism, the violence, the torture, the corruption. What would I do with this knowledge? Would I have the courage not to be a Good American and turn away?

. . .

In April 1967, Columbia SDSers read in the *Spectator* that U.S. Marine recruiters would be on campus for two days, looking for prospective officers. We took this as a direct provocation: The Vietnam War was coming to Morningside Heights.

SDS had been exposing and challenging the university's involvement with the war since the previous fall. Along with the sit-in at the Naval ROTC class that I participated in, we had led a successful referendum campaign to keep Columbia College from sending students' rank in class to local draft boards. Presumably, they would use this information to draft the poorer students. In the atmosphere of urgency before the referendum, I had ceased attending classes to help organize forums and dorm meetings. Though we won the referendum and the faculty subsequently voted to withhold the rankings, the majority of the students were driven more by self-interest—staying out of the army—rather than by a principled opposition to the government's policies in Vietnam.

In February a splinter group of SDS, people associated with the Maoist Progressive Labor Party (PL) had sat in to block recruiters from the Central Intelligence Agency from interviewing potential employees. The recruiters left, but sixteen people received warning letters from the university for participating. My friend JJ joined the sit-it, but I stayed with the majority of the SDS chapter that had voted against disrupting the recruiting. I was swayed by the arguments of Ted Kaptchuk, the chapter chairman, and his vice chairman, Ted Gold, who felt that the disruption would polarize the campus against us because there was not a general understanding of why recruiting for the CIA was wrong. We were scared of being politically isolated from other students.

Still, the Progressive Labor Party hard-core faction and its supporters ignored the vote and staged the sit-in. A bitter debate around the issue of disruption broke out on campus among faculty and students. Most of the faculty, both liberals and conservatives, believed in the "neutral" and "objective" character of the university. They did not want to see its normal functioning disturbed because of "external" political issues. Further, several senior faculty members were refugees from Nazi Germany. They identified SDS's antiwar activities with the actions of Nazi students at German universities in the thirties. This was a frightening image, even to us in SDS. "What if every small ground had the power to silence whomever they wanted—such as you?" asked the old liberals. "Isn't there an absolute right to free speech?"

I found myself in many heated arguments with my professors and other students about whether Columbia was participating in the war by allowing recruiting. "Suppose the Nazi SS came to a German university to recruit. Would you be silent and just let them?" I'd ask. "The Nuremberg Trials [of Nazi leaders after the end of World War II] established that it is the legal and moral responsibility of the individual not to comply with orders that constitute war crimes." I also argued that the interruption of the "normal" recruiting function at the university—which appears to be free speech—was a much smaller evil than the enormous one that the recruitment served, the war.

After a long spring of debate, the issues of complicity and disruption were coming back again, along with the U.S. Marines. The first day their recruiters appeared, SDS mustered around two hundred students to "confront" them. Actually, we just milled around in the dorm lobby where the marines had a table. Our exact intention was ambiguous: Even we didn't know what we would do. Opposing us was a group of about fifty right-wing and ROTC students—whom we called "jocks," whether they were athletes or not—protecting the marines by standing in front of them with their arms folded.

The two sides started pushing and shoving in the small lobby. "Fucking jock," some of our guys taunted. "Commie puke," we got in return. An SDSer was hit with a punch; we got our licks in, too. A college dean was urging on the jocks from the sidelines. I stayed with the SDS front line, facing off with a jock. We glared at each other, neither of us wanting to throw the first punch. Deep down I knew I was no fighter, but I would try my best to defend the cause. Just as the tension was reaching its peak, the campus police waded into the crowd to separate us. An official announced that the marine recruiting was over for the day. We had won.

About thirty of us SDSers went to the back room of the West End Bar to lick our wounds, plan for the next day, and celebrate our victory with a beer. We decided to mobilize everyone we could for the second day's confrontation: Tomorrow we would hold a peaceful demonstration against the marines and against the university's support for their recruiting.

That night we called everyone on our phone lists, put out leaflets to the forms and the campus, and made announcements on the university radio station, WKCR. We also organized ourselves into a contingent of marshals, with white armbands, to keep order. I was a marshal.

The next day I was astounded to count more than eight hundred students marching in opposition to the marines. It was the largest antiwar demonstration yet at Columbia. The hourlong picket line that filled the small quadrangle between John Jay Residence Hall, where the recruiters were, and Hamilton Hall, the main college classroom building, felt like a celebration. We sang freedom songs from the civil-rights movement: "Just like a tree that's planted by the wa-aw-ter, / We shall not be moved." We chanted, "What do you want? Marines out! When do you want it? Now!"

We had never before mobilized an antiwar demonstration on campus with that many people. Our confrontational tactics had worked: We'd forced people to choose sides and take a stand against the war. It was a lesson we wouldn't forget.

. . .

A week or so later, Jeff Jones of the New York City Regional Office of SDS, a happy-go-lucky long-haired blond surfer from Southern California improbably misplaced in Manhattan, told me that Secretary of State Dean Rusk would be given an award by the Foreign Policy Association, a true establishment organization. The presentation would take place at a black-tie dinner at the New York Hilton on Sixth Avenue. Rusk was one of the main architects and apologists of the war. I immediately saw a chance to redeem myself and the Columbia chapter.

The large coalition known as Vietnam Peace Parade Committee called a legal, peaceful demonstration to be held across the street from the Hilton. New York Regional SDS put out a leaflet that hinted at something different:

> EMBROIL THE NEW YORK HILTON (6TH AVE. AND 53RD ST.)
> REVOLUTION BEGINS: NOV. 14, 5–5:30 PM

Before the demonstration we distributed plastic bags of cow blood to remind onlookers of the blood being spilled in Vietnam. The police had announced an official protest area about two blocks from the entrance to the Hilton, were no one would see the demonstration, but we wanted no part of police restrictions. Our goal was to disrupt the banquet from outside by stopping traffic.

For several joyous hours that warm fall evening, I ran with my "affinity group," including Sue, through the midtown streets, stopping traffic, banging on limos, dousing them with cow's blood, and grappling with the police, who were out in force. Screaming and yelling, we actually did block the streets. We had little concern for bystanders inconvenienced by our demonstration; in fact, our goal was to disrupt people's normal lives in order to compel them to consider the war. What they were probably considering was how much they despised us from inconveniencing their commute, but that thought didn't occur to me until years later.

I was having a great time, running and shouting and beating on cars. After all the discussions and arguments and peaceful protests, this was actually doing something physical against the "masters of war." But then suddenly I found myself pushed against a newsstand by a plainclothes cop with a walkie-talkie. Right behind him were four uniformed cops whom he directed to grab and handcuff me. I was caught, but I didn't care. As I waited to be driven off, I looked out from the backseat of a squad car at Jeff Jones and Sue, standing on the sidewalk, laughing, hugging, waving bye-bye to me. Jeff had held back at the demonstration because he was set to fly off to Cambodia the next day on the first leg of a trip to North Vietnam to meet "the enemy."

This was my first time in jail—the Tombs, the House of Detention for Men, at 100 Centre Street in lower Manhattan. I saw in a grimy holding cell with dozens of other young people picked up off the streets that evening. As newcomers arrived, they told us that they had formed roving bands that had rampaged all the way down to Times Square, stopping traffic and breaking windows in hit-and-run actions for several more hours. We had successfully disrupted much of midtown to protest Dean Rusk and the war.

In that holding cell was a guy named Abbie Hoffman, who was already a well-known political street organizer as well as a civil-rights veteran. He would go on to found the Yippies and then become a fugitive. Abbie's wild curly hair and enormous Jewish nose dominated his face, but it was his infectious humor and spirit that attracted people. I once heard Abbie described as the "pied piper of the counterculture." That night in jail, we sang. He and I knew the same folk songs, including, I remember, "The Salvation Army Song": "Throw a nickel on the drum, same another drunken bum. / Thrown a nickel on the drunk and you'll be saved." We sang all sorts of leftist anthems popular in folk circles at the time: Woody Guthrie songs from the Depression, like "Dough Re Mi"; Joe Hill's Wobbly anthem, "Pie in the Sky"; and Pete Seeger's version of the song from the Spanish Civil War "Viva la Quince Brigada." With unrelenting energy—in retrospect, manic—Abbie rapped nonstop between songs to the younger cellmates about the need for resistance, for building a movement. He probably didn't remember me from that encounter, but I sure remembered him.

Very early the next morning, I was arraigned in the night court along with two other Columbia SDSers, Ron Carver and Ted Gold, the vice chairman of the chapter, on the charge of incitement to riot. Then we were released. I was proud of the charge: I thought incitement to riot was better than mere disorderly conduct or some such petty offense. That first arrest was a badge of courage.

When my case came up a few weeks later, my volunteer lawyer told me to plead guilty to the lesser charge of disorderly conduct. He had neither the desire nor the ability to wage a political defense, which would have involved arguing the necessity to break the law in the interest of stopping a greater evil. The judge gave me a lecture on courtroom decorum—"Don't sling your coat over your shoulder, this isn't a supermarket"—and on what he called, "legitimate and lawful protest." Then I was unconditionally released.

My lenient sentence was only just, I thought. Dean Rusk and the members of the Foreign Policy Association, not the protesters, were the ones who should have been arrested for war crimes. As for the question of "legitimate and lawful protest," I was convinced by now that were needed more, not less, militant disruption of business as usual, like the Pentagon and Rusk demonstrations, in order to grow the movement and stop the war.

. . .

DRAWING CONCLUSIONS:

- What does Rudd's memoir reveal about the factors that led many young college students to embrace radical politics in the late 1960s?

3.3 JEFFERSON AIRPLANE—AN EXAMPLE OF THE COUNTERCULTURE

Among the best sources of evidence for understanding the youth counterculture of the 1960s is the "psychedelic" rock music that became one of its defining characteristics. Rock performers such as the Beatles, the Rolling Stones, the Doors, Jimi Hendrix, and Janis Joplin not only fostered a sense of common identity that stood at odds with the American mainstream, but also helped spread the counterculture to beyond the confines of urban enclaves, such as San Francisco's Haight-Ashbury neighborhood and New York's Greenwich Village, where it was born.

San Francisco's Jefferson Airplane was among the most aggressively countercultural of the psychedelic rock bands of the 1960s. Founded by a group of folk musicians seeking to explore electrified rock music, Jefferson Airplane combined experimental sounds with songwriting that lampooned the cultural mainstream and celebrated alternative ways of living. Their breakthrough record was the 1967 album *Surrealistic Pillow*, which included such hit songs as "Somebody to Love" and "White Rabbit." An examination of the sounds, lyrics, and album cover art of Jefferson Airplane offers a window into the worldview of the so-called hippies.

GUIDING QUESTIONS:

- For each song, ask yourself what the song is about.
- What portrait does each song paint of mainstream culture?
- What does each song celebrate about the counterculture?
- How would you describe the tone or sentiment of each song?

"SOMEBODY TO LOVE"

WORDS AND MUSIC BY DARBY SLICK (1967)

When the truth is found
To be lies
And all the joy
Within you dies

Don't you want somebody to love?
Don't you need somebody to love?
Wouldn't you love somebody to love?
You better find somebody to love

When the garden flowers
Baby, are dead, yes
And your mind, your mind
Is so full of red

Don't you want somebody to love?
Don't you need somebody to love?
Wouldn't you love somebody to love?
You better find somebody to love

Your eyes, I say your eyes
May look like his
Yeah, but in your head, baby
I'm afraid you don't know where it is

Don't you want somebody to love?
Don't you need somebody to love?
Wouldn't you love somebody to love?
You better find somebody to love

Tears are running
They're all running down your dress
And your friends, baby
They treat you like a guest
Don't you want somebody to love?
Don't you need somebody to love?
Wouldn't you love somebody to love?
You better find somebody to love

"3/5 OF A MILE IN 110 SECONDS"
WORDS AND MUSIC BY MARTY BALIN (1967)

Do away with people blowing my mind
Do away with people wasting my precious time
Take me to a simple place
Where I can easily see my face
Maybe, baby I'll see that you were kind
Know I love you baby, yes I do
Know I love you baby, yes I do

Do away with people laughing at my hair
Do away with people frowning on my precious prayers
Take me to a circus tent
Where I can easily pay my rent
And all the other freaks will share my cares
Know I love you baby, yes I do
Know I love you baby, yes I do

Do away with things that come on obscene
Like hot rods, beauty queens, real fine nicotine
Sometimes it buys for 65 dollars
Prices like that make a grown man holler
'specially when it's sold by a kid who's only 15
Know I love you baby, yes I do
Know I love you baby, yes I do

3/5's of a mile in 10 seconds . . .

"WHITE RABBIT"
WORDS AND MUSIC BY GRACE SLICK (1967)

One pill makes you larger
And one pill makes you small
And the ones that mother gives you
Don't do anything at all
Go ask Alice
When she's ten feet tall

And if you go chasing rabbits
And you know you're going to fall
Tell 'em a hookah smoking caterpillar
Has given you the call to
Call Alice
When she was just small

When the men on the chessboard
Get up and tell you where to go
And you've just had some kind of mushroom
And your mind is moving low
Go ask Alice
I think she'll know
When logic and proportion
Have fallen sloppy dead
And the White Knight is talking backwards
And the Red Queen's "off with her head!
"Remember what the doormouse said;
"Feed YOUR HEAD . . .
Feed your head"

"WILD TYME (H)"
WORDS AND MUSIC BY PAUL KANTNER (1967)

It's a wild time!
I see people all around me changing faces!

It's a wild time!
I'm doing things that haven't got a name yet,
I need love, your love.
It don't matter if it's rain or shine.

It's a wild time, it's a wild time,
I see love all the time, I see love all the time,
I'm here for you any old time,
Stay here, play here.
Make a place for yourself here.

I want to be with you, no matter what I do,
what doesn't change is the way
I feel for you today.
Times just seem so good.
I do know that I should be here with you this way,
and it's new, and it's new, and it's all so new.
I see changes, changes all around me are changes.
It's a wild time, It's a wild time.

"LATHER"

WORDS AND MUSIC BY GRACE SLICK (1968)

Lather was thirty years old today,
They took away all of his toys.
His mother sent newspaper clippings to him,
About his friends who had stopped being boys.
There was Howard C. Green,
Just turned thirty-three,
His leather chair waits at the bank.
And Sergeant Dow Jones,
Twenty-seven years old,
Commanding his very own tank.

But Lather still finds it a nice thing to do,
To lie about nude in the sand,
Drawing pictures of mountains that look like bumps
And thrashing the air with his hands.

But wait, ol' Lather's productive you know,
He produces the finest of sound,
Putting drumsticks on either side of his nose,
Snorting the best licks in town,

But that's all over . . .

Lather was thirty years old today
And lather came foam from his tongue.
He looked at me, eyes wide, and plainly say,
"Is it true that I'm no longer young?"

And the children call him famous,
What the old men call insane.
And sometimes, he's so nameless,
That he hardly knows what game to play,
Which words to say.

And I should have told him, "No, you're not old."
And I should have let him go on . . . smiling . . . babywide.

"TRIAD"

WORDS AND MUSIC BY DAVID CROSBY (1968)

You want to know how it will be
Me and him OR you and me

You both stand there your long hair flowing
Your eyes alive your mind still growing
Saying to me—"What can we do now that we both love you,"
I love you too—I don't really see
Why can't we go on as three

You are afraid—embarrassed too
No one has ever said such a thing to you
Your mother's ghost stands at your shoulder
Face like ice—a little bit colder
Saying to you—"you cannot do that, it breaks
All the rules you learned in school"
I don't really see
Why can't we go on as three

We love each other—it's plain to see
There's just one answer comes to me
—Sister—lovers—water brothers
And in time—maybe others
So you see—what we can do—is to try something new—
If you're crazy too—
I don't really see
Why can't we go on as three.

DRAWING CONCLUSIONS:

- Taken together, what messages do the songs and music of Jefferson Airplane convey?
- What can we learn about the counterculture from the music and lyrics of Jefferson Airplane?

COVER OF THE 1969 JEFFERSON AIRPLANE ALBUM *VOLUNTEERS*

Because vinyl record albums were relatively large in size, album cover art became an important element in the marketing of records to consumers. For psychedelic rock bands, album cover art also became a vehicle to promote countercultural themes and imagery. This trend is epitomized by the cover art for Jefferson Airplane's 1969 album *Volunteers*, which presented listeners with a mock newspaper full of countercultural themes. A close examination of the cover art for *Volunteers* offers a revealing window into the counterculture of the 1960s.

GUIDING QUESTIONS:

- For each image, describe in detail what you see. What are the people doing? What objects do you see? What does the text say?
- What does each image convey? Do not read too much into them—focus on your immediate reactions.
- What is the overall tone of the album cover art for *Volunteers*?

Front of the album cover.

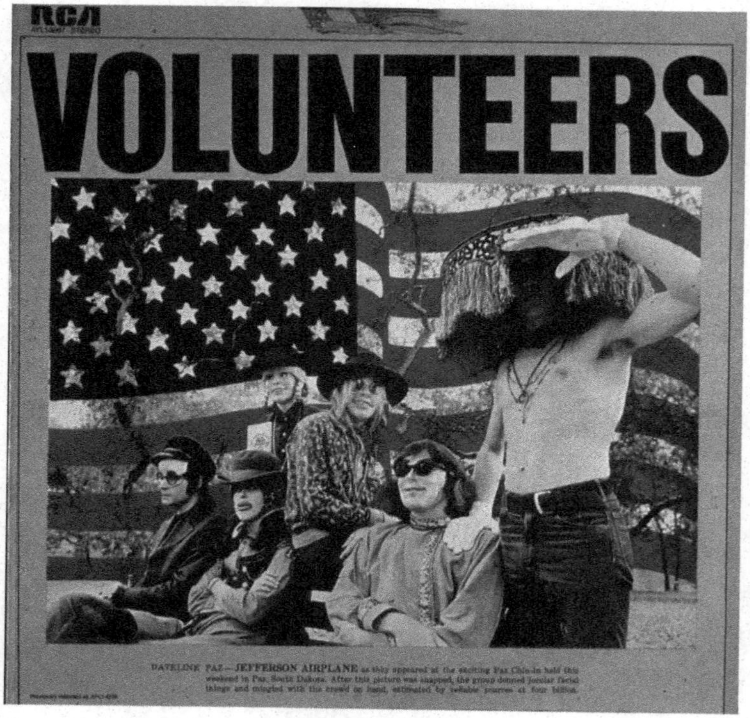

FIGURE 1 Volunteers- Front of the Album Cover
Source: Volunteers. Jefferson Airplane. RCA Victor, 1969.

Back of the album cover.

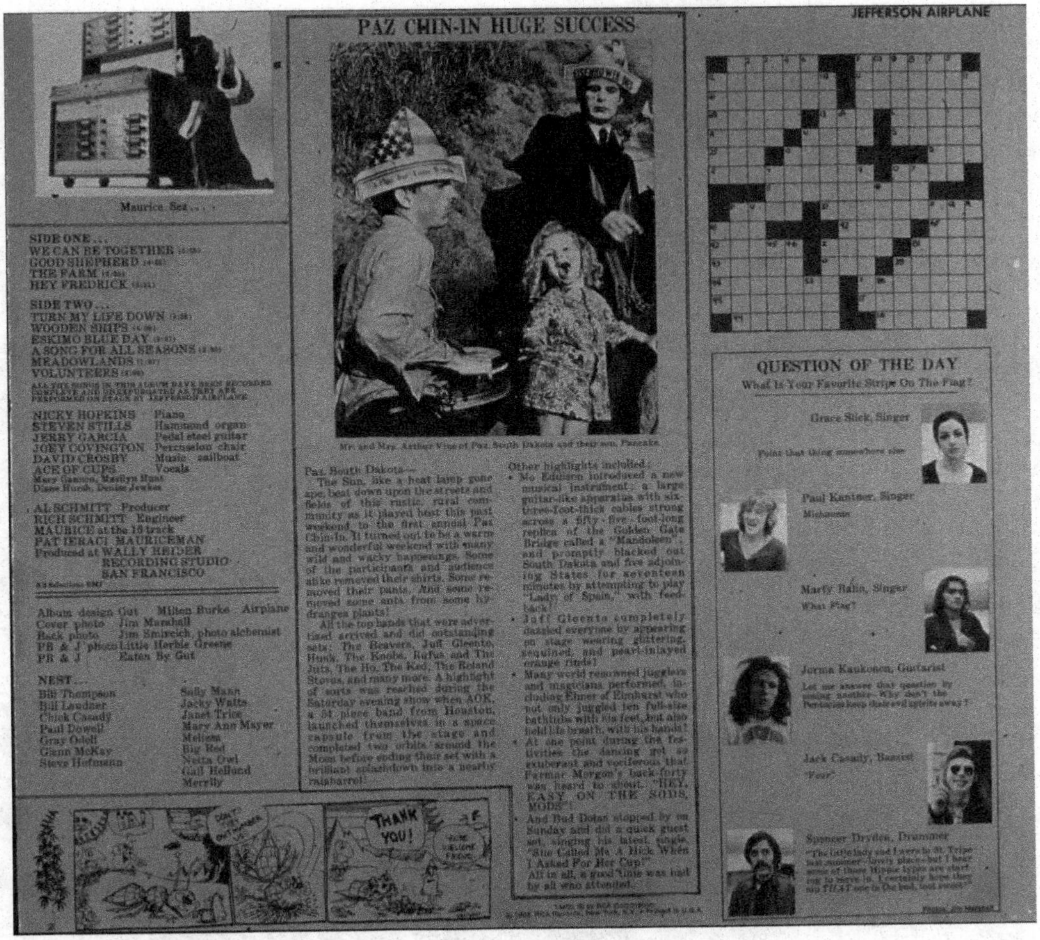

FIGURE 2 Volunteers-Back of the Album Cover
Source: Volunteers. Jefferson Airplane. RCA Victor, 1969.

Back of the album cover: details.

FIGURE 3 Volunteers-Back of the Album Cover-Details-Paz Chin-in Huge Success
Source: Volunteers. Jefferson Airplane. RCA Victor, 1969.

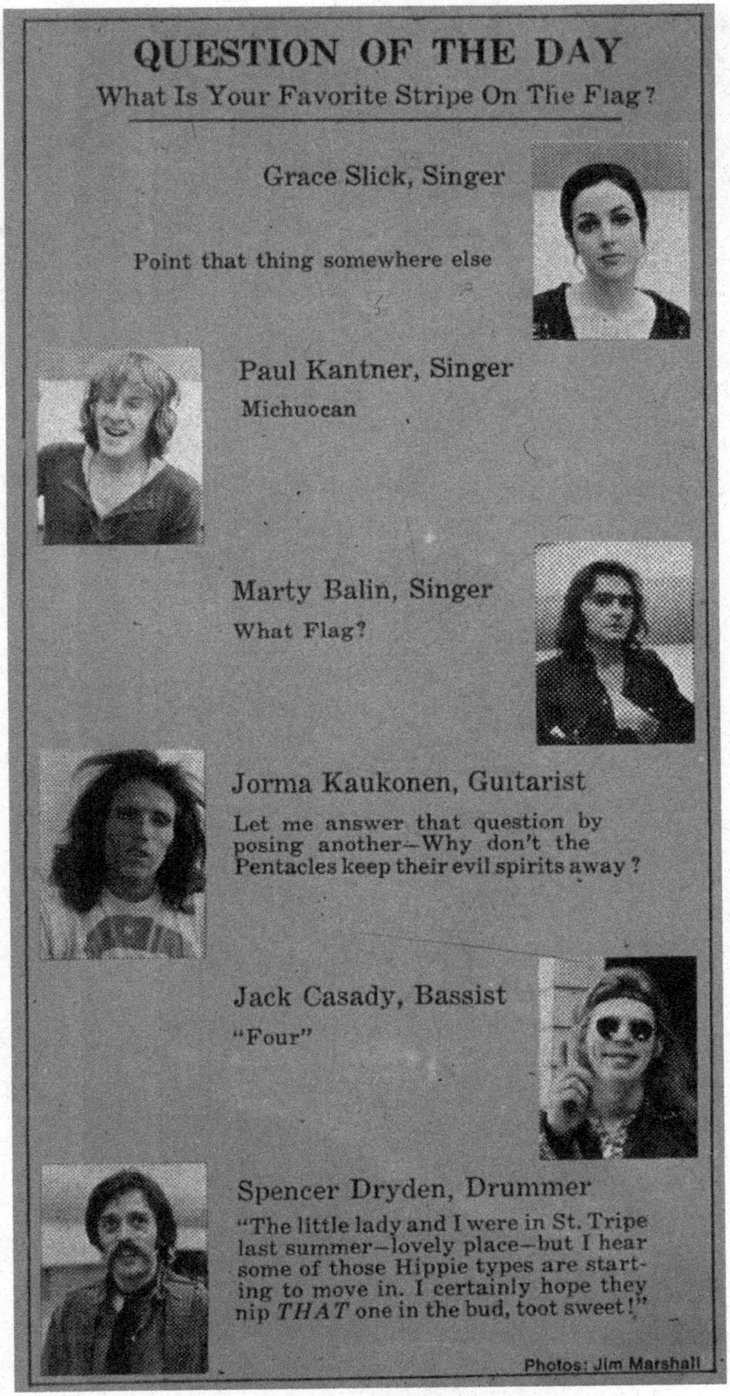

FIGURE 4 Volunteers-Back of the Album Cover-Details-Question of the Day
Source: Volunteers. Jefferson Airplane. RCA Victor, 1969.

FIGURE 5 Volunteers-Back of the Album Cover-Details-Comic Strip
Source: Volunteers. Jefferson Airplane. RCA Victor, 1969.

DRAWING CONCLUSIONS:

- What messages does the cover art for *Volunteers* convey?
- What can we learn about the counterculture from the cover art for *Volunteers*?

THE EXPERIENCE OF VIETNAM

In the late 1950s, the United States become involved in a civil war within the Southeast Asian country of Vietnam. The roots of this conflict lay in a successful war of independence that Vietnamese nationalists waged against France (their colonial ruler) in the 1940s and 1950s. (The United States government had backed France in its unsuccessful effort to maintain Vietnam as a colony.) Concerned that the Vietnamese nationalist movement was led by communists, the United States government worked with anti-communist forces in the country to establish an anti-communist regime in the southern part of Vietnam. From the late 1950s until 1975, the goal of US policy in Vietnam was to maintain an independent anti-communist "South Vietnam."

By 1965, the forces fighting to create a single, united, independent Vietnam (who were largely the same forces that had fought for independence from France) had come close to overthrowing the South Vietnamese government. In response, the United States government began to send large numbers of military personnel to Vietnam in an effort to preserve the South Vietnamese government. By 1968, there were about 500,000 US military forces in the country.

At first, relatively few of those serving in Vietnam doubted the wisdom and necessity of the war. As the conflict dragged on, however, and the prospects for success became uncertain, doubts arose among servicemen and women. While many continued to have faith in the war effort, others came to question it. Faced with the horrors of war (and aware of the divisions at home), many struggled to reconcile conflicting feelings about what they saw and experienced in Vietnam. Veterans returned to a deeply divided country profoundly affected by their wartime experiences—experiences that those at home often struggled to understand.

4.1 RECOLLECTIONS AND LETTERS FROM VIETNAM (1967–1970)

These documents come from letters sent home and from postwar recollections of people who served in Vietnam during the latter years of the war. The selections chosen focus on how soldiers, sailors, airmen, and marines felt about what they had experienced in Vietnam as well as their feelings toward the war and the divisions back home that the war had fostered. As you read these materials, consider how the things experienced in Vietnam may have contributed to the divisions that Americans lived through in the late 1960s.

GUIDING QUESTIONS:

- How did their wartime experiences affect those who served in Vietnam?
- What range of feelings toward the war and toward US policy in Vietnam is expressed in the documents? What sentiments are expressed toward the anti-war protests and other forms of social disorder at home?

BRIAN DELATE

Brian Delate served as an Army helicopter door gunner in Vietnam from March 1969 to March 1970.

Before I went over I knew a couple of friends that came back. I asked, "What was it like?" and they didn't know how to explain it and I didn't know what I was asking. And when I came back I ended up being the same way. Almost mute.

I tried to explain to people. I'm a verbal person, so I really wanted people to understand what I had gone through. My parents gave me a cocktail party. They didn't know what else to do. They gave me a cocktail party like it was a graduation party. And they realized in the middle of the party, they both did and I guess that's why I love them so much, that they really had made a mistake.

I was starting to get loaded, and this lady friend of my mother's said to me, "Well, did you kill anybody?" She's got a martini and a cigarette. She had no idea what she was asking. She was somebody who I'd looked up to for years as a kid. I said, "You have no idea of the dimension of your question. You just threw that out like, 'Did you ever deliver newspapers as a kid?'" I started staring her right in the eyes: "Do you realize what you're asking? Do you have any idea of the nature of your question?" And I let, I just split and thought, "Oh, man."

DOUGLAS ANDERSON

Douglas Anderson served as a Marine Corpsman in Vietnam from February 1967 to February 1968. (ARVN is an abbreviation for the Army of the Republic of Vietnam, the army of the South Vietnamese government. The Viet Cong, or "VC," was the insurgent military force seeking to topple the South Vietnamese government and to create a single unified Vietnamese state.)

It's taken me twelve years—it'll be thirteen in March—to assimilate the gap between what I thought I would see and what I did see. First of all, I'm not a heroic type of individual. I don't believe that I got up and ran under fire as much as I did to get to people.

From Brian Delate - Al Santoli, *Everything We Had: An Oral History of the Vietnam War* (New York: Random House, 1981), 117. Douglas Anderson - Al Santoli, *Everything We Had: An Oral History of the Vietnam War* (New York: Random House, 1981), 59–60.

I don't believe I made myself do those things. But I did. But what really bothered me were some of the things that I saw that were not compatible with the ideas that I'd been brought up to believe in, in terms of being a member of the military and fighting for a country that heroically helped defeat the Germans and the Japanese and was supposed to be the good guy and all of that.

I saw cruelty and brutality that I didn't expect to see from our own people against the villagers. It took me a while in country to realize why it was happening. In this type of fighting it was almost impossible to know who the enemy was at any one time. Children were suspect, women were suspect. Frequently the ARVNs themselves were on two payrolls. Their army was heavily infiltrated with Viet Cong or people who were politically ambivalent, who could change sides as easily as changing clothes.

When, for example, we would patrol an area of villages for a number of weeks and continue to lose men to booby traps, and the people in the villages who pretended not to know anything about these booby traps walked the same trails we did day after day without stepping on them, it became obvious that these people were well informed by the VC where the booby traps were.

One must understand that it's very easy to slip into a primitive state of mind, particularly if your life is in danger and you can't trust anyone. It was difficult for me to assimilate both sides of the picture, that maybe some of these villagers really were enemy. In one case I saw a young man, probably eighteen years old, push an old man into his family bunker inside his hootch and throw a grenade in after him. We'd been hit a lot that week and pressure had been building. It wasn't anything that happened that day. But I remember this guy distinctly because he had a tattoo of a little red devil on his left arm and he had his shirt off when he threw the old man into the bunker and threw the grenade in after him. This is something that I blocked from my memory for twelve years. There are several of these memory blocks that are coming back to me now that I had just put right out of my mind. And I think it's probably my association with other veterans that is bringing these things up.

STEPHEN A. HOWARD

Stephen A. Howard served at an Army combat photographer in Vietnam from January 1968 to August 1969.

I was going on nineteen when I got drafted. I had graduated from high school the year before, and I was working as an engineering assistant in this drafting firm. My mother went to the bus station with me to see me off to Fort Bragg for basic training, and she said, "You'll be back a man."

I didn't feel anything about Vietnam one way or the other. When you are black and you grow up in urban America in a low-income family, you don't get to experience a lot—if your parents protect you well. My mother did. My mother raised all four of us. She was a hospital maid, then she went to G. C. Murphy's company. And now she's director of security for the stores in Washington, D.C.

Mom is not college educated, so all she knows is what the propaganda situation is. She programmed us to be devoted to duty, to God, state, and country. She said you got to do all these good things—like military service—to be a citizen here in America. "You're not white," she would say, "so you're not as good as they are, but you got to work hard to strive to be as good as they are." And that's what you're brought up to believe.

I guess I knew that Martin Luther King was against the war. But I couldn't relate to what he was doing about it or even about discrimination because I wasn't old enough. Nor was my mother in a position to explain to me that whole power struggle was all about.

I was just brought up to believe that when the opportunity presents itself to you to stretch yourself out, you do it. Subconsciously or consciously you're trying to satisfy your mother's dreams even before you deal with what you even want to do.

From Stephen A. Howard - Wallace Terry, *Bloods: An Oral History of the Vietnam War by Black Veterans* (New York: Random House, 1984), 123–124, 133–134.

Mom wanted us to be better, to be middle class. She was looking forward to me being something. To going to Vietnam. To being a man.

. . .

This psychological thing, we try to suppress it. But it kills us quicker than if somebody just walked up to you and put a bullet in your head. 'Cause it eats away at your inner being. It eats away at everything that you ever learned in life. Your integrity. Your word. See, that's all you have.

Vietnam taught you to be a liar. To be a thief. To be dishonest. To go against everything you ever learned. It taught you everything you did not need to know, because you were livin' a lie. And the lie was you ain't have no business bein' there in the first place. You wasn't here for democracy. You wasn't protecting your homeland. And that was what wear you down. We were programmed for the fact as American fighting men that we were still fighting a civilized war. And you don't fight a civilized war. There's nothing civilized about—about war.

I think we were the last generation to believe, you know, in the honor of war. There is no honor in war.

My mama still thinks that I did my part for my country, 'cause she's a very patriotic person.

I don't.

ROBERT PETERSON

Robert Peterson served as an Army infantry staff sergeant in Vietnam from October 1966 to August 1967.

Chu Lai, August 1, 1967

Folks & Kids

Greetings from riot-free Vietnam. I'm beginning to feel relatively safe over here considering the outbursts in Newark, Detroit, etc. I guess my tour of duty will prepare me for stateside living. I wish they'd turn our platoon loose on those rioters—we'd clean them up in a hurry, using a few tactics we picked up over here, which I'm sure these rabble-rousers have never seen. It sure is hell to read about the killings and lootings back home—people taking undue advantage of the freedoms we are guaranteeing them. If they don't like our country, send them to another one and let them try to make it—but no, they can only riot and protest in a country like ours, in a time when we need support, we get nothing but violence and anti-everything riots. Damn 'em all! . . .

2 months or less.
Miss you all
Son & brother
Robert

LYNDA VAN DEVANTER

Lynda Van Devanter served as an Army nurse at two evacuation hospitals from June 1969 to June 1970. (The Montagnards are a minority ethnic group in Vietnam that the United States military and the South Vietnamese sought to enlist as allies in the war.)

24 July 1969

Dear Family,

Things go fairly well here. Monsoon is very heavy right now—haven't seen the sun in a couple of weeks. But this makes the sky that much prettier at night when flares go off. There's a continual mist in the air which makes the flares hazy. At times they look like falling stars; then sometimes they seem to shine like crosses.

At 4:16 A.M. our time the other day, two of our fellow Americans landed on the moon. At that precise moment, Pleiku Air Force Base, in the sheer joy and wonder of it, sent up a whole skyful of flares—white, red, and green. It was as if they were daring the surrounding North Vietnamese Army to try and tackle such a great nation. As we watched it from the emergency room door, we couldn't speak at all. The pride in our country filled us to the point that many had tears in their eyes.

It hurts so much sometimes to see the paper full of demonstrators, especially people burning the flag. Fight fire with fire, we ask here. Display the flag, Mom

---

From Robert Anderson - Michael E. Stevens, *Voices from Vietnam* (Madison: State Historical Society of Wisconsin, 1996), 107–108.
From Lynda Van Deventer - Bernard Edelman, *Dear America: Letter Home from Vietnam* (New York: Norton, 2002), 220–221.

and Dad, please, every day. And tell your friends to do the same. It means so much to us to know we're supported, to know not everyone feels we're making a mistake being here.

Every day we see more and more why we're here. When a whole Montagnard village comes in after being bombed and terrorized by Charlie, you know. These are helpless people dying every day. The worst of it is the children. Little baby-sans being brutally maimed and killed. They never hurt anyone. Papa-san comes in with his three babies—one dead and two covered with frag wounds. You try to tell him the boy is dead—"fini"—but he keeps talking to the baby as if that will make him live again. It's enough to break your heart. And through it all, you feel something's missing. There! You put your finger on it. There's not a sound from them. The children don't cry from pain; the parents don't cry from sorrow; they're stoic.

You have to grin sometimes at the primitiveness of these Montagnards. Here in the emergency room, doctors and nurses hustle about fixing up a little girl. There stands her shy little (and I mean little—like four feet tall) papa-san, face, looking down at the floor, in his loin cloth, smoking his long marijuana pipe. He has probably never seen an electric light before, and the ride here in that great noisy bird (helicopter) was too much for him to comprehend. They're such characters. One comes to the hospital and the whole family campus out in the hall or on the ramp and watches over the patient. No, nobody can tell me we don't belong here. . . .

Love,
Lynda

HECTOR RAMOS

Hector Ramos served a Sergeant with the Air Force Security Police in Vietnam from January 1969 to February 1970.

[August 1969]

Dear Yolanda,

. . . Things are picking up around here. We're starting to train the Vietnamese to do our jobs so they can take over when the time comes for the Air Force to pull out.

The Army's 9th Infantry Division has pulled out already, and the Navy's river patrol force is just about taken over by the Vietnamese Navy. The local people are not very enthusiastic about our leaving because, for one reason, they don't want to lose all the money they are making off the American GIs.

We cannot blame them for wanting a way of life that they have never had, and a continuation of the war is not going to bring any solution. They do not want to fight, they're tired of suffering, and they've finally realized this is more a political war with no gains for the common people. It's a complicated problem. I just can't begin to go into it without ending up with a book. I've always felt that if the North would agree to a peaceful settlement, both North and South could make more progress towards helping their people, whether it be under a communist or democratic system, than by killing each other. I've learned only one lesson from this and that is if man has been fighting his fellow man since the beginning of time, he will continue to do so, and the United States, as powerful as it may be, cannot play the role of God and solve all the problems of the world, and sometime I wonder if there really is a God.

Well, now, I'll be leaving for Hong Kong on the 14th to REST MY BONES. Really, Yolanda, I need a rest. What I'm really interested in is buying some tailor-made suits and a coat. I'll be getting you your ring in Hong Kong also. I want to see if I can find something special that no one else has. OK? . . .

I'll write again soon. I have to write to the kids.

Love,
Chicky

JOSEPH MORRISSEY

Joseph Morrissey served as a staff sergeant with an Army airmobile unit in Vietnam from July 1969 to May 1970.

Oct. 1969

From Hector Ramos - Bernard Edelman, *Dear America: Letter Home from Vietnam* (New York: Norton, 2002), 221–222.
From Joseph Morrissey - Bernard Edelman, *Dear America: Letter Home from Vietnam* (New York: Norton, 2002), 223–224.

Hello Brother,

How are you treating life these days? Have you gotten a grip on those Merrimack students yet? . . .

This place is sort of getting to me. I've been seeing too many guys getting messed up, and I still can't understand it. It's not that I can't understand this war. It's just that I can't understand war period.

If you do not get to go to that big peace demonstration [on] October 15th I hope you do protest against war or sing for peace—I would. I just can't believe half of the shit I've seen over here so far. . . .

Do you know if there's anything wrong at home? I haven't heard from anyone in about two weeks, and I normally get 10 letters a week. You mentioned in your last letters that you haven't heard from them for a while either. I couldn't take sitting over [in] this place if I thought there was anything wrong at home.

Well, brother, I hope you can get to your students and start them thinking about life. Have you tried any marijuana lectures lately? I know they dig that current stuff.

I gotta go now. Stay loose, Paul, sing a simple song of freedom and I'll be seeing you come summer.

JOHN R. GMACK

John R. Gmack served as an Army infantryman, artillery observer, and radio operator in Vietnam and in Cambodia from February to May 1970. He died on May 28, 1970, from wounds sustained in a field accident.

May 21, 1970

Dear Mom & Dad:

. . . You asked what I thought about the demonstrations. Well I think most of them are good. After all the people who are demonstrating are the ones who have Vietnam to look forward to! They are also letting the "brass" know what many people over here think too!, because once you're in the army your ideas and thoughts don't mean anything!

So more power to 'em.

Not much more

Love

John

GREG LUSCO

Greg Lusco served in the Army's 101st Airborne Division in Vietnam from November 1968 to August 1970. He and nineteen fellow soldiers wrote the following letter that appeared in Greenfield (Massachusetts) *Recorder* on July 23, 1970. (In the Kent State University incident referenced in the letter, members of the Ohio National Guard opened fire on anti-war protests, leaving four individuals dead. NVA is an abbreviation for the North Vietnamese Army.)

[July 1970]

[Dear Editor:]

This letter I am writing is not only from me but quite a few of my friends. I just thought you might like it.

This letter is from the men who daily risk their lives in the air over the war-wrought land of Vietnam. It is the combined thoughts and beliefs of 1st and 2nd platoons, B Company, 159th Aviation Battalion, 101st Airborne Division, and you can believe me that a lot of our descriptive phrases are being omitted due to the grossness and obscenities of them.

The outburst of raw violence and malice spontaneously occurred when the following quotation was read aloud to them from a letter: "We've had some memorial services for them at school and there's a movement for a strike." The quotation was in regards to the recent killings at Kent [State University] in Ohio. We are sorrowful and mourn the dead, but it grieves us no end and shoots pain into our hearts that the "biggest upset is over the kids who got killed at Kent [State]."

So why don't your hearts cry out and shed a tear for the 40-plus thousand red-blooded Americans and brave, fearless, loyal men who have given their lives so a bunch of bloody bastard radicals can protest, dissent and generally bitch about our private and personal war in Vietnam and now Cambodia?

During my past 18 months in hell I've seen and held my friends during their last gasping seconds before they succumbed to death. And not once, I repeat, and not one goddamn time did they chastise our country's involvement in Vietnam. Christ,

From John R. Gmack - Michael E. Stevens, *Voices from Vietnam* (Madison: State Historical Society of Wisconsin, 1996), 122.
From Greg Lusco - Bernard Edelman, *Dear America: Letter Home from Vietnam* (New York: Norton, 2002), 223–224.

we cheered when Nixon sent troops to Cambodia—we are praying we'll also see Laos.

And how in the hell do you think that we in Vietnam feel when we read of the dissension and unrest in our country caused by young, worthless radicals and the foremost runner of them all: the vile and disease-ridden SDS. This is what we feel like: We have an acute hatred, an unfathomable lust to maim, yes, even kill. You ask, "Is this towards the NVA and VC?" We answer, "Hell, no, it's for all you back in the World who are striving to make us feel like a piece of shit for fighting and dying for what we believe in—freedom."

Last month my company lost 12 good men and five more were torn up so bad that they have been sent back to the States. We shed true tears for these men. What did you do? Protest. In your feeble and deteriorating and filthy degenerate minds you have forced and caused these men to die for nothing. Do you place such a low value on our heads? We are trying to end the war so that our loved ones will never have to face the harsh realities of death in our own country.

Do not judge us wrongly. We are not pleading for your praise. All we ask is for our great nation to unite and stand behind President Nixon. Support us, help us end the war, damn it, save our lives. . . .

I am coming home soon. Don't shout and preach your nothingness to me. I am ashamed to be fighting to keep you safe, the rest of the loyal Americans. I am proud to give my life for you members of the SDS and your followers. I am returning to educate you on what it feels like to be in Nam. Yes, I am bringing the war home. We'll see if you're as good in fighting as you are in protesting.

Prepare yourselves—the makers are returning. May your children honor and respect our dead and chastise your actions.

We personally challenge you to come to Vietnam and talk with the VC and NVA in A Shau Valley. Let us know what they say, if you live.

We the undersigned are in full [agreement] with the forth-put statements. . . .

With love,
Greg Lusco
Phu Bai
South Vietnam

DRAWING CONCLUSIONS:

- What can we learn from these documents about the ways the experiences of those serving in Vietnam contributed to the social divisions of the late 1960s?

THE WOMEN'S MOVEMENT

For much of the twentieth century, most Americans subscribed to the idea that the public sphere (the sphere of business, work, politics, and government) was the proper sphere of men and that the private sphere (the sphere of home and family) was the proper sphere of women. While many Americans lived their lives in ways that were at odds with these assumptions, the idea of separate male and female spheres nonetheless served as a standard by why people were judged and by which people often judged themselves. The male breadwinner/female homemaker family, for instance, was held up as a norm to which all should aspire.

In the 1960s, a growing number of women (particularly younger college-educated women) began to openly challenge these gender norms. This "women's movement" took two primary forms. The first was a reinvigorated feminist movement that openly challenged laws and social practices that discriminated against women and that placed women in a subordinate social position. The second was the entry of large numbers of young women into previously male-dominated high-status professions, such as medicine, law, and business. The women's movement of the 1960s and 1970s challenged deeply rooted assumptions about gender in American culture and brought rapid changes to American gender roles.

5.1 WOMEN IN THE WORKFORCE

From the very beginnings of the industrial revolution, significant numbers of women have worked outside the home as part of the paid labor force. Over time, though, the patterns of women's labor force participation have changed significantly. The following tables and graphs document those changing patterns of women's labor force participation both before and after the re-emergence of an organized feminist movement in the late 1960s.

GUIDING QUESTIONS:

- What long-term patterns do you observe in the labor force participation of single and married women in the decades prior to the 1960s? What changes, if any, are there in these patterns following the 1960s?
- What patterns do you see in women's participation in higher education prior to the 1960s? What patterns do you see in women's employment in high-status professions prior to the 1960s? What changes, if any, do you see in these patterns after the 1960s?

TABLE 9 PERCENTAGE OF WOMEN IN WORK FORCE BY MARITAL STATUS

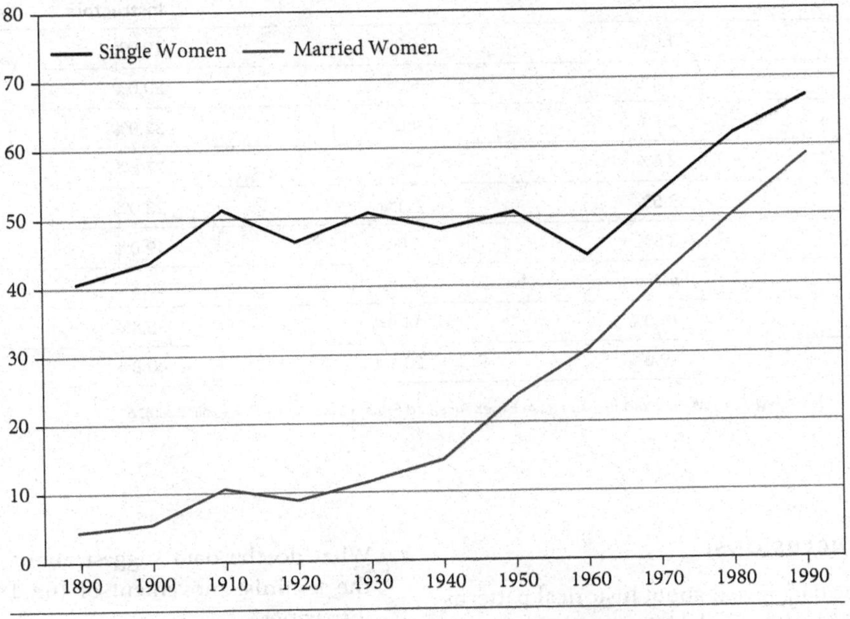

Data taken from Nancy Woloch, *Women and the American Experience*, 3rd Edition (Boston: McGraw Hill, 2000), 608.

TABLE 10 DEGREES GRANTED—PERCENTAGE FEMALE

	Bachelor/1st Professional Degrees	Doctorates
1900	19.1%	6.0%
1910	22.7%	9.9%
1920	34.2%	15.1%
1930	39.9%	15.4%
1940	41.3%	13.0%
1950	23.9%	9.6%
1960	35.3%	10.5%
1970	41.5%	13.3%
1980	47.3%	29.7%
1990	54.0%	37.0%

Data taken from Nancy Woloch, *Women and the American Experience*, 3rd Edition (Boston: McGraw Hill, 2000), 607.

TABLE 11 SELECTED PROFESSIONS—PERCENTAGE FEMALE

	Lawyers	Physicians	College Professors and Instructors
1910	1.0%	6.0%	19.0%
1920	1.4%	5.0%	30.0%
1930	2.1%	4.0%	32.0%
1940	2.4%	4.6%	27.6%
1950	3.5%	6.1%	23.0%
1960	3.5%	6.8%	19.0%
1970	4.7%	8.9%	28.3%
1982	14.0%	14.3%	35.4%
1991	19.0%	20.1%	40.8%

Data taken from Nancy Woloch, *Women and the American Experience*, 3rd Edition (Boston: McGraw Hill, 2000), 610.

DRAWING CONCLUSIONS:

- What do the data reveal about historical patterns of gender disparities in the labor market?
- What do the data suggest about the impact of the feminist movement of the 1960s on these disparities?

5.2 BETTY FRIEDAN, "THE PROBLEM THAT HAS NO NAME," FROM *THE FEMININE MYSTIQUE* (1963)

Journalist Betty Friedan was a 1942 graduate of Smith College, a prestigious private women's college in the state of Massachusetts. She continued to work as a writer following her 1947 marriage, but like many college-educated women of her generation she prioritized home and family over career. Her 1963 book, *The Feminine Mystique,* became a nationwide bestseller and is often credited with sparking the feminist movement of the 1960s. Some consider it the most influential American book of the twentieth century. In this first chapter of her book, Friedan suggests that American women (especially middle-class suburban women) were suffering from a "problem that has no name." In the rest of the book, Friedan argues that this problem was the result of cultural messages that taught American women to seek personal satisfaction solely in the roles of wife and mother, and she calls upon women to seek lives outside the home through the pursuit of careers and community involvement. Friedan's book, and the public reaction to it, offers a window into the thoughts and feelings that gave birth to a revived feminist movement in the United States.

GUIDING QUESTIONS:

- What, according to Betty Friedan, was the "problem that has no name"? Why does she believe this problem was significant?

THE FEMININE MYSTIQUE

1

THE PROBLEM THAT HAS NO NAME

The problem lay buried, unspoken, for many years in the minds of American women. It was a strange stirring, a sense of dissatisfaction, a yearning that women suffered in the middle of the twentieth century in the United States. Each suburban wife struggled with it alone. As she made the beds, shopped for groceries, matched slipcover material, ate peanut butter sandwiches with her children, chauffeured Cub Scouts and Brownies, lay beside her husband at night—she was afraid to ask even of herself the silent question—"Is this all?"

For over fifteen years there was no word of this yearning in the millions of words written about women, for women, in all the columns, books and articles by experts telling women their role was to seek fulfillment as wives and mothers. Over and over women heard in voices of tradition and of Freudian sophistication that they could desire no greater destiny than to glory in their own femininity. Experts told them how to catch a man and keep him, how to breastfeed children and handle their toilet training, how to cope with sibling rivalry and adolescent rebellion; how to buy a dishwasher, bake bread, cook gourmet snails, and build a swimming pool with their own hands; how to dress, look, and act more feminine and make marriage more exciting; how to keep their husbands from dying young and their sons from growing into delinquents. They were taught to pity the neurotic, unfeminine, unhappy women who wanted to be poets or physicists or presidents. They learned that truly feminine women do not want

From Betty Friedan, *The Feminine Mystique,* Norton Critical Edition (New York: W.W. Norton, 2013), 9–24.

careers, higher education, political rights—the independence and the opportunities that the old-fashioned feminists fought for. Some women, in their forties and fifties, still remembered painfully giving up those dreams, but most of the younger women no longer even thought about them. A thousand expert voices applauded their femininity, their adjustment, their new maturity. All they had to do was devote their lives from earliest girlhood to finding a husband and bearing children.

By the end of the nineteen-fifties, the average marriage age of women in America dropped to 20, and was still dropping, into the teens. Fourteen million girls were engaged by 17. The proportion of women attending college in comparison with men dropped from 47 per cent in 1920 to 35 per cent in 1958. A century earlier, women had fought for higher education; now girls went to college to get a husband. By the mid-fifties, 60 per cent dropped out of college to marry, or because they were afraid too much education would be a marriage bar. Colleges built dormitories for "married students," but the students were almost always the husbands. A new degree was instituted for the wives—"Ph. T." (Putting Husband Through).

Then American girls began getting married in high school. And the women's magazines, deploring the unhappy statistics about these young marriages, urged that courses on marriage, and marriage counselors, be installed in the high schools. Girls started going steady at twelve and thirteen, in junior high. Manufacturers put out brassieres with false bosoms of foam rubber for little girls of ten. And an advertisement for a child's dress, sizes 3–6x, in the *New York Times* in the fall of 1960, said: "She Too Can Join the Man-Trap Set."

By the end of the fifties, the United States birthrate was overtaking India's. The birth-control movement, renamed Planned Parenthood, was asked to find a method whereby women who had been advised that a third or fourth baby would be born dead or defective might have it anyhow. Statisticians were especially astounded at the fantastic increase in the number of babies among college women. Where once they had two children, now they had four, five, six. Women who had once wanted careers were now making careers out of having babies. So rejoiced *Life* magazine in a 1956 paean to the movement of American women back to the home.

In a New York hospital, a woman had a nervous breakdown when she found she could not breastfeed her baby. In other hospitals, women dying of cancer refused a drug which research had proved might save their lives: its side effects were said to be unfeminine. "If I have only one life, let me live it as a blonde," a larger-than-life-sized picture of a pretty, vacuous woman proclaimed from newspaper, magazine, and drugstore ads. And across America, three out of every ten women dyed their hair blonde. They ate a chalk called Metrecal, instead of food, to shrink to the size of the thin young models. Department-store buyers reported that American women, since 1939, had become three and four sizes smaller. "Women are out to fit the clothes, instead of vice-versa," one buyer said.

Interior decorators were designing kitchens with mosaic murals and original paintings, for kitchens were once again the center of women's lives. Home sewing became a million-dollar industry. Many women no longer left their homes, except to shop, chauffeur their children, or attend a social engagement with their husbands. Girls were growing up in America without ever having jobs outside the home. In the late fifties, a sociological phenomenon was suddenly remarked: a third of American women now worked, but most were no longer young and very few were pursuing careers. They were married women who held part-time jobs, selling or secretarial, to put their husbands through school, their sons through college, or to help pay the mortgage. Or they were widows supporting families. Fewer and fewer women were entering professional work. The shortages in the nursing, social work, and teaching professions caused crises in almost every American city. Concerned over the Soviet Union's lead in the space race, scientists noted that America's greatest source of unused brain-power was women. But girls would not study physics: it was "unfeminine." A girl refused a science fellowship at Johns Hopkins to take a job in a real-estate office. All she wanted, she said, was what every other American girl wanted—to get married, have four children and live in a nice house in a nice suburb.

The suburban housewife—she was the dream image of the young American woman and the envy, it was said, of women all over the world. The American housewife—freed by science and labor-saving appliances from the drudgery, the dangers of childbirth and the illnesses of her grandmother. She was healthy, beautiful, educated, concerned only about her husband, her children, her home. She had found true feminine fulfillment. As a housewife and mother, she was respected as a full and equal partner to man in his world. She was free to choose automobiles, clothes, appliances, supermarkets; she had everything that women ever dreamed of.

In the fifteen years after World War II, this mystique of feminine fulfillment became the cherished and self-perpetuating core of contemporary American culture. Millions of women lived their lives in the image of those pretty pictures of the American suburban housewife, kissing their husbands goodbye in front of the picture window, depositing their station wagons full of children at school, and smiling as they ran the new electric waxer over the spotless kitchen floor. They baked their own bread, sewed their own and their children's clothes, kept their new washing machines and dryers running all day. They changed the sheets on the beds twice a week instead of once, took the rug-hooking class in adult education, and pitied their poor frustrated mothers, who had dreamed of having a career. Their only dream was to be perfect wives and mothers; their highest ambition to have five children and a beautiful house, their only fight to get and keep their husbands. They had no thought for the unfeminine problems of the world outside the home; they wanted the men to make the major decisions. They gloried in their role as women, and wrote proudly on the census blank: "Occupation: housewife."

For over fifteen years, the words written for women, and the words women used when they talked to each other, while their husbands sat on the other side of the room and talked shop or politics or septic tanks, were about problems with their children, or how to keep their husbands happy, or improve their children's school, or cook chicken or make slipcovers. Nobody argued whether women were inferior or superior to men; they were simply different. Words like "emancipation" and "career" sounded strange and embarrassing; no one had used them for years. When a Frenchwoman named Simone de Beauvoir wrote a book called *The Second Sex*, an American critic commented that she obviously "didn't know what life was all about," and besides, she was talking about French women. The "woman problem" in America no longer existed.

If a woman had a problem in the 1950's and 1960's, she knew that something must be wrong with her marriage, or with herself. Other women were satisfied with their lives, she thought. What kind of a woman was she if she did not feel this mysterious fulfillment waxing the kitchen floor? She was so ashamed to admit her dissatisfaction that she never knew how many other women shared it. If she tried to tell her husband, he didn't understand what she was talking about. She did not really understand it herself. For over fifteen years women in America found it harder to talk about this problem than about sex. Even the psychoanalysts had no name for it.

When a woman went to a psychiatrist for help, as many women did, she would say, "I'm so ashamed," or "I must be hopelessly neurotic." "I don't know what's wrong with women today," a suburban psychiatrist said uneasily. "I only know something is wrong because most of my patients happen to be women. And their problem isn't sexual." Most women with this problem did not go to see a psychoanalyst, however. "There's nothing wrong really," they kept telling themselves. "There isn't any problem."

But on an April morning in 1959, I heard a mother of four, having coffee with four other mothers in a suburban development fifteen miles from New York, say in a tone of quiet desperation, "the problem." And the others knew, without words, that she was not talking about a problem with her husband, or her children, or her home. Suddenly they realized they all shared the same problem, the problem that has no name. They began, hesitantly, to talk about it. Later, after they had picked up their children at nursery school and taken them home to nap, two of the women cried, in sheer relief, just to know they were not alone.

Gradually I came to realize that the problem that has no name was shared by countless women in America. As a magazine writer I often interviewed women about problems with their children, or their marriages, or their houses, or their communities. But after a while I began to recognize the telltale signs of this other problem. I saw the same signs in suburban ranch houses and split-levels on Long Island and in New Jersey and Westchester County; in colonial houses in a small Massachusetts town; on patios in Memphis; in suburban and city apartments; in living rooms in the Midwest. Sometimes I sensed the problem, not as a reporter, but as a suburban housewife, for during this time I was also bringing up my own three children in Rockland County, New York. I heard echoes of the problem in college dormitories and semiprivate maternity wards, at PTA meetings and luncheons of the League of Women Voters, at suburban cocktail parties, in station wagons waiting for trains, and in snatches of conversation overheard at Schrafft's. The groping words I heard from other women, on quiet afternoons when children were at school or on quiet evenings when husbands worked late, I think I understood first as a woman long before I understood their larger social and psychological implications.

Just what was this problem that has no name? What were the words women used when they tried to express it? Sometimes a woman would say "I feel empty somehow . . . incomplete." Or she would say, "I feel as if I don't exist." Sometimes she blotted out the feeling with a tranquilizer. Sometimes she thought the problem was with her husband, or her children, or that what she really needed was to redecorate her house, or move to a better neighborhood, or have an affair, or another baby. Sometimes, she went to a doctor with symptoms she could hardly describe: "A tired feeling . . . I get so angry with the children it scares me . . . I feel like crying without any reason." (A Cleveland doctor called it "the housewife's syndrome.") A number of women told me about great bleeding blisters that break out on their hands and arms. "I call it the housewife's blight," said a family doctor in Pennsylvania. "I see it so often lately in these young women with four, five and six children who bury themselves in their dishpans. But it isn't caused by detergent and it isn't cured by cortisone."

Sometimes a woman would tell me that the feeling gets so strong she runs out of the house and walks through the streets. Or she stays inside her house and cries. Or her children tell her a joke, and she doesn't laugh because she doesn't hear it. I talked to women who had spent years on the analyst's couch, working out their "adjustment to the feminine role," their blocks to "fulfillment as a wife and mother." But the desperate tone in these women's voices, and the look in their eyes, was the same as the tone and the look of other women, who were sure they had no problem, even though they did have a strange feeling of desperation.

A mother of four who left college at nineteen to get married told me:

> I've tried everything women are supposed to do—hobbies, gardening, pickling, canning, being very social with my neighbors, joining committees, running PTA teas. I can do it all, and I like it, but it doesn't leave you anything to think about—any feeling of who you are. I never had any career ambitions. All I wanted was to get married and have four children. I love the kids and Bob and my home. There's no problem you can even put a name to. But I'm desperate. I begin to feel I have no personality. I'm a server of food and a putter-on of pants and a bedmaker, somebody who can be called on when you want something. But who am I?

A twenty-three-year-old mother in blue jeans said:

> I ask myself why I'm so dissatisfied. I've got my health, fine children, a lovely new home, enough money. My husband has a real future as an electronics engineer. He doesn't have any of these feelings. He says maybe I need a vacation, let's go to New York for a weekend. But that isn't it. I always had this idea we should do everything together. I can't sit down and read a book alone. If the children are napping and I have one hour to myself I just walk through the house waiting for them to wake up. I don't make a move until I know where the rest of the crowd is going. It's as if ever since you were a little girl, there's always been somebody or something that will take care of your life: your parents, or college, or falling in love, or having a child, or moving to a new house. Then you wake up one morning and there's nothing to look forward to.

A young wife in a Long Island development said:

> I seem to sleep so much. I don't know why I should be so tired. This house isn't nearly so hard to clean as the cold-water flat we had when I was working. The children are at school all day. It's not the work. I just don't feel alive.

In 1960, the problem that has no name burst like a boil through the image of the happy American housewife. In the television commercials the pretty housewives still beamed over their foaming dishpans and *Time*'s cover story on "The Suburban Wife, an American Phenomenon" protested: "Having too good a time . . . to believe that they should be unhappy." But the actual unhappiness of the American housewife was suddenly being reported—from the *New York Times* and *Newsweek* to *Good Housekeeping* and CBS Television ("The Trapped Housewife"), although almost everybody who talked about it found some superficial reason to dismiss it. It was attributed to incompetent appliance repairmen (*New York Times*), or the distances children must be chauffeured in the suburbs (*Time*), or too much PTA (*Redbook*). Some said it was the old problem—education: more and more women had education, which naturally made them unhappy in their role as housewives. "The road from Freud to Frigidaire, from Sophocles to Spock, has turned out to be a bumpy one," reported the *New York Times* (June 28, 1960).

"Many young women—certainly not all—whose education plunged them into a world of ideas feel stifled in their homes. They find their routine lives out of joint with their training. Like shut-ins, they feel left out. In the last year, the problem of the educated housewife has provided the meat of dozens of speeches made by troubled presidents of women's colleges who maintain, in the face of complaints, that sixteen years of academic training is realistic preparation for wifehood and motherhood."

There was much sympathy for the educated housewife. ("Like a two-headed schizophrenic . . . once she wrote a paper on the Graveyard poets; now she writes notes to the milkman. Once she determined the boiling point of sulphuric acid; now she determines her boiling point with the overdue repairman. . . . The housewife often is reduced to screams and tears. . . . No one, it seems, is appreciative, least of all herself, of the kind of person she becomes in the process of turning from poetess into shrew.")

Home economists suggested more realistic preparation for housewives, such as high-school workshops in home appliances. College educators suggested more discussion groups on home management and the family, to prepare women for the adjustment to domestic life. A spate of articles appeared in the mass magazines offering "Fifty-eight Ways to Make Your Marriage More Exciting." No month went by without a new book by a psychiatrist or sexologist offering technical advice on finding greater fulfillment through sex.

A male humorist joked in *Harper's Bazaar* (July, 1960) that the problem could be solved by taking away woman's right to vote. ("In the pre-19th Amendment era, the American woman was placid, sheltered and sure of her role in American society. She left all the political decisions to her husband and he, in turn, left all the family decisions to her. Today a woman has to make both the family and the political decisions, and it's too much for her.")

A number of educators suggested seriously that women no longer be admitted to the four-year colleges and universities: in the growing college crisis, the education which girls could not use as housewives was more urgently needed than ever by boys to do the work of the atomic age.

The problem was also dismissed with drastic solutions no one could take seriously. (A woman writer proposed in *Harper's* that women be drafted for compulsory service as nurses' aides and babysitters.) And it was smoothed over with the age-old panaceas: "love is their answer," "the only answer is inner help," "the secret of completeness—children," "a private means of intellectual fulfillment," "to cure this toothache of the spirit—the simple formula of handing one's self and one's will over to God."

The problem was dismissed by telling the housewife she doesn't realize how lucky she is—her own boss, no time clock, no junior executive gunning for her job. What if she isn't happy—does she think men are happy in this world? Does she really, secretly, still want to be a man? Doesn't she know yet how lucky she is to be a woman?

The problem was also, and finally, dismissed by shrugging that there are no solutions: this is what being a woman means, and what is wrong with American women that they can't accept their role gracefully? As *Newsweek* put it (March 7, 1960):

> She is dissatisfied with a lot that women of other lands can only dream of. Her discontent is deep,

> pervasive, and impervious to the superficial remedies which are offered at every hand. . . . An army of professional explorers have already charted the major sources of trouble. . . . From the beginning of time, the female cycle has defined and confined woman's role. As Freud was credited with saying: "Anatomy is destiny." Though no group of women has ever pushed these natural restrictions as far as the American wife, it seems that she still cannot accept them with good grace. . . . A young mother with a beautiful family, charm, talent and brains is apt to dismiss her role apologetically. "What do I do?" you hear her say. "Why nothing. I'm just a housewife." A good education, it seems, has given this paragon among women an understanding of the value of everything except her own worth . . .

And so she must accept the fact that "American women's unhappiness is merely the most recently won of women's rights," and adjust and say with the happy housewife found by *Newsweek*: "We ought to salute the wonderful freedom we all have and be proud of our lives today. I have had college and I've worked, but being a housewife is the most rewarding and satisfying role. . . . My mother was never included in my father's business affairs . . . she couldn't get out of the house and away from us children. But I am an equal to my husband; I can go along with him on business trips and to social business affairs."

The alternative offered was a choice that few women would contemplate. In the sympathetic words of the *New York Times*: "All admit to being deeply frustrated at times by the lack of privacy, the physical burden, the routine of family life, the confinement of it. However, none would give up her home and family if she had the choice to make again." *Redbook* commented: "Few women would want to thumb their noses at husbands, children and community and go off on their own. Those who do may be talented individuals, but they rarely are successful women."

The year American women's discontent boiled over, it was also reported (*Look*) that the more than 21,000,000 American women who are single, widowed, or divorced do not cease even after fifty their frenzied, desperate search for a man. And the search begins early—for seventy per cent of all American women now marry before they are twenty-four. A pretty twenty-five-year-old secretary took thirty-five different jobs in six months in the futile hope of finding a husband. Women were moving from one political club to another, taking evening courses in accounting or sailing, learning to play golf or ski, joining a number of churches in succession, going to bars alone, in their ceaseless search for a man.

Of the growing thousands of women currently getting private psychiatric help in the United States, the married ones were reported dissatisfied with their marriages, the unmarried ones suffering from anxiety and, finally, depression. Strangely, a number of psychiatrists stated that, in their experience, unmarried women patients were happier than married ones. So the door of all those pretty suburban houses opened a crack to permit a glimpse of uncounted thousands of American housewives who suffered alone from a problem that suddenly everyone was talking about, and beginning to take for granted, as one of those unreal problems in American life that can never be solved—like the hydrogen bomb. By 1962 the plight of the trapped American housewife had become a national parlor game. Whole issues of magazines, newspaper columns, books learned and frivolous, educational conferences and television panels were devoted to the problem.

Even so, most men, and some women, still did not know that this problem was real. But those who had faced it honestly knew that all the superficial remedies, the sympathetic advice, the scolding words and the cheering words were somehow drowning the problem in unreality. A bitter laugh was beginning to be heard from American women. They were admired, envied, pitied, theorized over until they were sick of it, offered drastic solutions or silly choices that no one could take seriously. They got all kinds of advice from the growing armies of marriage and child-guidance counselors, psychotherapists, and armchair psychologists, on how to adjust to their role as housewives. No other road to fulfillment was offered to American women in the middle of the twentieth century. Most adjusted to their role and suffered or ignored the problem that has no name. It can be less painful, for a woman, not to hear the strange, dissatisfied voice stirring within her.

It is no longer possible to ignore that voice, to dismiss the desperation of so many American women. This is not what being a woman means, no matter what the experts say. For human suffering there is a reason; perhaps the reason has not been found because the right questions have not been asked, or pressed far enough. I do not accept the answer that there is no problem because American women have luxuries that women in other times and lands never dreamed of; part of the strange newness of the problem is that it cannot be understood in terms of the age-old material problems of man: poverty, sickness, hunger, cold. The women who suffer this problem have a hunger that food cannot fill. It persists in women whose husbands are struggling interns and law clerks, or prosperous doctors and lawyers; in wives of workers and executives who make $5,000 a year or $50,000. It is not caused by lack of material advantages; it may not even be felt by women preoccupied with desperate problems of hunger, poverty or illness. And women who think it will be solved by more money, a bigger house, a second car, moving to a better suburb, often discover it gets worse.

It is no longer possible today to blame the problem on loss of femininity: to say that education and independence and equality with men have made American women unfeminine. I have heard so many women try to deny this dissatisfied voice within themselves because it does not fit the pretty picture of femininity the experts have given them. I think, in fact, that this is the first clue to the mystery: the problem cannot be understood in the generally accepted terms by which scientists have studied women, doctors have treated them, counselors have advised them, and writers have written about them.

Women who suffer this problem, in whom this voice is stirring, have lived their whole lives in the pursuit of feminine fulfillment. They are not career women (although career women may have other problems); they are women whose greatest ambition has been marriage and children. For the oldest of these women, these daughters of the American middle class, no other dream was possible. The ones in their forties and fifties who once had other dreams gave them up and threw themselves joyously into life as housewives. For the youngest, the new wives and mothers, this was the only dream. They are the ones who quit high school and college to marry, or marked time in some job in which they had no real interest until they married. These women are very "feminine" in the usual sense, and yet they still suffer the problem.

Are the women who finished college, the women who once had dreams beyond housewifery, the ones who suffer the most? According to the experts they are, but listen to these four women:

> My days are all busy, and dull, too. All I ever do is mess around. I get up at eight—I make breakfast, so I do the dishes, have lunch, do some more dishes and some laundry and cleaning in the afternoon. Then it's supper dishes and I get to sit down a few minutes before the children have to be sent to bed. . . . That's all there is to my day. It's just like any other wife's day. Humdrum. The biggest time, I am chasing kids.
>
> Ye Gods, what do I do with my time? Well, I get up at six. I get my son dressed and then give him breakfast. After that I wash dishes and bathe and feed the baby. Then I get lunch and while the children nap, I sew or mend or iron and do all the other things I can't get done before noon. Then I cook supper for the family and my husband watches TV while I do the dishes.
>
> After I get the children to bed, I set my hair and then I go to bed.
>
> The problem is always being the children's mommy, or the minister's wife and never being myself.
>
> A film made of any typical morning in my house would look like an old Marx Brothers' comedy. I wash the dishes, rush the older children off to school, dash out in the yard to cultivate the chrysanthemums, run back in to make a phone call about a committee meeting, help the youngest child build a blockhouse, spend fifteen minutes skimming the newspapers so I can be well-informed, then scamper down to the washing machines where my thrice-weekly laundry includes enough clothes to keep a primitive village going for an entire year. By noon I'm ready for a padded cell. Very little of what I've done has been really necessary or important. Outside pressures lash me through the day. Yet I look upon myself as one of the more relaxed housewives in the neighborhood. Many of my friends

> are even more frantic. In the past sixty years we have come full circle and the American housewife is once again trapped in a squirrel cage. If the cage is now a modern plate-glass-and-broadloom ranch house or a convenient modern apartment, the situation is no less painful than when her grandmother sat over an embroidery hoop in her gilt-and-plush parlor and muttered angrily about women's rights.

The first two women never went to college. They live in developments in Levittown, New Jersey, and Tacoma, Washington, and were interviewed by a team of sociologists studying workingmen's wives. The third, a minister's wife, wrote on the fifteenth reunion questionnaire of her college that she never had any career ambitions, but wishes now she had. The fourth, who has a Ph.D. in anthropology, is today a Nebraska housewife with three children. Their words seem to indicate that housewives of all educational levels suffer the same feeling of desperation.

The fact is that no one today is muttering angrily about "women's rights," even though more and more women have gone to college. In a recent study of all the classes that have graduated from Barnard College a significant minority of earlier graduates blamed their education for making them want "rights," later classes blamed their education for giving them career dreams, but recent graduates blamed the college for making them feel it was not enough simply to be a housewife and mother; they did not want to feel guilty if they did not read books or take part in community activities. But if education is not the cause of the problem, the fact that education somehow festers in these women may be a clue.

If the secret of feminine fulfillment is having children, never have so many women, with the freedom to choose, had so many children, in so few years, so willingly. If the answer is love, never have women searched for love with such determination. And yet there is a growing suspicion that the problem may not be sexual, though it must somehow be related to sex. I have heard from many doctors evidence of new sexual problems between man and wife—sexual hunger in wives so great their husbands cannot satisfy it. "We have made woman a sex creature," said a psychiatrist at the Margaret Sanger marriage counseling clinic. "She has no identity except as a wife and mother. She does not know who she is herself. She waits all day for her husband to come home at night to make her feel alive. And now it is the husband who is not interested. It is terrible for the women, to lie there, night after night, waiting for her husband to make her feel alive." Why is there such a market for books and articles offering sexual advice? The kind of sexual orgasm which Kinsey found in statistical plenitude in the recent generations of American women does not seem to make this problem go away.

On the contrary, new neuroses are being seen among women—and problems as yet unnamed as neuroses—which Freud and his followers did not predict, with physical symptoms, anxieties, and defense mechanisms equal to those caused by sexual repression. And strange new problems are being reported in the growing generations of children whose mothers were always there, driving them around, helping them with their homework—an inability to endure pain or discipline or pursue any self-sustained goal of any sort, a devastating boredom with life. Educators are increasingly uneasy about the dependence, the lack of self-reliance, of the boys and girls who are entering college today. "We fight a continual battle to make our students assume manhood," said a Columbia dean.

A White House conference was held on the physical and muscular deterioration of American children: were they being over-nurtured? Sociologists noted the astounding organization of suburban children's lives: the lessons, parties, entertainments, play and study groups organized for them. A suburban housewife in Portland, Oregon, wondered why the children "need" Brownies and Boy Scouts out here. "This is not the slums. The kids out here have the great outdoors. I think people are so bored, they organize the children, and then try to hook everyone else on it. And the poor kids have no time left just to lie on their beds and daydream."

Can the problem that has no name be somehow related to the domestic routine of the housewife? When a woman tries to put the problem into words, she often merely describes the daily life she leads. What is there in this recital of comfortable domestic detail that could possibly cause such a feeling of desperation? Is she trapped simply by the enormous demands of her role as modern housewife: wife, mistress, mother, nurse, consumer, cook, chauffeur; expert on interior decoration, child care, appliance repair, furniture refinishing, nutrition, and education? Her day is fragmented as she rushes from dishwasher to washing machine to telephone to dryer to station wagon to supermarket, and delivers Johnny to the Little League field, takes Janey to dancing class, gets the lawnmower fixed and meets the 6:45. She can never spend more than 15 minutes on any one thing; she has no time to read books, only magazines; even if she had time, she has lost the power to concentrate. At the end of the day, she is so terribly tired that sometimes her husband has to take over and put the children to bed.

This terrible tiredness took so many women to doctors in the 1950's that one decided to investigate it. He found, surprisingly, that his patients suffering from "housewife's fatigue" slept more than an adult needed to sleep—as much as ten hours a day—and that the actual energy they expended on housework did not tax their capacity. The real problem must be something else, he decided—perhaps boredom. Some doctors told their women patients they must get out of the house for a day, treat themselves to a movie in town. Others prescribed tranquilizers. Many suburban housewives were taking tranquilizers like cough drops. "You wake up in the morning, and you feel as if there's no point in going on another day like this. So you take a tranquilizer because it makes you not care so much that it's pointless."

It is easy to see the concrete details that trap the suburban housewife, the continual demands on her time. But the chains that bind her in her trap are chains in her own mind and spirit. They are chains made up of mistaken ideas and misinterpreted facts, of incomplete truths and unreal choices. They are not easily seen and not easily shaken off.

How can any woman see the whole truth within the bounds of her own life? How can she believe that voice inside herself, when it denies the conventional, accepted truths by which she has been living? And yet the women I have talked to, who are finally listening to that inner voice, seem in some incredible way to be groping through to a truth that has defied the experts.

I think the experts in a great many fields have been holding pieces of that truth under their microscopes for a long time without realizing it. I found pieces of it in certain new research and theoretical developments in psychological, social and biological science whose implications for women seem never to have been examined. I found many clues by talking to suburban doctors, gynecologists, obstetricians, child-guidance clinicians, pediatricians, high-school guidance counselors, college professors, marriage counselors, psychiatrists and ministers—questioning them not on their theories, but on their actual experience in treating American women. I became aware of a growing body of evidence, much of which has not been reported publicly because it does not fit current modes of thought about women—evidence which throws into question the standards of feminine normality, feminine adjustment, feminine fulfillment, and feminine maturity by which most women are still trying to live.

I began to see in a strange new light the American return to early marriage and the large families that are causing the population explosion; the recent movement to natural childbirth and breastfeeding; suburban conformity, and the new neuroses, character pathologies and sexual problems being reported by the doctors. I began to see new dimensions to old problems that have long been taken for granted among women: menstrual difficulties, sexual frigidity, promiscuity, pregnancy fears, childbirth depression, the high incidence of emotional breakdown and suicide among women in their twenties and thirties, the menopause crises, the so-called passivity and immaturity of American men, the discrepancy between women's tested intellectual abilities in childhood and their adult achievement, the changing incidence of adult sexual orgasm in American women, and persistent problems in psychotherapy and in women's education.

If I am right, the problem that has no name stirring in the minds of so many American women today is not a matter of loss of femininity or too much education, or the demands of domesticity. It is far more important than anyone recognizes. It is the key to these other new and old problems which have been torturing women and their husbands and children, and puzzling their doctors and educators for years. It may well be the key to our future as a nation and a culture. We can no longer ignore that voice within women that says: "I want something more than my husband and my children and my home."

DRAWING CONCLUSIONS:

- What does Friedan's work, and the public response to it, suggest about the sources of dissatisfaction that gave rise to the feminist movement of the 1960s?

5.3 "NATIONAL ORGANIZATION FOR WOMEN BILL OF RIGHTS" (1967)

In 1966, a group of feminist activists (including Betty Friedan) founded the National Organization for Women (NOW), a group that was intended to function as a civil rights organization for women. To this day, NOW remains among the most influential feminist organizations in the United States. In the 1960s, it represented the more moderate wing of the feminist movement (often referred to a "liberal feminism"), in contrast to the more radical "women's liberation" organizations. NOW summed up their initial goals and demands in their 1967 Women's Bill of Rights.

GUIDING QUESTIONS:

- What sorts of issues did NOW emphasize in their 1967 Bill of Rights? What does this suggest about their assumptions regarding the nature of gender inequality and the steps required to eliminate it?

NATIONAL ORGANIZATION FOR WOMEN BILL OF RIGHTS

ADOPTED AT THE NOVEMBER 1967 NOW NATIONAL CONFERENCE

We Demand:

I. That the United States Congress immediately pass the Equal Rights Amendment to the Constitution to provide that "Equality of rights under the law shall not be denied or abridged by the United States or by any State on account of sex" and that such then be immediately ratified by the several States.

II. That equal employment opportunity be guaranteed to all women, as well as men by insisting that the Equal Employment Opportunity Commission enforce the prohibitions against sex discrimination in employment under Title VII of the Civil Rights Act of 1964 with the same vigor as it enforces the prohibitions against racial discrimination.

III. That women be protected by law to insure their rights to return to their jobs within a reasonable time after childbirth without loss of seniority or other accrued benefits and be paid maternity leave as a form of social security and/or employee benefit.

IV. Immediate revision of tax laws to permit the deduction of home and child care expenses for working parents.

V. That child care facilities be established by law on the same basis as parks, libraries and public schools adequate to the needs of children, from the pre-school years through adolescence, as a community resource to be used by all citizens from all income levels.

VI. That the right of women to be educated to their full potential equally with men be secured by Federal and State legislation, eliminating all discrimination and segregation by sex, written and unwritten, at all levels of education including college, graduate and professional schools, loans and fellowships and Federal and State training programs, such as the job Corps.

VII. The right of women in poverty to secure job training, housing and family allowances on equal terms with men, but without prejudice to a parent's right to remain at home to care for his or her children; revision of welfare legislation and poverty programs which deny women dignity, privacy and self-respect.

From Alexander Bloom and Wini Breines, eds., *"Takin' It to the Streets": A Sixties Reader* (New York: Oxford University Press, 1995), 474–475.

VIII. The right of women to control their own reproductive lives by removing from penal codes the laws limiting access to contraceptive information and devices and laws governing abortion.

DRAWING CONCLUSIONS:

- What can we learn about liberal feminism from NOW's Bill of Rights?

5.4 "REDSTOCKINGS MANIFESTO" (1969)

The late 1960s saw the emergence of a more radical wing of feminism that came to be known as women's liberation. Redstockings, founded in New York City in early 1969, was an important early women's liberation organization. Their 1969 Redstockings Manifesto became among the most influential documents of the women's liberation movement. The manifesto provides a window into the thinking of the women's liberation movement.

GUIDING QUESTIONS:

- What is the Redstockings analysis of the nature of gender inequality? What do they believe must happen for it to be eliminated?

REDSTOCKINGS MANIFESTO

JULY 7, 1969

I. After centuries of individual and preliminary political struggle, women are uniting to achieve their final liberation from male supremacy. Redstockings is dedicated to building this unity and winning our freedom.

II. Women are an oppressed class. Our oppression is total, affecting every facet of our lives. We are exploited as sex objects, breeders, domestic servants, and cheap labor. We are considered inferior beings, whose only purpose is to enhance men's lives. Our humanity is denied. Our prescribed behavior is enforced by the threat of physical violence.

Because we have lived so intimately with our oppressors, in isolation from each other, we have been kept from seeing our personal suffering as a political condition. This creates the illusion that a woman's relationship with her man is a matter of interplay between two unique personalities, and can be worked out individually. In reality, every such relationship is a *class* relationship, and the conflicts between individual men and women are *political* conflicts that can only be solved collectively.

III. We identify the agents of our oppression as men. Male supremacy is the oldest, most basic form of domination. All other forms of exploitation and oppression (racism, capitalism, imperialism, etc.) are extensions of male supremacy: men dominate women, a few men dominate the rest. All power structures throughout history have been male-dominated and male-oriented. Men have controlled all political, economic and cultural institutions and backed up this control with physical force. They have used their power to keep women in an inferior position. *All men* receive economic, sexual, and psychological benefits from male supremacy. *All men* have oppressed women.

IV. Attempts have been made to shift the burden of responsibility from men to institutions or to women themselves. We condemn these arguments as evasions. Institutions alone do not oppress; they are merely tools of the oppressor. To blame institutions implies that men and women are equally victimized, obscures the fact that men benefit from the subordination of women, and gives men the excuse that they are forced to be oppressors. On the contrary, any man is free to renounce his

From Alexander Bloom and Wini Breines, eds., *"Takin' It to the Streets": A Sixties Reader* (New York: Oxford University Press, 1995), 485–487.

superior position, provided that he is willing to be treated like a woman by other men.

We also reject the idea that women consent to or are to blame for their own oppression. Women's submission is not the result of brain-washing, stupidity or mental illness but of continual, daily pressure from men. We do not need to change ourselves, but to change men.

The most slanderous evasion of all is that women can oppress men. The basis for this illusion is the isolation of individual relationships from their political context and the tendency of men to see any legitimate challenge to their privileges as persecution.

V. We regard our personal experience, and our feelings about that experience, as the basis for an analysis of our common situation. We cannot rely on existing ideologies as they are all products of male supremacist culture. We question every generalization and accept none that are not confirmed by our experience.

Our chief task at present is to develop female class consciousness through sharing experience and publicly exposing the sexist foundation of all our institutions. Consciousness-raising is not "therapy," which implies the existence of individual solutions and falsely assumes that the male-female relationship is purely personal, but the only method by which we can ensure that our program for liberation is based on the concrete realities of our lives.

The first requirement for raising class consciousness is honesty, in private and in public, with ourselves and other women.

VI. We identify with all women. We define our best interest as that of the poorest, most brutally exploited woman.

We repudiate all economic, racial, educational or status privileges that divide us from other women. We are determined to recognize and eliminate any prejudices we may hold against other women.

We are committed to achieving internal democracy. We will do whatever is necessary to ensure that every woman in our movement has an equal chance to participate, assume responsibility, and develop her political potential.

VII. We call on all our sisters to unite with us in struggle.

We call on all men to give up their male privilege and support women's liberation in the interest of our humanity and their own.

In fighting for our liberation we will always take the side of women against their oppressors. We will not ask what is "revolutionary" or "reformist," only what is good for women.

The time for individual skirmishes has passed. This time we are going all the way.

DRAWING CONCLUSIONS:

- What can we learn about the ideas of the women's liberation movement for the Redstockings Manifesto?
- How do the ideas of women's liberation differ from the ideas of liberal feminists, such as though who drafted NOW's Bill of Rights? How are their ideas similar?

THE GAY AND LESBIAN MOVEMENT

Early in the morning of June 28, 1969, New York City police raided the Stonewall Inn, a bar catering to gay men and trans women in the city's Greenwich Village neighborhood. While the reasons for the raid remain cloudy to this day, it fit a pattern of police harassment of establishments serving a queer clientele both in New York and in other cities. The raid at Stonewall sparked street demonstrations in Greenwich Village (a neighborhood with a large queer population) that escalated into several days of rioting. While struggles for gay and lesbian equality predated Stonewall, the rebellion gave rise to a new and more militant type of gay liberation politics. For this reason, the Stonewall Rebellion is often considered the starting point for the modern LGBTQ movement. The struggle for gay and lesbian equality received less public attention than the other movements of the decade, such as the black civil rights movement, Back Power, the Women's Movement, and the New Left. Over time, however, the gay and lesbian movement that arose in the late 1960s has had a profound impact on the culture of the United States.

6.1 BARBARA GITTINGS COMES OF AGE (1972)

Barbara Gittings was born in 1932. The daughter of a US diplomat, she first began to question her sexuality while an undergraduate at Northwestern University. Gittings spent several years trying to make sense of her feelings and experiences before finally finding a home in the "homophile" movement—the early movement for gay and lesbian civil rights. In 1958, she established a New York City chapter of the Daughters of Bilitis, an organization that provided a safe space for lesbians while also challenging various forms of discrimination that lesbians faced. Gittings went on to become a prominent leader in the movement for LGBTQ equality. In this document, Gittings provides an account of her struggle to understand her own sexuality and her ultimate discovery of the homophile movement.

GUIDING QUESTIONS:

- What challenges did Gittings face as a young person in the 1950s discovering her identity as a lesbian woman?
- What importance did her discovery of the homophile movement play in her life?

BARBARA GITTINGS COMES OF AGE

"But that was the year I had to come to terms with my homosexuality, and it was rough. I'd had clues, I had been attracted to other girls while in high school—and one girl in particular—and I did sense that this was different, not the way it was supposed to be. But at that time I didn't fully realize the stigma against homosexuality."

At Northwestern Barbara became friends with another student in the college dorm. Then a rumor began to spread that they had a lesbian relationship. "It shocked me when I heard about it. It also did something for me. It told me that even though there was no truth to this particular rumor, there was a truth behind it—yes, I must be homosexual!"

To make sure, Barbara went to a woman psychiatrist in Chicago. The doctor agreed that Barbara was homosexual and offered to try to change her. "She took it for granted that change was what I wanted, and so did I. It was part of the culturally accepted outlook then that if you had homosexual tendencies, this was a great misfortune and should be corrected. But my allowance wasn't enough for regular visits." Barbara appealed to her father, but he refused to finance psychiatric treatment, asking her what problems she could possibly have that a priest couldn't help solve? She wouldn't explain." And my friend in the dorm told me that we'd have to see much less of each other because of the rumor. There was no one I could talk with."

Barbara began ignoring her courses and instead spent many hours in the libraries at Northwestern and in Chicago. "I went to texts on abnormal psychology, to encyclopedias, to medical books, to every book dealing with sex, as well as to whatever I could find under card catalog headings like 'sexual perversion.' I was so anxious to get to the material on homosexuality, I didn't even mind looking in categories like 'perversion' and 'abnormal.' And I half believed them anyway.

"But everything I found was so alien, so remote. It didn't give me any sense of myself or what

From Kay Tobin and Randy Wicker, eds., *The Gay Crusaders* (New York: Arno Press, 1975), 207–212.

my life and experience could be. It was mostly clinical-sounding—disturbance, pathology, arrested development—and it was mostly about men." She flunked out of Northwestern at the end of her freshman year. The only subject she had conscientiously pursued—other than homosexuality—was glee club.

"At seventeen I went home in disgrace for having failed in college. I felt I couldn't even tell my family why it had happened. I had nowhere to turn except back to the books. They were the only way I had to save myself. And then I started finding the novels of homosexuality, books like *Nightwood, The Well of Loneliness, The Unlit Lamp, Extraordinary Women*. At last here were lesbians shown as real people! They didn't exactly have lives of bliss, but at least they were functioning people and had their happinesses. They had more realism than all the case histories I'd read put together! I still feel enormous gratitude and affection for those early lesbian novels. Finding the fiction literature of my people was a godsend to me.

"When I got my own copy of *The Well of Loneliness*, I hid it in the junk pile that was my bedroom at home. But my father spotted it. I didn't know this until I got a letter from him in the mail. Mind you, we were living in the same house but he couldn't bring himself to discuss it with me! He wrote that it was a depraved and obscene book and that it was immoral for me to have it. He said it was my moral obligation to dispose of it permanently, that I must burn it! So I hid it better and told him I had destroyed it. Later we had an argument about the book and I defended it by saying it had excellent character portrayals and nature descriptions. My father retorted, they always say that about obscene books.

"Around this time I signed up for a university extension night course in—guess what?—abnormal psychology. There I met a woman who'd been in high school with me a couple years earlier. In our talks after class and in note-passing during class, she managed, awkwardly, to let me know she was gay and interested in me, and I awkwardly let her know I felt the same way. With her I had my first affair." Barbara's attitude toward her orientation took another turn for the better. "My desire for the relationship and its rewards definitely outweighed the worried and confused feelings I still had." The relationship was short-lived, but for Barbara it confirmed her growing feeling that lesbian love was right for her.

Soon after the affair ended, Barbara acted decisively to reorganize her life. At eighteen she left home without explanation to live on her own in central Philadelphia. She got a room in a rooming house, bought a hot plate, and learned to like plain cooked vegetables and boiled eggs. She found a job clerking in a music store. She joined American Youth Hostels to go hiking and later became a bicycling and canoeing enthusiast as well. Just as important, she found a choral group to sing in. Six months after she'd left home, when it was obvious that her lifestyle was a settled if unconventional one, her father wrote, in his own words, "relieving you of the onus of your disobedience" in running away from home. Barbara adds, "My father wasn't really as severe as these incidents make him sound. I think I was his favorite child. Underneath he seemed to like my independent spirit."

It proved easier for Barbara to move out of the world of debutante parties than into the gay world she longed for. "On weekends, dressed as a boy, I'd hitch rides with truckers up Route 1 to New York City to go to the gay bars. At first I didn't know of any gay bars in Philadelphia. I had a lot of trouble getting plugged into the gay community. I spent agonized years trying to find a comfortable social life, and the bars were the only place I had to start looking. Since I didn't have much money and didn't like to drink anyway, I'd hold a glass of ice water and pretend it was gin on the rocks. I'd get into conversation with other women but I'd usually find we didn't really common interests, we just happened both to be gay. I just didn't run into any lesbians who shared my interests in books and hostel trips and baroque music. They all seemed to groove on Peggy Lee and Frank Sinatra and nothing older! It was only later, in other settings, that I found gay people I was really congenial with. In those days I felt there was no real place for me in the straight culture, but the gay bar culture wasn't the place for me either. It was a painful and confusing time in my life.

"I wore drag because I thought that was a way to show I was gay. It's changed now, but in the early

50's there were basically two types of women in the gay bars, the so-called butch ones in short hair and plain masculine attire and the so-called femme ones in dresses and high heels and makeup. I knew high heels and makeup weren't my personal style, so I thought, well, I must be the other kind! And I dressed accordingly. What a waste of time and energy! I was really a mixed-up kid.

"The only other models, the only other images of homosexual people I had to look to were in the books, and there too, much was made of differentiating both lesbians and male homosexuals into masculine and feminine types. This differentiating is disappearing very fast today, not only for gays but for straights too. Nowadays people generally feel freer to look and act whatever way they feel most comfortable, and they don't so readily follow set patterns.

"It was risky as well as inappropriate for me to be in drag. One night in Philadelphia, I left a mixed bar with a male gay acquaintance, and outside there were two marines who put on brass knuckles and attacked my friend. "We'd beat you up too, sonny, if you weren't wearing glasses," one told me. When they left, I took my companion to the hospital where he had thirteen stitches put in his face."

Saturdays in New York Barbara spent combing musty Fourth Avenue secondhand bookstores looking for more gay fiction. "In most of the novels homosexuality brought suffering or downright tragedy. Even so, they represented a history, a people, a sense of community. For me, these books were a large part of my early liberation. My sense of myself as a lesbian came from the fiction literature, certainly not from psychiatry-drenched texts."

Soon she had the beginnings of a valuable collection. She gave up methodically building it only when she discovered in the late 50's that a few other book buffs were way ahead of her—such as Dr. Jeannette Foster, author of *Sex Variant Women in Literature*, and Gene Damon, current editor of the lesbian-feminist magazine *The Ladder*. Barbara maintains that Gene Damon "almost certainly has the most extensive private collection of gay literature in the country, particularly lesbian literature, with many rare items." Barbara's book collecting today concentrates on non-fiction as she keeps tabs on all the current pro and con materials on homosexuality. Most of her fiction collection lies tucked away in cartons.

In her early twenties Barbara had her first serious love relationship and at last entered a milieu where she learned that drag and role-playing were not necessary to lesbian life. While visiting a straight friend at Swathmore College, Barbara met several gay women at the school. One in turn introduced her to a black writer and poet. Barbara was immediately attracted to this woman—"she was a very warm person, and very self-determining"—and soon they entered a difficult affair that lasted half a year. The two planned to go to Mexico together. Barbara (who by then was working for the architectural firm) gave notice on her job, got a visa and started packing. Unexpectedly her lover chose to end the affair, leaving alone for Mexico. "I fell apart in a way," says Barbara. Advancing lame excuses to her boss for her change in plans, Barbara begged (successfully) for her job back and returned to a workaday existence.

Finally she found the gay movement. "I had sought out Donald Webster Cory, author of *The Homosexual in America*, and he told me of the Mattachine Society in San Francisco. For my vacation in 1956 I flew to the West Coast and showed up at the Mattachine office with a rucksack on my back. I'd planned to do some hiking out there. And I did—right over to Daughters of Bilitis which the Mattachine men told me about. It was an exciting time to arrive. They were just planning their first issue of *The Ladder*. The dozen or so women I met there, including Phyllis Lyon and Del Martin, provided me with a much better sense of lesbianism and the lesbian community than I'd ever had before."

Barbara was enthusiastic enough to become a founder and key organizer of DOB's first chapter on the East Coast, in New York City. "We formed in late 1958 with the help and encouragement of the Mattachine Society of New York, which gave us meeting space and other support. At the time there were no newspapers, not even the *Village Voice*, that would take ads for gay groups. So all *Ladder* subscribers within a big radius of New York were notified. Eight of ten showed up, and that's how we started. I was elected the first chapter president and served for 3 years. Almost every weekend for many months I took the bus—I was no longer hitching rides!—from Philadelphia to New York to keep the chapter rolling. We had a busy schedule of Gab-n-Java sessions, buffet suppers, business meetings, and lectures. And we built up a mailing list of nearly 300." Barbara also did most of the work on their newsletter, including stenciling and mimeographing after hours at her office, then typing and stuffing envelopes to ensure absolute security for those on the mailing list.

"I've always been a joiner," she admits. "Some people just like to get in there and pitch. And at that time, the idea that there were organizations of the people I identified with most closely was extremely appealing. Still, I didn't have then the strong movement or cause orientation that I have now. It seemed enough that gay people were getting together, never mind why, in a setting order than the bars."

Barbara reviews the evolution of the gay movement during the late 50s and 60s. "At first we told ourselves we were getting together to learn more about the nature of homosexuality and to let other people know. We looked for 'sympathetic' psychiatrists and lawyers and clergymen who would say things that made us feel a bit better about ourselves. In retrospect, I think this was a very necessary stage to go through. The movement we have today could not have developed if there hadn't been this earlier effort to get over the really severe feelings of inadequacy about being gay that most of our people had.

"Also we talked about doing something, such as getting laws changed, to ease things a little. Later we began to claim we were entitled to some rights. I recall that a homosexual bill of rights was the subject of an early gay group conference on the West Coast, and the bill of rights proved so controversial the delegates from one group walked out of the meeting. There was still a strong feeling that if we spoke nicely and reasonably and played by the rules of the game, we could persuade heterosexuals that homosexuals were all right as human beings."

DRAWING CONCLUSIONS:

- What can we learn from Gittings's account about the experiences of gay and lesbian people in the post–World War II period and the factors that contributed to growing sense of gay and lesbian identity?

6.2 MARK SEGAL, EXCERPT FROM *AND THEN I DANCED: TRAVELING THE ROAD TO LGBT EQUALITY* (2015)

Born in 1951, Mark Segal grew up in public housing as one of the few Jews in a predominantly Italian-American Catholic neighborhood in Philadelphia. After graduating high school, he moved to New York City, arriving just shortly before the 1969 Stonewall Rebellion. After participating in the Stonewall events, Segal helped to found the Gay Liberation Front, a gay liberation organization that embodied the new militant spirit inspired by Stonewall. Segal also created Gay Youth, the country's first LGBTQ youth organization. He went on to pursue work as a journalist and established the publication *Philadelphia Gay News*. In this excerpt from his autobiography, Segal describes life as a gay teenager in Philadelphia and his move to New York.

GUIDING QUESTIONS:

- What challenges did Segal face as a gay youth in the 1960s?
- Why did Segal move to New York? What did he find there?

AND THEN I DANCED: TRAVELING THE ROAD TO LGBT EQUALITY

(EXCERPT)

MARK SEGAL

When I was younger, maybe five or six years old, my cousin Norman was sixteen. His father discovered that he was gay, gave him a major beating, and threw him out of the house. Cousin Norman was the family member whom nobody mentioned. One day, I was in the backseat of my parents' Studebaker while they were discussing him and I somehow picked up on the fact that he was a guy who liked guys—a fegeleh. It was rarely brought up in the family and this clued me in to the dynamic that silence was preferred on this topic. Talk or no talk, I knew that whatever it all meant, I too was a fegeleh. And I knew never to speak about it.

As a teenager, I read in *TV Guide* one afternoon that on his PBS talk show, David Susskind was going to interview "real life homosexuals." A new word different from fegeleh, somehow I knew it also referred to me. I just knew it. In the fifties and sixties, those words were rarely used, you were a sinner in religious circles; you were a criminal in legal situations; you were insane in the psychiatric community; and you were unemployable by city, state, and federal governments. Pretty much a life of condemnation awaited you. If people found out the word homosexual applied to you, chances were you would lose your job, your family, be subjected to electrical shocks, and lose everything else you valued, so most remained inside a closet within a closet. I didn't know all of this as a kid, but I knew it was a dangerous subject to discuss. This would all change later on, but in the early sixties there weren't many places to turn if such a life was yours.

From Mark Segal, *And Then I Danced: Traveling the Road to LGBT Equality* (New York: Akashic Books, 2015), 25–28.

My parents had given me a nine inch portable black-and-white television set for my bar mitzvah. It was all the rage back then, an itty-bitty set with big round batteries. The David Susskind show came on at late at night and I remember taking my TV up to my room, making my bedcovers into a tent, and watching the show. There was a man from the Mattachine Society in New York talking about gay people. I thought to myself, There are homosexuals in New York. There are people like me. Then and there I knew I would move to New York.

It was awhile before I took action, but that night a plan began to form in my head. I was going to be with people like me. For a long while I had no idea how I'd do it, but it eventually came to me. Radio Corporation of America (RCA) had a technical institute that taught high school students how to be television cameramen. That was my ticket. It broke my father's heart since he really wanted me to go to college, and Mom always said I'd make a great lawyer. But the only thing that mattered to me then was to be with my own kind and there were none of us in Philadelphia, at least none that I knew. In New York I would become part of a new breed of gay men who didn't slide easily into the popular and unfortunate stereotypes of the times—and that would work to my advantage.

On May 10, 1969, the day after grades were finalized, I moved to New York on the pretense that I would start technical school in September. My parents drove me up, dropped me off, and I got a room at the YMCA. I dressed up in my best clothes and set off for a gay evening, probably expecting that my gay brothers and sisters would line up to embrace me and welcome me into their community. The problem was, I had no idea where to go. There were certainly no neon signs pointing to the gay area. It seemed the place to start my search was Greenwich Village, which according to the network news was the counter-cultural hub of the 1960s. Getting off the subway in the Village, I had an unhappy, lonely feeling. Leaving the security of home, finding myself in a strange place with no prospects of a job and little money, was a bit daunting. Yet my search was on. It didn't begin very well, though, and that first night I returned to my tiny four-dollar sweatbox room, exhausted and unsuccessful in finding my people.

After a few days of looking around, I came across a Village dance bar, the Stonewall, a mob-owned dive. As it turned out, two boys who I'd met at the YMCA from Saint Cloud, Minnesota, were there that night as well.

That first week, remembering the Susskind show with real live homosexuals, I also looked up Mattachine Society in the telephone book and went to their office. I had no idea what to expect. All I knew about them from the television show was that they worked on keeping gay people from getting fired. I walked out of the office about fifteen minutes later with a guy named Marty Robinson, who would later become one of the most unsung heroes of the gay movement. Marty was young and evidently frustrated in his dealings with Mattachine. He said, "You don't want to be involved with these old people. They don't understand gay rights as it's happening today. Look what's happening in the black community. Look at the fight for women's rights. Look at the fight against the Vietnam War."

It was 1969 and Mattachine became old. They were men in suits. We were men in jeans and T-shirts. So he told me that he and others were going to start a new gay rights movement, one more in tune with the times. Marty was creating an organization called the Action Group and I became an inaugural member. We didn't know exactly what we were going to do or what actions we might pursue, but none of that mattered. Others at that time were also creating gay groups to spark public consciousness, similar to the groups feminists were establishing. It deserves to be said right here and right now that the feminist movement was pivotal in helping to shape the new movement for gay rights.

Groups across New York worked independently of each other, but all with the same goal of defining ourselves rather than accepting the labels that society had branded us with. We were on the ground floor of the struggle for equality, and though some might have seen it as a sexual revolution, we saw it as defining ourselves. Years later a friend would remark, "Mark was so involved with the sexual revolution that he didn't have time to participate." The Action Group would hold meetings walking down Christopher Street—our outdoor office, so to speak. We didn't have a headquarters.

Then, just a little over a month after I arrived, on June 28, 1969, Stonewall happened.

DRAWING CONCLUSIONS:

- What can we learn from Segal's account about the experiences of queer youth in the 1960s and the factors that contributed to growing sense of rebellions among queer people?

6.3 HOMOPHILE FREEDOM SONG (1966)

The late 1950s and 1960s saw the growth of a gay and lesbian civil rights movement (known as the "homophile" movement) in many ways modeled on the black civil rights movement of the period. Using methods similar to the black civil rights movement, the homophile movement sought to change laws and social practices that discriminated against gays and lesbians. Between 1965 and 1969, the homophile movement held an annual July 4th picket at Independence Hall in Philadelphia in support of gay and lesbian rights. This "Homophile Freedom Song" was composed for the 1966 Independence Hall picket and was sung to the tune of the "Battle Hymn of the Republic."

GUIDING QUESTIONS:

- What specific changes in laws and social practices does the "Homophile Freedom Song" call for?
- What factors are cited in the song as inspiration for the homophile movement?

"HOMOPHILE FREEDOM SONG" (1966)

Mine eyes have seen the struggles of the Negroes and the Jews,
I have seen the counties trampled where the laws of men abuse,
But you crush the homosexual with anything you choose,
Now we are marching on.
CHORUS:
Glory, glory, hallelujah,
Glory, glory, hallelujah,
Glory, glory, hallelujah,
Now we are marching on.
Your masquerading morals squad has twisted all we've said,
You've put peepholes in our bathrooms, and made laws to rule our bed,
We ask you to treat us fairly but you always turn your head,
Now we are marching on. (Chorus)
In your so-called "Great Society" you've given us no place,
We bring to you our problems, and you stand and slap our face,
How can you boast of freedom and ignore this great disgrace,
Now we are marching on. (Chorus)
Now we've asked, and begged, and pleaded for the right to have a life,
Free to choose the one we love, and free from man-made strife,
But you turn around and stab us with your legislative knife,
Now we are marching on. (Chorus)
We've been drowned out by injustice till our whispers can't be heard,
You have shattered all our dreams and hopes and yet we never stirred,
But we're rising in a chorus and you'll soon hear every word,
Now we are marching on. (Chorus)
The civil rights you took for us we want them back again.
We will talk and write and picket, until we see you bend,

From *Homosexual Citizen*, September 1966, 14–15.

If you do not give them freely, we will
take them in the end,
Now we are marching on. (Chorus)

DRAWING CONCLUSIONS:

- What does the "Homophile Freedom Song" reveal about the goals of the homophile movement?
- What does the song reveal about the factors that contributed to the rise of the movement?

6.4 DICK LEITSCH, "THE HAIRPIN DROP HEARD AROUND THE WORLD" (1969)

In the mid- to late 1960s, Dick Leitsch was president of the Mattachine Society, a prominent homophile organization. Leitsch lived in New York City and witnessed the events of the Stonewall Uprising. He published the following widely read account of the uprising, which was published in the *Mattachine Society of New York Newsletter* shortly after the events described.

GUIDING QUESTIONS:

- What exactly sparked the demonstrations outside the Stonewall Inn early on the morning of Saturday, June 28, 1969?
- Why did the demonstrations escalate into a neighborhood-wide riot in New York's Greenwich Village?

"THE HAIRPIN DROP HEARD AROUND THE WORLD"

DICK LEITCSH

The first gay riots in history took place during the predawn hours of Saturday and Sunday, June 28–29, in New York's Greenwich Village. The demonstrations were touched off by a police raid on the popular Stonewall Club, 53 Christopher Street. This was the last (to date) in a series of harassments which plagued the Village area for the last several weeks.

Plainclothes officers entered the club at about 2 a.m., armed with a warrant, and closed the place on grounds of illegal selling of alcohol. Employees were arrested and the customers told to leave. The patrons gathered on the street outside, and were joined by other Village residents and visitors to the area. The police behaved, as is usually the case when they deal with homosexuals, with bad grace, and were reproached by "straight" onlookers. Pennies were thrown at the cops by the crowd, then beer cans, rocks, and even parking meters. The cops retreated inside the bar, which was set afire by the crowd.

A hose from the bar was employed by the trapped cops to douse the flames, and reinforcements were summoned. A melee ensued, with nearly a thousand persons participating, as well as several hundred cops. Nearly two hours later, the cops had "secured" the area.

The next day, the Stonewall management sent in a crew to repair the premises, and found that the cops had taken all the money from the cigarette machine, the jukebox, the cash register, and the safe, and had even robbed the waiters' tips!

Since they had been charged with selling liquor without a license, the club was reopened as a "free store," open to all and with everything being given away, rather than sold.

A crowd filled the place and the street in front. Singing and chanting filled Sheridan Square Park, and the crowds grew quickly.

At first, the crowd was all gay, but as the weekend tourists poured in the area, they joined the crowd. They'd begin by asking what was happening. When they were told that homosexuals were protesting the closing of a gay club, they'd become very sympathetic, and stay to watch or join in. One middle-aged lady with her husband told a cop that he should be ashamed of himself. "Don't you know that these people have no place to go, and need places like that

Originally published in *The Mattachine Society of New York Newsletter* (July 1969). Reprinted in *The Stonewall Reader* (New York: Penguin Books, 2019), 99–104.

bar?" she shouted. (Several hours later, she and her husband, with two other couples, were seen running with a large group of homosexuals from the night-sticks brandished by the TPF.)

The crowds were orderly, and limited themselves to singing and shouting slogans such as "Gay Power," "We Want Freedom Now," and "Equality for homosexuals." As the mob grew, it spilled off the sidewalk, overflowed Sheridan Square Park, and began to fill the roadway. One of the six cops who were there to keep order began to get smart and cause hostility. A bus driver blew his horn at the meeting, and someone shouted, "Stop the Bus!" The crowd surged out in to the street and blocked the progress of the bus. As the driver inched ahead, someone ripped off an advertising card and blocked the windshield with it. The crowd beat on the sides of the (empty) bus and shouted, "Christopher Street belongs to the queens!" and "Liberate the street."

The cops got the crowd to let the bus pass, but then the people began a slow-down-the-traffic campaign. A human line across the street blocked traffic, and the cars were let through one at a time. Another car, bearing a fat, gouty-looking cop with many pounds of gilt braid, chauffeured by a cute young cop, came through. The fat cop looked for all the world like a slave owner surveying the plantation, and someone tossed a sack of wet garbage through the car window and right on his face. The bag broke and soggy coffee grounds dripped down the lined face, which never lost its "screw you" look.

Another police car came through Waverly Place, and stopped at the corner of Christopher. The occupants just sat there and glared at the crowd. Suddenly, a concrete block landed on the hood of the car, and the crowd drew back. Then, as one person, it surged forward and surrounded the car, beating on it with fists and dancing atop it. The cops radioed for help, and soon the crowd let the car pass.

Christopher Street, from Greenwich to Seventh Avenues, had become an almost solid mass of people—most of them gay. No traffic could pass, and even walking the few blocks on foot was next to impossible. One little old lady tried to get through, and many members of the crowd tried to help her. She brushed them away and continued her determined walk, trembling with fear and murmuring, "It must be the full moon, it must be the full moon."

Squad cars from the Fifth, Sixth, Fourth, and Ninth Precincts had brought in a hundred or so cops, who had no hope of controlling the crowd of nearly two thousand people in the streets. Until this point, the crowd had been, for the most part, pleasant and in a jovial mood. Some of the cops began to become very nasty, and started trouble. One boy, evidently a discus thrower, reacted by bouncing garbage can lids neatly off the helmets of the cops. Others set garbage cans ablaze. A Christopher Street merchant stood in the doorway of her shop and yelled at the cops to behave themselves. Whenever they would head in her direction, she'd run into the shop and lock the door.

The focus of the demonstration shifted from the Stonewall to "The Corner"—Greenwich Avenue and Christopher Street. The intersection, and the street behind it, was a solid mass of humanity. The Tactical Police Force (TPF) arrived in city buses. 100 of them debarked at The Corner, and 50 more at Seventh Ave. and Christopher.

They huddled with some of the top brass that had already arrived, and isolated beer cans, thrown by the crowd, hit their vans and cars now and again. Suddenly, two cops darted into the crowd and dragged out a boy who had done absolutely nothing. As they carried him to a waiting van brought to take off prisoners, four more cops joined them and began pounding the boy in the face, belly, and groin with night sticks. A high shrill voice called out, "Save our sister!" and there was a general pause, during which the "butch" looking "numbers" looked distracted. Momentarily, fifty or more homosexuals who would have to be described as "nelly," rushed the cops and took the boy back into the crowd. They then formed a solid front and refused to let the cops into the crowd to regain their prisoner, letting the cops hit them with their sticks rather than let them through.

(It was an interesting sidelight on the demonstrations that those usually put down as "sissies" or "swishes" showed the most courage and sense during the action. Their bravery and daring saved many people from being hurt, and their sense of humour and camp helped keep the crowds from getting nasty or too violent.)

The cops gave up on the idea of taking prisoners, and concentrated on clearing the area. They rushed both ways on Greenwich, forcing the crowds into 10th Street and 6th Avenue, where the people circled the blocks and reentered Christopher. Then the cops formed a flying wedge, and with arms linked, headed down Greenwich, forcing everyone in front of them into side streets. Cops on the end of the wedge broke off and chased demonstrators down the side streets and away from the center of the action.

They made full use of their night sticks, brandishing them like swords. At one point a cop grabbed a wild Puerto Rican queen and lifted his arm to bring a club down on "her." In his best Mario Montez voice, the queen challenged, "How'd you like a big Spanish dick up your little Irish ass?" The cop was so shocked he hesitated in his swing and the queen escaped.

At another point, two lonely cops were chasing a hundred or more people down Waverly Place. Someone shouted out that the queens outnumbered the cops and suggested catching them, ripping off their clothes, and screwing them. The cops abandoned the chase and fled back to the main force for protection.

The police action did eventually disperse the crowds, many of whom abandoned the cause and headed to the docks for some fun. By 2:30, nearly two hours after the bus had been delayed, the area was again peaceful. Apart from two to three hundred cops standing around the area, it looked like an unusually dull Saturday night.

Then, at 3 a.m. the bars closed, and the patrons of the many gay bars in the area arrived to see what was happening. They were organized and another attempt was made to liberate Christopher Street. The police, still there in great numbers, managed to break up the demonstrations. One small group did break off and attempt to liberate the IND subway station at Sixth Avenue and Waverly Place, but the police, after a hurried consultation as to whether they could act on the "turf" of the Transit cops, went in and chased everyone out.

By 5:30 a.m., the area was secure enough that the TPF police were sent home, and the docks were packed tight with homosexuals having the time of their lives. After all, everything was perfectly "safe"—all the cops were on "The Corner"!

In all, thirteen people were arrested on Saturday morning—7 of them employees of the Stonewall. Four more were arrested on Sunday morning, and many more were detained then released. Apparently, only four persons were injured ... all of them cops. Three suffered minor bruises and scratches, and one a "broken wrist" (it was not specified whether it was the kind of "broken wrist" that requires a cast, or the kind that makes it noisy to wear a bangle bracelet ... we presume it was the former).

Sunday night saw a lot of action in the Christopher Street area. Hundreds of people were on the streets, including, for the first time, a large leather contingent. However, there were never enough people to outnumber the large squads of cops milling about, trying desperately to head off any trouble.

The Stonewall was again a "free store" and the citizenry was treated to the sight of the cops begging homosexuals to go inside the bar that they had chased everyone out of a few nights before.

Inasmuch as all the cops in town seemed to be near The Comer again, the docks were very busy, and two boys went to the Charles Street station house and pasted "Equality for Homosexuals" bumper stickers on cop cars, the autos of on-duty cops, and the van used to take away prisoners.

One of the most frightening comments was made by one cop to another, and overheard by a MSNY member being held in detention. One said he'd enjoyed the fracas. "Them queers have a good sense of humor and really had a good time," he said. His "buddy" protested "aw, they're sick. I like nigger riots better because there's more action, but you can't beat up a fairy. They ain't mean like blacks; they're sick. But you can't hit a sick man."

DRAWING CONCLUSIONS:

- What can we learn from Leitch's account about both the short-term and long-term factors that contributed to the Stonewall Rebellion of 1969?

6.5 THOMAS LANIGAN-SCHMIDT, "1969 MOTHER STONEWALL AND THE GOLDEN RATS" (1989)

Thomas Lanigan-Schmidt is a visual artist who participated in the Stonewall Rebellion. In the following text (prepared for 1989 art exhibition marking the twentieth anniversary of the rebellion), Lanigan-Schmidt reflects upon the meaning and significance of Stonewall.

GUIDING QUESTIONS:

- What can we learn from Lanigan-Schmidt's text about the experiences of queer youth in the 1960s?
- What was the importance of gay-friendly spaces like Greenwich Village and the Stonewall Inn to queer youth in the 1960s?

DRAWING CONCLUSIONS:

- What can we learn from Lanigan-Schmidt's text the factors that contributed to the Stonewall Rebellion of 1969?

1969 Mother Stonewall and the Golden Rats
© 1989 By Thomas Lanigan-Schmidt

We sat on the curb-gutter around the corner from a Dance-Bar called The STONEWALL. He had wounds sutured up and down his arms. The army had rejected him for being "a queer". His father had thrown him out of the house through a glass door. I'd left home for the last time too. I was supposed to be on a ditch-digging, road repair, summer job crew with a bunch of jerks I'd gone to school with (they would've buried me alive, just for the fun of it). So, I up and went to New York City with just the clothes on my back. One Queen had an enormous burn-scar covering her* face and most of her* body. Her* mother didn't want men to "be tempted" by her son's beauty. We lived in cheap hotels, broken down apartments, abandoned buildings or on the streets. Home was where the heart is. Some were able to get menial jobs. Some of us were on welfare. Some of us hustled. And some of us pan-handled (begged for money in the streets). Food was where you found it. Many of us had gotten thrown out of home before finishing high school. WE WERE STREET RATS. Puerto Rican, Black, Northern and Southern whites, "Debby the Dyke" and a Chinese queen named "JADE EAST". The sons and daughters of postal workers, welfare mothers, cab drivers, mechanics and NURSES Aids (just to name a few). Until properly introduced it was de rigueur argot to call everybody "MISS THING," (after this, it was discretionary USAGE). I strongly objected when a queen called "Opera Jean" called me "MARY" (but I'm a man!?) "MARY, GRACE, ALICE, whats the Difference, Afterall, we're all sisters? Aren't We?" (ONE IN ESSENCE and UNDIVIDED). She* was head-strong, so I stopped complaining. I ended up being named "VIOLET" by a black queen named "NOVA".

WE ALL ENDED UP TOGETHER AT A PLACE CALLED THE STONEWALL. SAFE and SOUND. All you had to do was find an empty beer, so the waiter would think you bought a drink, and the night was yours. A replica of a wishing well stood near the back bar of one of the two large rooms painted black. The juke box played a lot of Motown music. We DANCED. The Air Conditioners seemed not to work at all because the place was always so crowded. We were happy. This place was the "ART" that gave form to the feelings of our heartbeats. Here the consciousness of knowing you "belonged" nestled into that warm feeling of finally being HOME. And Home engenders Love-and-Loyalty quite naturally. So, We loved the Stonewall.

The cops (singular and Plural) were generically known as "Lily Law," "Betty Badge", "Patty Pig" or "The Devil with the blue Dress on". That night Betty Badge got carried away. It was not only a raid but a bust. Mother STONEWALL WAS being VIOLATED. They forcibly entered her with nightsticks. The lights went on. It wasn't a pretty sight (How would children feel seeing their mother raped right before their eyes? Their home broken into and looted!? The Music Box Broken. The Dancing stopped. The replicated Wishing Well SMASHED?). No, this wasn't a 1960's Student Riot. Out there were the streets. There were no Nice Dorms for sleeping. No school CAFETERIA for certain food. No affluent PARENTS to send us checks. The was a ghetto riot on home turf. We already had our WAR WOUNDS. This was just another battle. Nobody thought of it as History, Herstory, MY-Story, Your-Story or our-story. We were being denied a place to dance together.. Thats ALL. The total charisma of a revolution in our ~~consciousn~~ CONSCIOUSNESS rising from the gutter to the gut to the heart and the mind was here. Non-existence (or Part existence) was coming into being, and being into becoming. Our Mother Stonewall was giving birth to a New ERA and we were the midwives.

THAT NIGHT The "Gutter (STREET) RATS" shone like the brightest Gold! And like that baby born in a feed-troft (a manger) or found by Pharoes daughter in a basket floating down the river NILE, the mystery of history happened again in the Least likely of Places.

* She
* "Queen argot, generic pronoun, in this case refers to a male person.

Please Xerox a few copies and give to friends

FIGURE 6 Mother Stonewall and the Golden Rats
Source: Thomas Lanigan-Schmidt, Mother Stonewall and the Golden Rats, 1989, Xerox photocopy. Courtesy of the artist and Pavel Zoubok Fine Art

THE CONSERVATIVE BACKLASH

For much of the 1960s, social and cultural movements that challenged the status quo (such as the civil rights movement, the New Left, the counterculture, and black power) commanded the attention of the country. Many Americans sympathized with these movements. Many more viewed them with growing anger and frustration. Toward the end of decade, this animosity exploded in a "conservative backlash" that rocked American politics and culture. This backlash took many forms, among the most important of which was support for candidates for public office who promised to crack down on protesters, rioters, and hippies. The conservative backlash helped propel Richard Nixon into the presidency in 1968 and drove his landslide re-election victory in 1972. Anger toward the social movement of 1960s also fed a new kind of conservative politics that culminated in the election of President Ronald Reagan on a platform that directly challenged the expansive liberalism that had characterized American politics in the post–World War II era. As with the other movements of the 1960s, the legacies of the conservative backlash can be seen up until the present day. Understanding the sources of the conservative backlash can therefore help us make sense of many elements of contemporary American politics and culture.

7.1 WHITE ATTITUDES ON ISSUES OF RACE

Central to the conservative backlash of the late 1960s was antipathy toward the racial liberation movements of the time. To understand the widespread white hostility toward movements for racial justice, it is helpful to delve into the racial attitudes of white Americans. Fortunately, there is a wealth of public opinion survey data available from the time period with which to explore white racial attitudes. The data presented here are taken from Angus Campbell's *White Attitudes Toward Black People*, published in 1971.

GUIDING QUESTIONS:

- How did white Americans people tend to view government efforts to address racial inequalities? How did their views tend to differ from those of black Americans?
- How did white Americas tend to view the movements for racial justice of the time? How did their views tend to differ from those of black Americans?
- How did white Americans tend to view interracial contact?
- To what extent did white Americans tend to acknowledge the existence of racial discrimination as a reality in American life?

TABLE 12 AMERICAN ATTITUDES TOWARD ISSUES OF RACE

The following are results of public opinion polls taken among black and white Americans nationwide in 1964, 1968, and 1970.

Some people feel that if Negroes* are not getting fair treatment in jobs the government in Washington ought to see that they do. How do you feel about it? Should the government in Washington see to it that Negroes get fair treatment in jobs or leave these matters to the states and local communities?

	White			Black		
	1964	1968	1970	1964	1968	1970
See to it they get fair treatment	33%	33%	—	87%	84%	—
It depends	8%	7%	—	3%	1%	—
Leave to the states	44%	46%	—	5%	9%	—
Don't know	4%	2%	—	1%	1%	—
Not interested enough to have an opinion	11%	12%	—	4%	5%	—

Some people say that the government in Washington should see to it that white and Negro children are allowed to go to the same schools. Others claim that this is not the government's business. Do you think the government in Washington should:

	White			Black		
	1964	1968	1970	1964	1968	1970
See to it that white and Negro children go to the same schools	38%	33%	41%	68%	84%	84%
It depends	7%	7%	10%	4%	3%	3%
Stay out of this area as it is none of its business	42%	48%	36%	12%	6%	7%

* In the 1960s, the term "Negro" remained in common use, even among some African American leaders.

Continued

	White			Black		
	1964	1968	1970	1964	1968	1970
Don't know	3%	1%	1%	7%	3%	1%
Not interested enough to have an opinion	10%	11%	12%	9%	4%	5%

As you know, Congress passed a law that says that Negroes should have the right to go into any hotel or restaurant they can afford, just like anybody else. Some people feel that this is something the government in Washington should support. Others feel the government should stay out of the matter. Should the government support the right of Negroes:

			White			Black
	1964	1968	1970	1964	1968	1970
To go to any hotel or restaurant they can afford	41%	48%	56%	88%	90%	93%
It depends	4%	3%	4%	1%	1%	1%
Stay out of this matter	43%	37%	27%	35	4%	2%
Don't know	2%	2%	1%	0%	0%	0%
Not interested enough to have an opinion	10%	10%	12%	8%	5%	4%

Which of these statements would you agree with: White people have a right to keep Negroes out of their neighborhoods if they want to, or Negroes have a right to live wherever they can afford to, just like anybody else?

	White			Black		
	1964	1968	1970	1964	1968	1970
White people have a right to keep Negroes out	29%	24%	21%	2%	1%	2%
Negroes have a right to live wherever they can afford to	53%	65%	67%	89%	96%	97%
It depends, don't know	18%	11%	12%	9%	3%	1%

Are you in favor of desegregation, strict segregation, or something in between?

	White			Black		
	1964	1968	1970	1964	1968	1970
Desegregation	27%	31%	35%	72%	72%	78%
Something in between	46%	48%	44%	20%	19%	19%
Strict segregation	24%	16%	17%	6%	5%	3%
Don't know	3%	5%	4%	2%	4%	0%

In the past few years, we've heard a lot about civil rights groups working to improve the position of the Negro in this country. How much real change do you think there has been in the position of the Negro in the past few years: a lot, some, or not much at all?

	White			Black		
	1964	1968	1970	1964	1968	1970
A lot	38%	49%	54%	57%	61%	41%
Some	39%	35%	33%	31%	32%	45%
Not much at all	20%	15%	10%	11%	6%	14%
Don't know	3%	1%	3%	1%	1%	0%

Some say the civil rights people have been trying to move too fast. Others feel they haven't pushed fast enough. How about you, do you think that the civil rights leaders are trying to push too fast, are going too slowly, or are they moving at about the right speed?

	White			Black		
	1964	1968	1970	1964	1968	1970
Too fast	68%	68%	57%	10%	6%	7%
About right	21%	23%	30%	62%	62%	52%
Too slowly	3%	4%	6%	23%	28%	39%
Don't know	8%	5%	7%	5%	4%	2%

During the past year or so, would you say that most of the actions Negroes have taken to get the things they want have been violent, or have most of these actions been peaceful?

	White			Black		
	1964	1968	1970	1964	1968	1970
Most have been violent	61%	73%	61%	18%	26%	25%
Some violent, some peaceful	4%	3%	3%	6%	7%	3%
Most have been peaceful	23%	17%	25%	64%	58%	61%
Don't know	12%	7%	11%	12%	9%	11%

Do you think the actions Negroes have taken have on the whole helped their cause, or on the whole have hurt their cause?

			White			Black
	1964	1968	1970	1964	1968	1970
Helped	21%	21%	25%	72%	66%	78%
Both helped and hurt	4%	3%	4%	1%	7%	3%
Hurt	63%	69%	62%	14%	16%	11%
Don't know	12%	7%	9%	13%	11%	8%

The following are results of a survey conducted among white residents of fifteen American cities in 1968. The survey was limited to individuals living within the city limits. A parallel survey of the suburban communities surrounding two of the cities, however, indicated that attitudes among white suburban residents were similar to those of white city residents.

White Attitudes Toward Interracial Contact

1. Suppose you had a job where your supervisor was a qualified Negro. Would you mind that a lot, a little, or not at all?
   Mind a lot—4%
   Mind a little—8%
   Mind not at all—86%
   Don't know—2%

2. If you had small children, would you rather than only had white friends, or would you like them to have Negro friends too, or wouldn't you care one way or the other?
   Only white friends—33%
   Negro friends too—19%
   Don't care one way or other—46%
   Don't know—2%

3. If a negro family with about the same income and education as you moved next door to you, would you mind it a lot, a little, or not at all?
   Mind a lot—19%
   Mind at little—25%
   Mind not at all—49%
   Already Negro family next door—4%
   Don't know—3%
4. Who do you think you could more easily become friends with, a Negro with the same education and income as you or a white person with a different education and income than you?
   White person—49%
   Negro person—23%
   No difference—5%
   Don't know—23%

White Perceptions of Discrimination Against Negroes

1. Do you think that in [CITY] many, some, or only a few Negroes miss out on good housing because white owners won't rent or sell to them?

Many—38%
Some—30%
Only a few—22%
None—4%
Don't know—6%

2. Do you think that in [CITY] many, some, or only a few Negroes miss out on jobs and promotions because of racial discrimination?

Many—22%
Some—34%
Only a few—26%
None—12%
Don't know—6%

3. It is sometimes said that the things we have just been talking about, such as unnecessary roughness and disrespect by the police, happen more to Negroes in [CITY] than to white people. Do you think this is definitely so, probably so, probably not so, or definitely not so?

Definitely—9%
Probably—29%
Probably not so—30%
Definitely not so—26%
Don't know—6%

4. On the average, Negroes in [CITY] have worse jobs, education, and housing than white people. Do you think this is due mainly to Negroes being discriminated against, or mainly due to something about Negroes themselves?

Mainly due to discrimination—19%
Mainly due to Negroes themselves—56%
A mixture of both—19%
Don't know—6%

White Sympathy with the Black Protest

1. Some Negro leaders are talking about having non-violent marches and demonstrations in several cities in 1968. Do you think such demonstrations are different from the riots, or that there is no real difference?
   Are different—60%
   Are not different—35%
   Don't know—5%
2. Do you think Negroes are justified in using orderly marches to protest against discrimination? IF YES: If that doesn't help, do you think Negroes are justified in protesting through sit-ins?
   Marches and sit-ins both justified—28%
   Marches justified by not sit-ins—39%
   Neither marches nor sit-ins justified—27%
   Don't know—6%

3. Some people say these disturbances (in Detroit and Newark) are mainly a protest against unfair conditions. Others say they are mainly a way of looting and things like that. Which of these seems more correct to you?
   Mainly protest—44%
   Mainly looting—28%
   Some of both—24%
   Don't know—4%
4. Do you think the large disturbances like those in Detroit and Newark were planned in advance, or that there was some planning but not much, or weren't planned at all?
   Planned in advance—48%
   Some planning—36%
   Not planned at all—11%
   Don't know—5%
5. Some say that Negroes have been pushing too fast for what they want. Others feel they haven't pushed fast enough. How about you—do you think Negroes are trying to push too fast, are going too slowly, or are moving at about the right speed?
   Too fast—67%
   Too slowly—7%
   About right speed—22%
   Don't know—4%

All data from Angus Campbell, *White Attitudes Toward Black People* (Ann Arbor: University of Michigan Press, 1971).

DRAWING CONCLUSIONS:

- What can we learn about white racial attitudes from this public opinion survey data?
- What insight does this data give you into the sources of the conservative backlash?

7.2 AMERICAN ATTITUDES TOWARD SOCIAL DISORDER

In early 1971, a pair of public opinion survey researchers named Albert Cantrill and Charles Roll carried out a pair of public opinion surveys designed to "attain a sense of the basic hopes and fears of the American people and to explore their views on such issues as national unrest and the war in Indochina." The data that Cantrill and Roll gathered are an invaluable source of information regarding the perspectives of Americans in the wake of the upheavals of the 1960s. Their data on American attitudes toward social disorder are particularly useful for analyzing the sources of the conservative backlash. Cantrill and Roll found that certain groups of Americans tended to emphasize the systemic causes of social disorder while other groups of Americans tended to blame the protesters themselves for the disorders.

GUIDING QUESTIONS:

- How concerned did Americans tend to be in the early 1970s about the spread of social disorder?
- Which groups of Americans were most likely to blame protests for the spread of social disorder?
- Which groups of Americans were most likely to blame systemic problems for the spread of social disorder?

TABLE 13 AMERICAN ATTITUDES TOWARD SOCIAL DISORDER

There has been a lot of talk in the news recently about unrest in our country and ill-feeling between groups. In general, how concerned are you about this unrest and ill-feeling? Do you think it is likely to lead to a real breakdown in this country or do you think it is likely to blow over soon?

	Likely to Lead to Breakdown	Likely to Blow Over Soon	Don't Know
National Average	47%	38%	15%

Choose one or two of the following reasons that are mainly responsible for this unrest and ill-feeling.

Our traditional way of doing things is not working and some basic changes are needed if we are to work together	34%
Some young people have gotten out of hand and have no respect for authority	32%
The protests are largely communist inspired	31%
Our leaders in government and business are not trying hard enough to solve the problems we face and people are losing confidence in them	31%
Some Negroes and other minorities are making unreasonable demands	31%
Many of the problems our country faces are so big that we can't agree on how to solve them	19%
Can't say	7%

The responses were grouped into two categories:

- Those dealing with protesters (Responses #2, #3, and #5)
- Those dealing with systemic problems (Responses #1, #4, and #6)

Population Groups More Likely to Blame Demonstrators for Unrest	
	Points by Which Total for "Protest-Related" Reasons Exceeds Total for "System-Related" Reasons
The grade school educated	+41
People in farmer-headed households	+41
Those 50 years of age or over	+40
The high school educated	+25
Residents of municipalities under 50,000 in population	+22

Population Groups More Likely to Blame Conditions for Unrest	
	Points by Which Total for "System-Related" Reasons Exceeds Total for "Protest-Related" Reasons
The college educated	+53
Non-whites	+45
Those twenty-one to twenty-nine years of age	+41
People in household headed by professional and business people	+23

From Albert H. Cantril and Charles W. Roll, Jr., *The Hopes and Fears of the American People* (New York: Universe Books, 1971), 31–35.

DRAWING CONCLUSIONS:

- What can we learn from this data about American attitudes toward social disorder?
- What insight does this data give you into the sources of the conservative backlash?

7.3 RICHARD ROGIN, "JOE KELLY HAS REACHED HIS BOILING POINT" (1970)

While hostility toward the social movements of the 1960s was felt in many segments of the country, it was particularly pronounced among blue-collar white Americans—those without a college degree. For many, street brawls that broke out in New York City in May of 1970 between anti-war demonstrators and workers at the World Trade Center construction site came to symbolize the growing gulf between the protest movements and blue-collar white America. Curious to understand the sources of the conservative backlash, journalist Richard Rogin conducted an in-depth interview with Joe Kelly, a New York City construction worker who participated in May 1970 attack on anti-war demonstrators. In June 1970, the *New York Times* published Rogin's profile of Kelly under the title, "Joe Kelly Has Reached His Boiling Point."

GUIDING QUESTIONS:

- What is Kelly's view of the war in Vietnam?
- What is Kelly's view of anti-war demonstrators?
- What are Kelly's views on issues of race?
- What are Kelly's own personal values and life goals?

"When you were still up on Broadway you could hear the ruckus, the hollering. The peace demonstrators trying to outshout the construction workers. The construction workers hollering, 'U.S.A., all the way' and 'We're Number One.' And the peace demonstrators screaming up there that the war was unjust and everything else, right by the Treasury Building on Broad Street there.

"There was just a lot of hollering and screaming going back and forth until whoever the individual was—oh, he was no spring chicken, he was forty, forty-five years old—that spit on the flag. I was maybe four or five rows back in with the construction workers. I saw him make a gesture, you know, a forward motion. That was it. That was the spark that ignited the flame. It came out in the roar of the crowd. 'He spit on the flag! He spit on the flag!' And of course the construction worker got up there on top of the monument and he gave him and he gave him a good whack and off came the guy's glasses and I guess he followed his glasses off the pedestal there.

"And then there just seemed to be a rush, a mob scene. The chant then was, 'Get the flags up on the steps where they belong. It's a government building.' And they can say what they want about the New York Police Department, they coulda had the National Guard there with fixed bayonets and they would not have held the construction workers back then.

"When we first went up on the steps and the flags went up there, the whole group started singing 'God Bless America' and it damn near put a lump in your throat. It was really something. I could never say I was sorry I was there. You just had a very proud feeling. If I live to be a hundred, I don't think I'll ever see anything quite like that again."

William H. Chafe and Harvard Sitkoff, eds. *A History of Our Times: Readings on Postwar America* (New York: Oxford University Press, 1983), 277–289.

Joe Kelly's big chin and right hand tremble as he is caught in the deep, remembered passions of that noontime on Friday, May 8. He is thirty-one years old, a brawny 6 feet 4 inches, 210 pounds, blue eyes and receding red hair under his yellow plastic construction helmet decorated with U.S. flag decals and "FOR GOD AND COUNTRY."

It is now late afternoon, nearly two weeks later, and we are sitting in a gray wooden construction shanty on the sprawling World Trade Center site in lower Manhattan where he works. Joe is a well-liked, skillful mechanic in an intricate and demanding trade, elevator construction—installing the elevators and the heavy complex machinery to make the cars run.

On that violent day, soon after he came down for his half-hour lunch break from the forty-second floor of the soaring red steel skeleton of Tower A—another high, seemingly timeless, world which will rise 110 stories overlooking New York and the industrial hinterlands of New Jersey, where men walk almost casually on springy planks laid over open steel now seventy flights up—Joe Kelly reached his "boiling point." He found he could not "sit back" any longer, and he became a demonstrator for the first time in his life. Though "not much of a shouter," and a strong believer that violence solves nothing, he also shouted and threw his first punch in more than ten years.

During that long menacing midday several hundred construction workers, accused by reporters of using metal tools as weapons, were joined by office workers on a rampage through lower Manhattan. They beat up and injured seventy antiwar protesters and bystanders, including four policemen. With cries of "Kill the Commie bastards," "Lindsay's a Red," and "Love it or leave it," they surged up to City Hall. There they forced the flag, which had been lowered to half-staff in mourning for the four dead Kent State students, to be raised again. Then, provoked by peace banners, they stormed through Pace College across the street. It was a day that left New York shaken.

His face taut with fury, Mayor John V. Lindsay went on television to call the workers' attacks "tough and organized" though the unions promptly denied any influence. But he lashed out even more strongly at the outnumbered police whom many witnesses had accused of inadequate preparations and of standing by tolerantly during the assaults on the peaceful rally. Only six arrests were reported. He charged the police with failing as "the barrier between [the public] and wanton violence."

Others called the workers bullies or Nazi brownshirts. "We have no control over what they want to call us," says Joe Kelly. "But I think that the large majority of people, going as high as 85 to 90 percent, are more than happy. Not so much for the violence but for the stand that we took. And now they're standing up, the construction worker is only an image that's being used. The hardhat is being used to represent all of the silent majority."

It was the wild start of two weeks of almost daily noon-hour, flag-waving, bellicose, damn-Lindsay (the most common signs called him a Communist or a faggot) and praise-Nixon counter-marches through downtown New York, which Joe Kelly enthusiastically joined. Some of his fellow workers even happily lost an hour's pay for marching too long after lunch. Despite the fact that many of the men returned late following Friday's slugfest, none were docked. "I was going to dock one man who came back an hour and a half late," says Frank Pike, general elevator construction foreman, "but he said, 'I saw these kids spit on the flag. What could I do? How could I dock the man?"

The union word had come down: "Demonstrate all you want but be careful, no violence." Others say that the union tried to stop the men from all informal demonstrations. In any event, there was no more major violence; thousands of helmeted police patrolled the streets.

The construction workers loaded their unfinished skyscrapers with huge U.S. flags and their hardhats became a national symbol of fervent support for the Nixon Administration and its Indochina war policy. President Nixon was even presented with a hardhat at a White House ceremony. The climax came on May 20 when an estimated one hundred thousand construction workers and longshoremen sang and chanted from City Hall to Battery Park in a massive display of jingoistic sentiment probably unparalleled during the uncertain years of the Vietnam conflict.

That day Joe Kelly was given the honor of carrying the gold-fringed American flag with the gold eagle, its wings outspread, on the top of the pole, leading a contingent of hundreds of his fellow workers from Local No. 1, International Union of Elevator Constructors. With his yellow helmet on, he marched, resolutely serious-faced, rarely showing a thin smile, ignoring the pretty secretaries leaning over the police barriers. He displayed the training he received when he was an M.P. with an Army honor guard stationed in Heidelberg, West Germany. Around him Broadway boomed with the chants: "We're Number One," "U.S.A., all the way," "God Bless America" and "You're a Grand Old Flag." "Yankee Doodle" and "Over There" blared forth. The workers cheered and whistled through the applause from spectators and the shower of ticker tape and computer cards from high office windows.

They marched to the green lawns of Battery Park, with the breeze coming off the upper bay cooling a hot blue day. Joe Kelly's friends came up to him and shook his hand, saying: "Beautiful." "Like a champ, Joe." Joe clenched and unclenched the fingers of his right hand, which had held the flagpole for two hours. "I feel fine," he said. "This is terrific. It'll wake a few people up. This will happen not only down here but in the rest of New York and across the country now." The first thing to happen, though, was that Frank Pike docked himself and all the elevator constructors an hour's pay for parading instead of working. A few men never made it back to the job that afternoon.

Within the next few weeks in belligerent defense of Nixon's Southeast Asia policies, nearly twenty thousand construction workers paraded (and pummeled antiwar spectators) in St. Louis, and several hundred workers scuffled with students holding a peace rally at Arizona State University in Tempe.

Joe Kelly is proud, confident, and outspoken in the old American style. He is almost mystically proud of his flag, his country, the Establishment, and eager to end the Indochina war by striking more aggressively, though the details of young soldiers and innocent civilians sadden him. He is determined to be on guard against Communism and to crush it wherever it threatens his nation. Joe is convinced that a subversive conspiracy of teachers, influenced by foreign powers, is brainwashing the students to Communist beliefs. Distressed by the hippie lifestyle of so many youths, he is also furious at student radicals who burn and shut down schools which his taxes pay for and which most of his fellow workers cherish because they never had a chance to go to them. He is a stalwart charter member of Richard Nixon's silent majority, a devout Roman Catholic and fiercely loyal to his President, whose office he regards with almost holy respect.

"The Pope to the Catholic Church is the same as the President to the American people," he says. "He's the one who decides. He's infallible when he speaks of religion as far as the Catholic Church goes. I'm not saying Nixon is infallible. But he's Commander in Chief of the Armed Forces. He's in charge."

Vietnam: "I just hope that these people give Nixon the play to go in there in Cambodia and knock the living hell out of their supply lines. If this is what it takes to stop the loss of American lives, well, let's go the hell in there and get it over with."

My Lai massacre: "I don't believe anybody in the United States, nice and cozy, has a right to judge them [the accused] until everything comes out in the trial."

Kent State: "They [the National Guardsmen] must have felt their lives were threatened; that's why they shot."

Inflation: "I have faith in Nixon. I think he'll curb inflation, given the chance."

High taxes: "If this is what it takes to run this country, I don't mind paying them. You couldn't live anyplace else like you do here."

The flag: "I think of all the people that died for that flag. And somebody's gonna spit on it, it's like spitting on their grave. So they better not spit on it in front of me. You think you could get it better someplace else—well, then, don't hang around here, go there."

Unemployment: "I don't know where they're getting these figures from [up to a five-year high for all jobs and 11.9 percent in construction] because here in New York you got a [construction] boom going on."

Joe Kelly has what used to be faithfully accepted as the old-fashioned, authentic American credentials: he is hard-working, conscientious, obedient and trusting in authority, an adherent of law and order, patriotic, sentimental, gentle and affectionate with his loved ones, angry and determined to right wrongs as he sees them, moderately compassionate, a believer in the virtues of his way of life.

To the antiwar protesters and others grieving and critical over America's present course in Indochina and what they perceive as unfeeling repressive policies at home, he probably appears as an anachronism. To them, he is Joe Kelly, yesterday's comic-book hero, a relic from the somehow simpler, self-righteous days of the old world wars when, with a grin and a wave and a song, Americans marched off to solve the world's problems. "The Jack Armstrong of Tower A," one of his fellow workers called him approvingly.

Joe Kelly and millions of Americans like him would not share the gloomy conclusion of John W. Gardner, a Republican and chairman of the National Urban Coalition, that the country is disintegrating. They see a country in momentary disarray, under stress, but they retain a sturdy optimism. They know but do not suffer the dark fear that a complex and subtle civil war is wasting the land with hate and with overt and invisible violence: white against black, conservatives against liberals, workers against students, old against young, fathers against sons. Even the old hawks of organized labor now face opposition within their own ranks over the Indochina war.

America heaves against the old grain. The kids are on the loose trying to shake off the crusty habits of the country the way a snake sheds its skin. The antis feel depressed by their own Government, if not worse, and sense mendacity everywhere.

The kids, Joe Kelly thinks, ought to feel lucky to be in America where they have the legitimate right to dissent and stage peaceful demonstrations. If they did the equivalent of burning draft cards or desecrating the flag in Russia or China, they would, he says, be shot down in the street.

"These kids," he says, "they can do as they feel like. I mean burn, loot, steal, do anything they feel like in the name of social reform. But can the average Joe Blow citizen go out and do this?" A crime is a crime, he says, even if it's for social reform, and he argues that there is a double standard of justice for students, especially in New York.

What about the kids' mockery of the Puritan ethic? "If they don't want to educate themselves or go out and work hard for a living and make a few dollars, spend a few dollars, and save a few dollars for a rainy day, that's their prerogative. But in general, again, this has been bred into them somewhere. This is not the American way."

Joe Kelly never thought the picture presented by his hardworking life would need any defense. There is his pretty blonde wife, Karen; two strawberry-blonde daughters, Robin Lynn, four, and Kerry Ann, one and a half, and now a newborn son, James Patrick. "I had two cheerleaders," he says, "now I got a ballplayer." There is also a collie named Missy and a newly bought brick-and-shingle, two story, $40,000 house on an irregular 50 by 100 foot lot, tastefully furnished, with a modern kitchen ("All you can get for two arms"), and a freshly sodded lawn on one of those breezy Staten Island streets with the gulls overheard, children pedaling red tricycles, the hum of an electric mower, and a man hosing down a gleaming red Dodge Challenger, all the residents of the neighborhood blue-collar whites, doing well.

Joe Kelly and his neighbors, the steamfitter, the bus driver, the policeman, the TV color processor, have worked too hard to get to that street to give it all up. They have had too many peace protests, too many moratoriums, too many harsh laments and shouted obscenities against their country, too many rock-throwings and strikes and fires on campuses where they want their children to make it, too many bombings and too many Vietcong flags waving down the streets of their city, too many long-haired youths and naked boys and girls, too many drugs, too much un-Americanism, not to feel angry and resentful.

Joe Kelly sits on his plastic-covered orange couch in front of his new Motorola Quasar color TV console and seethes as he watches the six o'clock news day after day. What really galls him, he says, is what he considers small groups of radical students closing down schools. "In California," he says, "they burned a bank to the ground. You just watch and boil. Who do these university presidents, responsible people, think they have an obligation to? The students are burning something every day. They're taking over something in the chancellor's office every day."

And then that Friday morning, Joe Kelly mounted his turquoise Triumph 500-cc. motorcycle, rode down to the ferry slip, read *The Daily News* and had a coffee as the ferry crossed to Manhattan, then rode his motorcycle again to his job. When he walked into the shanty on the building site, he heard that a shoving incident the previous day between peace demonstrators and construction workers elsewhere in the downtown area had triggered the men from a number of skyscrapers to action. For the workers, "it was the straw that broke the camel's back," he recalls. Spontaneously, Joe says, perhaps a quarter of the World Trade Center's 212 elevator constructors decided to go down the seven blocks and "see what this peace demonstration was all about."

"My partner, Tommy, he climbed up on top of the light stanchion down on Wall Street and planted the flag up there, right in front of the Treasury Building, to a great round of applause. The flags were up on the top steps. The construction workers and the Wall Street workers, they had the steps of the Treasury Building filled and the demonstrators were now down in the street.

"And they started to chant in unison '—, no, we won't go,' and they just kept it up. And all of a sudden, just the same as the movement had started up onto the steps, the movement started back down off the steps. This chant that they kept up, it just raised the anger to a degree that it just seemed that everybody would just want to get down there and disperse them. When I say, 'disperse,' I don't mean physically take these kids and manhandle them, but just to break them up, break up the group and break up this chant because it just seemed so un-American.

"I guess the average construction worker is what you would call a flag-waver. You can call me a flag-waver any day of the week. I think that's just something to be proud of, to be a flag-waver, to be proud of your country. And these kids just kept it up and kept it up.

"As the movement started down off the steps, again there was a certain amount of them [protesters] that wanted to stand their ground, and they're dealing with men that work with iron and steel every day of the week and do manual labor every day of the week, and they just made a mistake. They just never heard about that discretion business. I will say this: there was as many of these antiwar demonstrators whacked by Wall Street and Broadway office workers as there were by construction workers. The feeling seemed to be that the white-collar-and-tie-man, he was actually getting in there and taking as much play on this thing as the construction worker was.

"This was something. Listen. I'm thirty-one years old. I'd never witnessed anything like this is my life before, and it kinda caught me in awe that you had to stop and see what was going on around you. It was almost unbelievable. This was the financial district of New York City, probably the financial district of the world, and here was this mass clash of opposite factions, right on Wall Street and Broad, and you could hardly move, there were so many people taking part in this aside from the five hundred construction workers. It was just something that you had to stand back and blink your eyes and actually look a second and third time, and you couldn't believe that this was actually taking place in that particular area.

"There was one kid came after me, I don't know why. He just came flying out of the crowd. I don't claim to be a violent person. I couldn't possibly remember the last time I ever struck anybody. It had to be at least ten years ago, maybe twelve years ago. And for some reason this guy picked out somebody and it just happened to be me. He came running at me with arms flailing and I gave him a whack and back he went. He went down, I know that, and I just figured he wouldn't be back for more."

. . . Joe attends noon Mass on Sundays and he also coaches basketball and baseball teams in a boy's league in Blessed Sacrament parish. (After the Army, he spent three years as a weekend counselor at an orphanage on Staten Island.) His reading consists of *The Daily News*, the *Advance*, the sports section of *The New York Post* and *Popular Mechanics* magazine. The Kellys go out to the movies perhaps every six weeks and may stop in afterward for "a couple of drinks in a nice, quiet, respectable place." Once a week his wife leaves him at home when she goes to play bingo. There is usually a Christmas party for the men on the job, and Otis [Elevator Co.] throws a picnic in the summer. Recently, the elevator constructors and their wives had a $20-a-couple dinner dance at the Commuter's Café on Cortlandt Street, across from the Trade Center site . . .

On television, Joe enjoys Johnny Cash and Jackie Gleason and sometimes Dean Martin. He likes to be in bed by 11 p.m. Before he was married, Joe played basketball four nights a week in a community-center league. With family responsibilities, his heavy work schedule, and his relative slowness of foot today, he has cut it out completely. "I go down once in a while to watch and eat my heart out," he says.

Joe gets his extravocational workouts now around the house, putting in sod, helping to grade the backyard for a large above-ground plastic swimming pool for the children, planting two blue spruces and yews and rhododendrons in the front.

The Kellys haven't been able to take any vacations, though Joe has had two weeks off yearly and will get three weeks under the new contract starting this summer (there was either a strike, or they were saving for the house, or the children were too small). Perhaps twice a summer they drive down to the New Jersey shore around Belmar in their 1967 English Ford station wagon and go swimming.

Why does he work so hard? "A lot of people ask me that," he says. "I wanted the house. Right? I wanted something nice for the wife and the kids, someplace where the kids could grow up and have their own backyard. They wouldn't have to be running out in the street. And now I have the house and I want it fixed up nice. And maybe when it is fixed up nice, I'll relax a bit." Meanwhile, he is at the "boiling point."

"My belief is, physical violence doesn't solve a damn thing. One party has to sway the other party to his belief and then the argument is settled. I honestly don't believe that there will be any more physical violence in New York City. I think that one Friday and it's over with. I don't like to see anybody get bounced. I saw some of those kids go down and I didn't think they were gonna get up. I certainly don't agree with them. I would much rather prefer grabbing them by the head of the hair and taking a scissors and cutting their hair off, something that was much less violent but you still would have gotten your message across.

"Up at City Hall it became obvious that they had better get that flag back up to the top of the mast. Within a few minutes the flag went back up and everybody seemed nice and happy and again they started singing, 'God Bless America' and the national anthem and again it made you feel good. Not that I like seeing those four kids out in wherever it was, Kent, get killed. I don't like to see anybody get beat up, never mind lose their life.

"I don't think Mayor Lindsay has the right to put that flag at half-staff. That flag represents this country, so the leading representative of the country, who is President Nixon to me, is the only one that has the power or the right to raise or lower a flag."

Joe Kelly says he never even asked what his father's politics were, believing it to be a man's private affair. How did he arrive as a militant member of the no-longer-silent majority? What brought him to believe that Communism was undermining America from within?

"Two people stand out in my mind," Joe says, "why I'm taking part. Joe McCarthy often said, beware of this school system; they're going to infiltrate, brainwash the kids. And Khrushchev in 1960 banging on the UN table. He said they wouldn't have to take over the country physically, they'd do it from within." Though he was only a youngster during McCarthy's heyday, Kelly says: "It's something I've read somewhere along the line." He feels that the students are only dupes in the hands of subversive teachers who, Joe hints, are under the control of foreign powers. In some way, the bad teachers had to be weeded out, he says.

Joe Kelly first voted in 1960, when he chose John F. Kennedy over Nixon for President because he was impressed with Kennedy's performance in the TV debates. Though he still reveres President Kennedy, he wouldn't vote that way again. By 1964 he had swung to the right and voted for Goldwater over Johnson. In the 1965 and 1969 New York mayoral races, he voted the Conservative party line for William F. Buckley, Jr., and John Marchi. He cast his ballot for Nixon for President in 1968.

It was the Goldwater campaign that crystallized Joe's feeling about the war in Vietnam. "I think that it all goes back again, like history repeating itself, to Hitler," he says. "When Hitler kept marching into these countries and, instead of just fighting Hitler's country, you were fighting all these countries after a while. You just can't let Communism take over everything around you because when they got everything around you, they're gonna come after you."

Three men who command his admiration now are John Wayne, Vice-President Agnew, and Chicago Mayor Richard Daley. In fact, Joe wishes New York could borrow Daley for six months to give the city a stiff dose of law and order. He has complete disdain for Mayor Lindsay. He believes Lindsay has turned New York into "welfare city" and is trying to be the champion of welfare recipients and the young antiwar generation in a bid for the Presidency. "Do what you want in Lindsay's city—" he says caustically, "burn the schools. He's got to raise the budget this year to pay for what they burned down."

Of the recent influx of minority workers into his once closely bound union, he says: "They're here to stay, entitled to. But if they're going to work with us, if we go up on the iron and risk our lives walking it, by God, they have to go along with us. There've been several instances in the city where they've refused because they didn't have to."

As for a black family living on his street, he is adamantly against it, feeling that panic-selling would drive down the value of his property. "I had to bust my backside for five years to get that down payment for that house," he says. "I am not interested in seeing all that go down the drain."

It is on this precious ground—his home and his family—that he takes a defiant, mildly worried stand. He would like his daughters to go to college or nursing school and his son to get as much schooling as possible, to become a doctor or a lawyer—"something where he can use his head to make a living, not his back like his old man does."

While his wife hopes and prays that her daughters will never wear their hair straight and long like the hippies and that her children's minds will be protected in parochial schools despite the danger of lay teachers, Joe Kelly tells a story about a neighbor's friend's son, a boy of sixteen.

"This boy," he says, "came home from school one day and told his father he was a bum, that he was part of the Establishment. And this fellow was a World War II veteran, decorated several times and wounded twice. And he just turned around and he gave the kid a good whack and I guess he broke his jaw or broke his nose and the father was in a turmoil. This is his own flesh and blood talking to him.

"I cannot imagine having my kids come home and tell me I'm a bum because I believe in the Establishment—and there is nobody that believes in the Establishment more than I do. The more I see of this stuff, the closer I try to become to my kids. I believe that my way is correct, the Establishment way, law and order first, and this is what I'm gonna do my damndest to breed into them so that they don't get some other off-the-wall ideas."

Joe says that if his children ever called him a bum because he believes in the flag, they'd better leave his house. "I would do everything to control myself not to hit them. I mean, this is what I brought into the world. But it's awful hard. I certainly can see that man flying off the handle and whacking the kid. Oh, yeah, he certainly did regret it. But his big question is, Where did his kid get this trend of thinking?"

Joe Kelly doesn't believe that melees such as the memorable one at noon on May 8 are any solution. So his answer, he says reflectively, is to arm himself with education, engage in dialogue.

"When they throw a point at you," he says, "be able to talk to them on their theories on socialism, Communism. This is the best way—to talk them out of the stuff instead of just saying it's un-American or using your fists."

Ironically, Mayor Lindsay has said much the same thing: "Perhaps their [the construction workers'] demonstrations, in the end, will help us break through to a new dialogue in which we not only talk, but listen."

DRAWING CONCLUSIONS:

- What explains Kelly's animosity toward the social movements of the 1960s?
- What can we learn about the conservative backlash from Rogin's profile of Kelly?

7.4 SPIRO AGNEW QUIPS

A former governor of the state of Maryland, Spiro Agnew was elected vice president of the United States in 1968 as Richard Nixon's running mate. Embracing the role of Richard Nixon's political "attack dog," Agnew became known as a voice of the "silent majority" through his biting and satirical attacks on hippies, radicals, anti-war protesters, and black power militants. Agnew's quips offer a window into the conservative backlash and its political uses.

GUIDING QUESTIONS:

- Who are the targets of Spiro Agnew's quips? What is Agnew's critique of these targets?
- Who is the intended audience for Agnew's quips? What is his message to that audience?

SPIRO AGNEW QUIPS

"In the United States today, we have more than our share of the nattering nabobs of negativism. They have formed their own 4H Club—the hopeless, hysterical hypochondriacs of history."

—*Speech in San Diego, California, September 11, 1970*

"This is the criminal left that belongs not in a dormitory, but in a penitentiary. The criminal left is not a problem to be solved by the Department of Philosophy or the Department of English—it is a problem for the Department of Justice. . . . Black or white, the criminal left is interested in power. It is not interested in promoting the renewal and reforms that make democracy work; it is interested in promoting those collisions and conflict that tear democracy apart."

—*Speech at a Florida Republican dinner, April 28, 1970*

"A spirit of national masochism prevails, encouraged by an effete corps of impudent snobs who characterize themselves as intellectuals."

—*Denouncing anti-war demonstrations to a Republican fundraiser in New Orleans, October 19, 1970*

"Freedom of speech is useless without freedom of thought. And I fear that the politics of protest is shutting out the process of thought, so necessary to rational discussion. We are faced with the Ten Commandments of Protest:

Thou Shalt Not Allow Thy Opponent to Speak.
Thou Shalt Not Set Forth a Program of Thine Own.
Thou Shalt Not Trust Anybody Over Thirty.
Thou Shalt Not Honor Thy Father or Thy Mother.
Thou Shalt Not Heed the Lessons of History.
Thou Shalt Not Write Anything Longer than a Slogan.
Thou Shalt Not Present a Negotiable Demand.
Thou Shalt Not Accept Any Establishment Idea.
Thou Shalt Not Revere Any but Totalitarian Heroes.
Thou Shalt Not Ask Forgiveness for Thy Transgressions,
Rather Thou Shalt Demand Amnesty for Them."

—*Speech to governors and their families, December 3, 1969*

"Yippies, Hippies, Yahoos, Black Panthers, lions and tigers alike—I would swap the whole damn zoo for the kind of young Americans I saw in Vietnam."

—*Speech in St Louis, Missouri, February 1970*

DRAWING CONCLUSIONS:

- What is Agnew's critique of the social movements of the 1960s?
- How is Agnew using the conservative backlash to his and President Nixon's own political advantage?

From William H. Chafe and Harvard Sitkoff, eds., *A History of Our Times: Readings on Postwar America* (New York: Oxford University Press, 1983), 277–289.

ADDITIONAL RESOURCES

Anderson, Terry. *The Movement and the Sixties: Protest in America from Greensboro to Wounded Knee*. New York: Oxford University Press, 1995.

Collier, Peter, and David Horowitz. *Destructive Generation: Second Thoughts about the Sixties*. New York: Summit Books, 1989.

Evans, Sarah. *Personal Politics: The Roots of Women's Liberation in the Civil Rights Movement and the New Left*. New York: Knopf, 1979.

Gitlin, Todd. *The Sixties: Yeas of Hope, Days of Rage*. New York: Random House, 1987.

Hodgson, Godfrey. *America in Our Time: From World War II to Nixon, What Happened and Why?* Garden City, NY: Doubleday, 1976.

Isserman, Maurice, and Michael Kazin. *America Divided: The Civil War of the 1960s*. New York: Oxford University Press, 2000.

O'Neill, William L. *Coming Apart: An Informal History of America in the 1960s*. Chicago: Ivan R. Dee, 2005.

Peniel E., Joseph. *Waiting 'til the Midnight Hour: A Narrative History of Black Power in America*. New York: Henry Holt, 2006.

Perlstein, Rick. *Nixonland: The Rise of a President and the Fracturing of America*. New York: Scribner, 2008.

Report of the National Advisory Commission on Civil Disorders. Washington, DC: Government Printing Office, 1968.

Report of the President's Commission on Campus Unrest. Washington, DC: Government Printing Office, 1970.

Rosen, Ruth. *The World Split Open: How the Modern Women's Movement Changed America*. New York: Viking, 2000.

Stein, Marc. *Rethinking the Gay and Lesbian Movement*. New York: Routledge, 2012.

Tamarkin, Jeff. *Got a Revolution: The Turbulent Flight of Jefferson Airplane*. New York: Atria Books, 2003.

Weisbrot, Robert. *Freedom Bound: A History of America's Civil Rights Movement*. New York: Norton, 1990.

INDEX